the Mountainway
of the
Navajo

Painting, *The Fire Dance*, by Robert Chee

Leland C. Wyman

the
Mountainway
of the
Navajo

with a myth of the Female Branch recorded
and translated by Father Berard Haile, OFM

The University of Arizona Press / Tucson, Arizona

About the Author . . .

LELAND C. WYMAN, outstanding non-Indian authority on Navajo religion, with the eminent Franciscan scholar of Navajo culture, the late Father Berard Haile, has been responsible for English-speaking readers having access to numerous major ceremonials of the Navajo people, such as Beautyway, the Windways, Red Antway, Blessingway, and several others that preceded the Mountainway volume. Wyman, a Ph.D. in biology from Harvard, taught and did research in physiology at Boston University for four decades, meanwhile engaging in many cross-disciplinary projects. In the early 1930s he began to write on Navajo ceremonialism and mythology, and soon teamed up with anthropologists and other specialists to publish on Navajo medicine, ethnobotany, ethnoentomology, psychology and art.

THE UNIVERSITY OF ARIZONA PRESS

I. S. B. N.-0-8165-0412-1

L. C. No. 74-83333

*To all who have contributed, directly
or indirectly, to my research with the Navajos during
the past four decades — colleagues and coworkers,
students, museum officials, Navajos, and my wife*

Contents

ILLUSTRATIONS

TABLES

Foreword

FOR TWO SCORE YEARS Leland C. Wyman, a man of insatiable curiosity and boundless energy who always makes it a point to finish what he has begun, has been the Boswell of Navajo Indian ceremonialism. His quest has been to understand—to the extent that one who is not himself a native-born participant of the culture can ever understand—the Navajo "way." Once earning the knowledge and having been granted the wisdom he has shared the results of his labors with an English-reading audience, thereby lengthening the body of Navajo thought throughout a considerable part of the entire world and making permanent that which might otherwise have disappeared with the deaths of those who were bearers of the traditions. This is not to say that Navajo ceremonialism and the cosmology which underlies it are in danger of extinction. Both, however, are in a continual state of change such that yesterday's beauty and truth are ever in danger of becoming today's forgotten past and a prelude to our own demise.

Leland Wyman would forestall, if not prevent, such a demise. In doing so he is himself part of a tradition, one which began with the Navajo studies of Washington Matthews and which was carried on by Father Berard Haile, Gladys Reichard, and by a select few other non-Indians who were able to share in a Navajo world view.

The Navajo "way" is made up of many lesser "ways," most of them outwardly expressed in chants, ritual poetry, drama, pictorial art (especially sandpaintings), and ceremonial paraphernalia. Wyman has been a cosmographer who has attempted to map for us complex and inter-twined networks: Blessingway, Beautyway, Shootingway, Red Antway, Windways, Flintway, and Upward-Reaching Way, to mention a few.

In the present volume we are told briefly about the Navajo people and their ceremonial system that we might better understand the Mountain-Top-way (Mountain Chant) in terms of its various branches, phases, and ritual. Arthritic conditions and mental disturbances among Navajos can sometimes be attributed to influences from mountain animals, primarily the bear. The Mountain

Chant is used to treat diseases brought on by such causes. In what follows we learn of the ceremonies which comprise the chant; of the spectacular public performance of the final night known as the Corral or Fire Dance; of the songs, including translations into English of nineteen examples; and of the preparation and disposition of prayersticks.

Here, too, are illustrations of thirty-two Mountainway sandpaintings and an in-depth analysis of their symbols and designs. We share in a discussion of the mythology of Mountainway based on eight variations of the myth by different Navajo authors and of how these legends connect with those in related ceremonials. This includes special attention given to the story of the Pueblo War which serves as an introduction to the myths of Beautyway and Female Mountainway and of the Enemyway rite. Other stories are analyzed, and there is a short note on the geography of the Mountainway myths.

As well as Wyman's contribution to our understanding of Mountainway, we are given for the first time in print the myth of the Female Mountain-Top-way told by Yucca Patch Man as recorded and translated by Father Berard Haile. There is also "Raised by the Owl" told by River Junction Curley, recorded and translated by Father Berard.

What began in 1934 as a study by Wyman of a Navajo patchwork cloak has continued in his piecing together what appears to non-Navajos to be the patchwork of their "ways." His efforts, moreover, may well mark the closing of an era and the beginning of a new one in our understanding of the lifeway of another people. As increasing numbers of Navajos become literate, in their own language as well as in English, they are becoming the authors to preserve their traditions in writing and to interpret themselves to others as they see fit. But oncoming generations of literate Navajos will always be grateful that some of their non-literate forbears consented to share their knowledge and wisdom in the roles of teacher and consultant with those who sought understanding. Were it not for the tradition whose exemplars are Berard Haile and Leland Wyman, much which otherwise might forever have been lost from human heritage has been rescued for the sustenance of all our descendants.

BERNARD L. FONTANA
Ethnologist
Arizona State Museum

Acknowledgments

WHENEVER A NAVAJO MYTH is published the author of the work in which it appears is making use of the property of the Navajo Indian who dictated it to the recording individual. I wish to express my profound thankfulness, therefore, for the gifts of their intangible property to the numerous native authors of the myths and makers of the drypaintings which I have consulted. I am also mindful of the labors of the recorders and translators of the myths and of the artists who put the drypaintings into permanent form. Especial remembrance should be set down, of course, for Yucca Patch Man and River Junction Curly, the authors of the two myths presented in this volume, and Father Berard Haile who recorded and translated them, and also for Franc Johnson Newcomb who copied more Navajo drypaintings than any other person. I am also keenly aware of the kindness and helpfulness of the Navajo Indians with whom I have lived and worked and who have instructed me in their lore. My thanks also go to the Franciscan Fathers of Saint Michaels, Arizona, and to Father Roger Huser, Minister Provincial of St. John Baptist Province of Cincinnati, Ohio, for giving me permission to publish Father Berard's translations of the two myths mentioned. Bernard L. Fontana of the Arizona State Museum at the University of Arizona also should be commended for his enterprise in bringing about the transfer of Father Berard's notes and manuscripts to the Special Collections of the University of Arizona Library. I wish to express my own thanks to the various people who have been head of the Special Collections during my years of work for making my use of materials both easy and pleasant, and especially to Phyllis Ball who has always acceded to requests for assistance with prompt cheerfulness. A copy of one of the myths mentioned above, *Raised by the Owl*, had been deposited by Father Berard in the Department of Anthropology of the University of Chicago, and as long ago as 1957 Fred Eggan of that department had sent me the copy of this manuscript for study and possible publication.

The initial stimulus for this book came out of a conversation some years ago with John D. Barrett, then Director of the Bollingen Foundation of New York City, when he suggested casually that I ought to prepare a sequel to *Beautyway* (Bollingen Series LIII). Later, when I found the myth of Female Mountainway among Father Berard's manuscripts, his suggestion began to take form because the myths of the two chants relate the adventures of two sisters and the tale of the Older Sister of the Mountain Chant myth is the most appropriate possible sequel to the story of the Younger Sister of Beautyway. Edward B. Danson, Director of the Museum of Northern Arizona, and various members of his staff most kindly provided various facilities and did much to further my work on this book, and similar acknowledgment goes to the late Kenneth E. Foster, former director of the Museum of Navaho Ceremonial Art in Santa Fe, and to Bertha P. Dutton, the subsequent director, for favors accorded me during the numerous periods when I was studying the manuscripts and reproductions of sandpaintings housed there. I am indebted to the Smithsonian Institution Press for permitting me to use an adaptation of some passages in their Contributions to Anthropology, Number 13. David P. McAllester of Wesleyan University revised Father Berard's translations of some of the songs of Mountainway, and for this I am most grateful.

I wish to thank the following individuals and institutions for permission to use as illustrations reproductions of sandpaintings or other paintings under their care or in their collections: Ture Bengtz, Director, The Art Complex Inc., Duxbury, Mass. (Fig. 1); Bertha P. Dutton, Director, Museum of Navaho Ceremonial Art, Santa Fe, New Mexico (Figs. 4–6, 8–11, 15–17, 19, 21, 25, 27 [Oakes Collection], 28, 30–34); Maud Oakes, Big Sur, California (for permission to use her painting of the porcupine as Fig. 27); Edna Robertson, Curator, Fine Arts Collection of the Museum of New Mexico, Santa Fe (Figs. 14, 23); Edward B. Danson, Director, Museum of Northern Arizona, Flagstaff (Figs. 2, 13, 22, 26 [Haile Collection]; 20, 29 [Reichard Collection]); Wilma Kaemlein, Curator of Collections, Arizona State Museum, Tucson (Figs. 3, 13, 18); the late Franc J. Newcomb, Albuquerque, New Mexico (Figs. 7, 24). Moreover, I have happy memories of many fruitful conversations with Franc Newcomb.

Frederick W. Maynard of the Department of Biology of Boston

University contributed his photographic skill in preparing the illustrations. My wife, Paula, with infinite patience did much to lighten immeasurably the long hours of analysis and writing, and helped with the correcting of the manuscript as well. Finally, I wish to express my appreciation to Boston University for providing a professor emeritus with space and the use of certain equipment, and to the University of Arizona Press for bringing about publication.

LELAND C. WYMAN
Boston University
Boston, Massachusetts

Introduction

The ceremony of . . . mountain chant—literally, chant towards (a place) within the mountains—is one of a large number practiced by the shamans, or medicine men, of the Navajo tribe. I have selected it as the first of those to be described, because I have witnessed it most frequently, because it is the most interesting to the Caucasian spectator, and because it is the best known to the whites who visit and reside in and around the Navajo country. Its chief interest to the stranger lies in the various public performances of the last night. Like other great rites of the shamans, it has its secret ceremonies of many days' duration in the medicine lodge; but, unlike the others, it ends with a varied show in the open air, which all are invited to witness.

Washington Matthews[1]

ALMOST A CENTURY HAS PASSED since Washington Matthews wrote these words. Prior to his studies little was known about Navajo religious practices and beliefs, but during the many years which have elapsed since he submitted his paper on the chant towards a place in the mountains to the Bureau of Ethnology, this work has remained the definitive account of this song ceremonial. Moreover, it also has the distinction of containing the first color reproductions of Navajo drypaintings. For the reasons stated by Matthews in the passage quoted above, the Mountain Chant together with the Night

---

[1] Matthews, 1887, p. 385. Dr. Washington Matthews was a United States Army physician stationed at Fort Wingate, New Mexico, in the 1880s when he made these studies.

[1]

Chant has stood out in the mind of the white man among the twenty-six or so ceremonial complexes with their more than forty branches, rituals, and so on, which were or still are practiced by the Navajo. In fact, non-Navajos on the whole know very little, if anything, about the other song ceremonials. As Matthews said, this is because the Mountain Chant and the Night Chant are the only ones commonly performed in recent years which have spectacular public performances with masked impersonators of supernatural beings or other acts.

Mountains loom large on Navajo horizons. The flat portions of the Navajo country are surrounded by majestic ranges and peaks. In their own cosmology, the Navajo's traditional habitat has as its boundaries the four sacred mountains of the cardinal directions. These peaks have a prominent place in the mythology and practice of the Blessingway rites which are the backbone of Navajo religion, holding a central position from which they control, in a way, all other ceremonials.[2] The one essential item of paraphernalia required for performing a Blessingway rite, which the Navajo say is in control of it, is the mountain soil bundle, containing pinches of soil from the summits of the sacred mountains. Blessingway, however, is concerned with specific mountain peaks, whereas the Mountain Chant deals with mountains in general.

The Navajo are not alone, of course, in their concern for mountains. Their Pueblo neighbors believe them to be the dwelling place of their kachinas, supernatural beings important in their religion. They assert that mountains have power, that they are great shrines or sanctuaries, that, perhaps, they themselves are supernatural beings or that at least the four sacred mountains of the directions are.[3] In fact all peoples seem to have a need, sometimes almost a craving, for mountains. There are few places on earth where human beings live that are without them, and if they are lacking, the people sometimes build high places, as the ancient inhabitants of the flat river valleys of Mesopotamia built their mountainlike ziggurats to serve as connecting links, both real and symbolic, between the gods in heaven and the mortals on earth.

The myth published by Matthews, a tale of the adventures of a Navajo man who was captured by the Ute Indians, is the legend of Male Mountainway (see below). The myth of Female Mountainway, a quite different story, tells the adventures of a Navajo girl

---

[2] Wyman, 1970a, pp. 16–25; see also Reichard, 1970, p. 452.

[3] Parsons, 1939, pp. 173, 195, 214.

trying to escape from Bear Man who pursued her relentlessly. In 1938 Father Berard Haile published the origin legend of the Navajo Enemyway, an Evilway [Ghostway][4] rite designed to alleviate troubles thought to be caused by the ghosts of dead aliens [non-Navajo]. An important part of this myth is *The Pueblo War* which begins the tale of two sisters whose favors were sought by unwanted suitors, Big Snake Man and Bear Man, but leaves them just as they separated, each to be pursued by her fearful follower. In 1957 Wyman published the story of the adventures of the younger sister who was pursued by the Snake Man, which became the basis for the Navajo chantway, Beautyway, but the fate of the older sister was left hanging in the air. In 1935 Father Berard had obtained an extensive text from Yucca Patch Man of Fort Defiance Coal Mine, Arizona, who was a singer of Female Mountainway. This myth which relates the adventures of the older sister and Bear Man has not been published and is the main concern of this volume, thus completing the published versions of the stories of these characters.[5] First, however, a brief account of the Navajo and their ceremonial system will provide a background for readers who are not familiar with these people.

The Navajo and Their Religion[6]

THE NAVAJO INDIAN TRIBE, the largest group of native Americans in the United States, numbering more than 130,000 individuals, continues to be one of the most rapidly growing ethnic groups in this country. Its members have overflowed the legal boundaries of their approximately 18 million acres of reservation and leased lands, some having been resettled on other reservations and others having relocated in some of our industrial centers. Their homeland —the severely eroded Colorado plateau country of the "four corners" region of northeastern Arizona, northwestern New Mexico, southwestern Colorado, and southeastern Utah—although containing some of the most beautiful scenic attractions in the world, is singularly inhospitable for those who have to make a living from it.

---

[4] The suffix "-way" is a translation of the ending of Navajo names for their ceremonials.

[5] Much briefer and less satisfactory myths, which are not translations of native texts but which were obtained in English through interpreters, have been published by Coolidge and Coolidge (1930), Wheelwright (1951), and O'Bryan (1956).

[6] The following section is adapted from the author's *Sandpaintings of the Navaho Shootingway and the Walcott Collection*, Smithsonian Contributions to Anthropology No. 13, pp. 1–6, courtesy of the Smithsonian Institution Press.

Attempts to cope with this situation have resulted in a relatively enormous number of acculturative changes in the last few decades, so that on their lands Navajo Indians now operate motels, restaurants, service stations, an industrial park (near Gallup, New Mexico), an $8 million lumber mill, extensive irrigation projects, and tribal parks patterned after our national parks and monuments. Moreover, they have attracted to their lands a number of small industries that employ Navajo labor. Among other projects is the establishment of a Navajo Community College on the reservation.

In spite of these changes and in spite of their having overcome to a large extent their distrust of the white man's medicine (most Navajo babies are now born in hospitals or in clinics), the Navajo have preserved the traditional cultural inventory of their body of beliefs and practices dealing with those segments of experience not subject to rational control—or what we would call their "philosophy" and their "religion." This cultural complex encompasses as well their system of medical theory and practice—a system which provides comfort, social security, potent psychotherapy, and some actual medical therapy to a people predisposed to worry over health. There is no doubt that it was this predisposition—exacerbated by the prevalence of disease, hard times, and the fear of ghosts and witchcraft—that caused the Navajo's religious practice to take the form of curing ceremonials. In nearly every one of their religious performances an actual patient is treated for a real or anticipated ailment. Their priests are also their doctors. There is no word in the Navajo language that can be translated as "religion," but this word from our own culture is the most convenient label for their beliefs concerning the dynamics of the universe and techniques for controlling them and their belief in what we would call "the supernatural," although they do not make it a separate category of thought as we do. Traditional Navajo ceremonialism may be undergoing, however, what will prove to be a losing battle with the peyote cult, the Native American Church of North America, a redemptive social movement which rejects local traditional culture and which in turn is rejected by cultural conservatives. In the 1950s the proportion of Navajo peyotists varied from zero to 80 percent of the population in different areas of the reservation, and today the proportion probably is much higher. The recent book by David F. Aberle (1966) provides the most extensive study of this question.

The core of Navajo religious philosophy is the belief that the universe is an orderly, all-inclusive, unity of interrelated elements in which the principle of reciprocity governs man's relations with these elements, which include other men. Thus, favor for favor and injury for injury, unless compensated for, are the keynotes that should guide man's behavior. Being all-inclusive, the universe contains both good and evil, not as abstract ethical concepts but as complementary components. Innumerable powers in it are indifferent or good when under control and in harmony with man, but they may be potentially evil when uncontrolled. Some, such as ghosts of the dead or certain beings or elements like snake, lightning, or coyote, have greater potentiality for evil than others; and some are predominantly good unless related to excessive activity. Improper contact with inherently dangerous powers — even though it be indirect, unintentional, or unconscious — or the breaching of traditional restrictions [taboos] may lead to illness, the price man pays for disturbance of the normal order, harmony, or balance among elements in the universe. Such a theory of evil is based on contagion rather than sin; for example, murder is potentially dangerous not because of the deed itself but because of contact with the dead. Likewise, excesses in gambling or in sexual activity — in fact, any excessive activity — are thought of as symptoms of disease amenable to ritual cure, and thus are not considered sins. Malevolent misuse of ritual knowledge by witches causes troubles that are especially difficult to deal with, sometimes being refractory to ceremonial treatment and requiring special techniques such as the sucking cure (see Haile, 1950). The witch, therefore, is hated and feared.

THE CEREMONIAL SYSTEM

THE MEANS for bringing dangerous elements under control, exorcising ghosts, restoring harmony, curing disease, and rendering the patient immune to further contamination from the same supernatural influences are the knowledge and correct performance of orderly procedures; that is, control by ritual. In a ceremonial, the Holy People, the supernatural beings invoked, are the judges of the completeness and correctness of the ritual, and if satisfied they are compelled by the ethic of reciprocity to restore universal harmony and thus cure the patient. Hence, prayers and offerings in Navajo ceremonials are invocatory and compulsive, to attract and obligate the holy ones, not to glorify or thank them.

Navajo ceremonials are conducted by trained specialists, called "singers," because the singing which accompanies every important act in the ritual is held to be the one essential element of the ceremonial. The singers learn by apprenticeship, ratifying their knowledge by payment to the teacher. A singer specializes in one or two [or at most half a dozen] complete chants, because each one is a vast complex of songs, prayers, ritual acts, plant medicines, material properties, and symbols. The chants have two-night, five-night, and some even nine-night forms. The singer is paid according to the elaborateness of the ceremonial, and by reciprocity he is compelled to perform if he accepts the fee. Conversely, it is the payment which insures the efficacy of the performance. The cost of a ceremonial may vary from the equivalent of twenty-five dollars for a two-night performance to several thousand dollars for a nine-night chant when hundreds of spectators must be hospitably fed by the sponsors — the patient and his kinsmen. Navajo singers do not belong to organized priesthoods, and they have no religious societies like their neighbors, the Pueblo Indians, and no religious calendar, but they carry out the ceremonials whenever they are needed. In fact, there is no sense of membership in anything like a church. One merely uses the ceremonials or one does not.

A singer is summoned by an intermediary, usually a kinsman of the patient, after the family has held a conference and decided upon the etiological factors causing the patient's illness — bad dreams, fear of the consequences of violated taboos, or other indication that he requires ritual aid. If it cannot determine which ceremonial is needed, the family may employ a diagnostician, a specialist in divination [usually not a singer] who interprets involuntary motions made by his hand while he is in a trancelike state [hand-trembling]. Sometimes, but not commonly, the older techniques of star gazing or listening, interpreting things seen or heard, are used. Unless there is urgency, the singer usually comes to the family's home [which has been emptied and swept for the chant] within four days. Only the traditional, roughly circular house [hogan][7] may be used. Square houses such as our own, which are becoming more and more common, will not suffice for the ceremony. The Navajos have never built towns like those of the Pueblos, but live in little family groups, often scattered far apart over the semidesert terrain.

---

[7] The word 'hogan' is an anglicization of the Navajo word for their house, a roughly circular or hexagonal structure of logs or stone, chinked with mud, with a central opening in the log roof for a smokehole. The doorway faces east. The family hogan is usually emptied and swept for a ceremonial, but sometimes when large sand-paintings are to be made or many visitors are expected, as in the great nine-night winter chants, Nightway and Mountainway, a special large hogan is built for the occasion.

The Navajo ceremonial system consists of two types of ceremonials, the chantways, performances in which the songs are accompanied by a rattle, and those in which a rattle is not used, which we call rites for lack of a single Navajo equivalent term for them. Among the latter are two song ceremonial complexes of great importance, the Blessingway rites and the Enemyway rite. Blessingway, regarded by the Navajo as the backbone of their religion and given historical precedence over all other ceremonials by them, controls all the chantways and provides a unifying force in Navajo culture. Comparatively short and simple, lasting only two nights, the Blessingway rites consist of songs, prayers, a ceremonial bath, and, sometimes, drypaintings. They are performed to maintain harmony, to avert misfortune, for good luck, to invoke blessings upon all of man's possessions and activities. A person who is sung over represents the group to be benefited. The Blessingway rites are used for the installation of tribal officers, for the departing or returning soldier, for the neophyte who is singing for the first time, for blessing a new house, for consecrating ceremonial paraphernalia, and to aid childbirth. The girl's adolescence rite and the wedding ceremony are Blessingway rites, and so was the obsolete rain ceremony. Every chant includes at least one Blessingway song to adjust possible mistakes and errors which might otherwise render the ceremonial ineffectual or even cause illness.

The Enemyway rite [sometimes included with the Evilway chants] is used to exorcise the ghosts of aliens [non-Navajos], and it makes much of war and violence. In fact, it belongs in the native category of ceremonials which may be translated Evilway, and in Navajo theory it should have nothing to do with Blessingway, which emphasizes peace and harmony, excluding all evil. Such rites are discussed in detail and three versions of the myth of Blessingway are presented in a publication by Wyman (1970a). It is possible that the understandably obsolescent hunting [Gameway], salt-gathering, and war rites drew upon Blessingway and Enemyway for their songs.

The Navajo think of certain ceremonials as "going together" or as "partner chants." They make such associations because of interrelations in the origin legends of the chants, efficacy against common etiological factors, procedures peculiar to the group, and so on. Although all Navajos in all regions do not group these ceremonials in precisely same way, the uniformity among the groupings and subgroupings of chants is striking enough to enable us to derive a classification from the remarks of informants (see Wyman and Kluckhohn, 1938).

Each of the chants used to cure illness is concerned with particular etiological factors that are thought to cause the disease or diseases for which the chant is believed to be efficacious. For instance, Red Antway, a chant in the Holyway group (see below) deals with ants, especially red ants, as etiological factors and is used for genitourinary troubles, skin diseases, and other ills. The Windways are employed for sicknesses thought to have been caused by winds, snakes, lightning, or cactus. The relationships of the various chants to particular etiological factors and diseases have been described in numerous publications.

Most of the chantways are dominated by a ritual or pattern of behavior governing procedure that is concerned with restoration and the attraction of good, a ritual which may be translated as Holyway. A few of them may also be performed according to Evilway [or Ghostway] ritual, characterized by acts designed to exorcise native ghosts and thus cure sickness caused by them, and, hopefully, to combat the effects of witchcraft. Such activities include big hoop and cincture or garment ceremonies, overshooting, blackening the patient, and lightning-herb, ashblowing, and brushing procedures (see Wyman, 1973, pp. 31–42, 58–62). A few may also be conducted according to Lifeway ritual, specialized for curing injuries resulting from accidents. A distinctive feature of Lifeway ritual is painting the patient red, the color of flesh and blood, symbolizing return to life and health. In addition there is a fundamental Evilway chant called Upward-reachingway and a fundamental Lifeway chant called Flintway (see Wyman and Kluckhohn, 1938). Formerly there were about twenty-three Holyway chantway systems, all for curing illnesses, to which — by elaboration according to male and female branches, ritual, and other considerations — about forty names for song ceremonials could be ascribed. Ten or eleven of these chantways are now extinct or obsolescent, and four or five are uncommon, leaving only eight that are well known and frequently performed.

Each chantway has special relations with certain groups of supernatural beings, although there is considerable overlapping. The organization of the Navajo pantheon presents perplexing problems. There is no evidence of a well-ordered hierarchy, although Reichard (1970) suggested that a sun cult is outstanding. Factors that complicate the picture are the equivalence of beings appearing under different names or as various actors in the myths, the multiplication of deities in time and space, duplication of functions among different deities, and, perhaps most important, the immanence of supernatural power. Animals, plants, mountains, and many natural phenomena are endowed with power. Even the seemingly most insignificant of these are indispensable; all are interdependent, being complementary parts of the whole. Animals and plants are conceived as capable of assuming human form at will, mountains have anthropomorphic inner forms, and even material objects such as arrows may be "people" (see Wyman, 1970a).

Among the Holy People [powerful and dangerous, not virtuously holy], Changing Woman is surely the most beloved. Her twin children, Monster Slayer and Born for Water, sired by the Sun, represent war power. First Man, First Woman, First Boy, and First Girl and their companions, Coyote, the exponent of irresponsibility, and Be'gochidi were prominent in early events on the earth just after the Emergence from the underworlds. Members of a group of Holy People led by Talking God and known as the Ye'i are impersonated by masked dancers in public performances of some ceremonials. The list of Holy People representing the powers in the world — Bear, Big Snake, Cactus People, Ant People, Thunders, Winds, and a host of others — is endless. Nearly every element in the universe may be thus personalized, and even the least of these personalizations, such as Big Fly and Cornbeetle Girl [tiny helpers and mentors], are as necessary for the harmonious scheme of things as is the great Sun.

The Navajo ceremonial system is sanctioned and explained in a large body of oral "literature" transmitted from generation to generation around family firesides (see Spencer, 1957; Wyman, 1962, pp. 29–58). This mythology consists of two major parts — the general Origin Myth, which includes the story of the Emergence from the underworlds (see Wyman, 1973, pp. 74–93), and the Origin Legends of the separate ceremonials that branch off from the Origin Myth at various points. These legends tell how the chant started and how it should be carried out. There are as many of these ceremonial myths as there are ceremonials and branches thereof, but they are not entirely independent. Besides the unique mythic motifs specific to given ceremonials, there are rather complex episodes [major motifs] that appear in the myths of two or more ceremonials, a host of simple incidents [minor motifs] that are common to many chantways, and some universal elements that are present in all or virtually all myths. Thus the Navajo's mythology, like their pantheon and, indeed, their universe, is a unit composed of interlocking parts, filled with vivid word imagery, fine ritual poetry, keen humor, and great imaginative power. The myth of Blessingway is one that is most intimately associated with the Origin Myth, being mostly concerned with the Post-Emergence Events and giving the origin of many elements of Navajo culture (see Wyman, 1970a). It is felt that a singer should know the myths pertaining to his specialty ceremonials, and that when relating one he should begin with the Origin Myth and tell it up to where the chant myth branches from it. Such knowledge is not, however, an indispensable part of a singer's equipment, although the best singers do learn the myths.

THE HOLYWAY CHANTS

HOLYWAY CHANTS may be categorized in seven subgroups: the Shooting Chant, Mountain Chant, God-Impersonators, Wind Chant, Hand-Tremblingway, and Eagle Trapping subgroups, and a grouping of three extinct ceremonials of uncertain affiliation. The Mountain Chant subgroup, one of the largest, contains the Mountainways, Beautyway, and the obsolescent or extinct Excessway and the related Mothway. The God-Impersonators subgroup includes the well-known Nightways, the related Big Godway, Plumeway, the obsolescent Coyoteway, and the extinct Dogway and Ravenway. The Wind Chant subgroup is made up of Navajo Windway and Chiricahua Windway. Hand-Tremblingway stands alone. The Eagle Trapping subgroup contains the uncommon or obsolescent Eagleway and Beadway.

The Shooting Chant subgroup contains the Shootingways, the less commonly performed Red Antway, Big Starway [performed today according to Evilway ritual], and the recently extinct Hailway and Waterway.

Red Antway is concerned with diseases coming from ants, horned toads, and, secondarily, from lightning and bears; such diseases are primarily of a genitourinary nature, although other conditions – such as gastrointestinal distress, skin diseases, sore throat, or rheumatism – may be treated by the chant (see Wyman, 1973, pp. 25–27). Big Starway, although probably concerned with heavenly bodies originally, being an Evilway chant, today is used to treat almost any illness supposed to be caused by the Ghosts of Navajos or by witches (see Wheelwright, 1956, pp. 106–110). The extinct Hailway and Waterway were used to treat injuries caused by frost or water.

The Windways may belong in the Shooting Chant subgroup instead of comprising a separate one, as there are numerous conformities among the major mythic motifs of the origin legends of the two subgroups (see Wyman, 1962, p. 46, table 2, pp. 48, 66). Moreover, among the etiological factors against which Navajo Windway is directed are snakes and sometimes lightning [Thunder], with which snakes [and arrows] are conceptually equated, and such factors are the main concern of Shootingway (see Wyman, 1962, pp. 20–21). Another ceremonial which seems to be closely related to Shootingway, again on the basis of the origin myths, is Flintway, the fundamental Lifeway chant, which Kluckhohn (1960, p. 69) did assign to the Shooting Chant subgroup (see also Wyman, 1962, p. 51). It may be significant that Shootingway frequently is performed according to Lifeway ritual.

A curing chant is made up of procedures that invoke and attract supernatural beings who can correct the harm done by them or by their earthly cognates, and other procedures that exorcise evil. Some of these ceremonies are more or less fixed, while others may be inserted, or omitted, or modified according to circumstances. Moreover, any of them may be modified internally according to the specific symbolism of the chant being given.

A typical Holyway chant consists of about twelve such ceremonies. It begins at sundown when the singer consecrates the hogan by placing cornmeal and sprigs of hard oak on or above the roof beams in the cardinal directions. Following this, and on each of the three succeeding evenings in a four-night or nine-night chant, there may be an unraveling ceremony, in which a certain number of bundles of herbs and feathers tied together with a wool string are applied to various parts of the patient's body and the string is pulled free, symbolizing release from harm. Then there is a short singing ceremony, sometimes accompanied by basket drumming [beating an inverted basket], that goes on for an hour or so.

The most spectacular feature of a Holyway chant is the sandpainting ceremony. It is performed once in a two-night ceremonial and four times — on successive days, and each time with a painting of a different design — in a five-night or nine-night chant. If the chant is to include this feature, a setting-out ceremony is performed just before dawn on the first morning. Bundle-prayersticks [wooden sticks decorated with painted symbols and feathers] are vertically inserted in a mound of earth in front of the door to the hogan to notify human and supernatural beings that a sandpainting is to be made. A fire is kindled with a firedrill, and coals from it are used to rekindle the fire throughout the chant. Then, just after dawn on each of the first four mornings a sweat and emetic ceremony drives away evil by internal and external purification. During that ceremony small sandpaintings, often of snakes, may be made at the cardinal points around the central fireplace, and another small sandpainting made northwest of the fire, on which the patient's basket of emetic is placed. Ritually prepared wooden pokers are laid beside the sandpaintings around the fire. Sweating, vomiting, and bathing in the warm herbal decoction [emetic] purify the patient and others who may wish to participate. After breakfast, invocatory offerings of "jewels" [bits of turquoise, etc.], painted reeds stuffed with tobacco ["cigarettes"], and/or painted wooden prayersticks are prepared to attract the Holy People. The patient holds these while repeating a long litany after the singer. Finally, a helper deposits the offerings in specified places away from the hogan.

In the forenoon of the last day a bath ceremony purifies the patient still further. Following this, or after the offering ceremonies on the other days, the sandpainting within the hogan is begun. When the picture has been completed, usually in the late forenoon or early afternoon, the bundle-prayersticks are brought in from the set-out mound and placed in upright position around the painting. Cornmeal then is sprinkled on the sandpainting by singer and patient.

On the last day only, the patient's body is painted from head to foot with symbolic designs by means of mineral pigments [figure painting], and in his hair are tied a feather plume and a shell or turquoise bead [token tying]. The bead becomes the patient's property, a mark of recognition for the Holy People and a protection from further danger. The patient then sits on some figure in the sandpainting; and the singer, after moistening his palms in herb medicine, applies sand from various parts of the painted figure's bodies to corresponding parts of the patient's body. Then he similarly applies the bundle-prayersticks and parts of his own body to the patient. Finally, the patient leaves the hogan; the sandpainting is erased; and the sand is carried outside and deposited to the north of the hogan.

The procedures in the ritual identify the patient with the Holy People represented in the painting who have been attracted to the scene to look at their painted likenesses. The patient absorbs their powers from the sands applied to him, exchanging evil for good, and becomes strong like them and immune to further harm. Indeed, for a time he is a Holy Person himself. That is why he must observe four days of ceremonial restrictions afterwards, lest he harm others through his acquired power.

There is an all-night singing on the final night, and at dawn the patient faces the east outside the hogan and "breathes in the dawn" four times. The ceremonial ends with a final prayer and a Blessingway song to avert the consequences of errors of omission or commission.

Optional ceremonies such as the ritual consumption of cornmeal mush or a meat decoction, or the performance of a shock rite (see Wyman, 1973, pp. 56–58), may be added at extra expense if requested by the patient. Public performances by teams of masked dancers impersonating the Holy People or other exhibitions — like a sacred vaudeville show [Dark Circle of Branches, "Corral Dance" or "Fire Dance"] — may occupy the final night of nine-night performances of some chants, such as Nightway and Mountainway.

Nearly every act throughout a ceremonial is accompanied by singing. The singer leads, shaking a rattle, while all who can join in. Most chants require knowledge of several hundred songs. Prayers are said at intervals; herbal medicines are prepared and administered to the patient; a bullroarer is whirled to imitate thunder; the singer's equipment is laid out on a calico spread and objects from it are applied to the patient; and expendable materials and objects are deposited somewhere outside the hogan where they can do no harm. Some ceremonies, such as the consecration of the hogan, the bath, figure painting, token tying, all-night singing, and the dawn procedures occur only once in any chant. Others are repeated four times in five-night or nine-night performances but are given only once in a two-night chant — except for the sweat-emetic ceremony, which must be performed four times, if at all. In a nine-night chant the short singing, setting-out, and sandpainting ceremonies are moved ahead, to the fifth to eighth days.

Branch, Phase, and Ritual
of Mountainway

MOUNTAIN-TOP-WAY [literally, Mountain-on-side], more conveniently called Mountainway, is one of a group of Navajo song ceremonials which Wyman and Kluckhohn called the Mountain Chant subgroup.[8] Besides the Mountainways this subgroup contains their sister chant, Beautyway, and the extinct Excessways [Prostitutionway] and Mothway. The interrelations of these chantways were discussed in the volume on Beautyway so such considerations need not be repeated here (Wyman, 1957, pp. 29–34). Various informants and authors have held that there are at least three branches of Mountainway, the Male, the Female, and the Cub branch.[9] Male and female branches of a ceremonial are not distinguished according to the sex of the patient being treated for either one may be sung over a man or a woman. Father Berard thought that the distinction depends upon the sex of the "author" of the chant, that is the protagonist of the myth. Since Matthews' myth has a hero while that of Yucca Patch Man has a heroine, he assumed that the former is the legend of Male Mountainway for the latter is, according to the informant, the myth of the female branch. Father Berard suggested, however, that the Old Woman's branch, listed by Wyman and Kluckhohn, and the Cub branch are references to the female bear and the cubs as etiological factors and not actually branches of Female Mountainway. This is also in line with the opinion of the

---

[8] Wyman and Kluckhohn, 1938, p. 5. As Reichard said (1970, p. 11), "the Mountain Chant is named for the dwelling place of the many spirits the chant invokes, summarized by Bear, Snake, and Porcupine."

[9] Coolidge and Coolidge, 1930, pp. 148, 202; Haile, 1946, introduction; 1950, p. 242. The Mountain-Shootingways listed as branches by Wyman and Kluckhohn (1938, p. 5) are not separate ceremonials but are phases of Shootingway, names for that chant when it includes a Dark Circle of Branches (Corral Dance, Fire Dance) performance on the final night of a nine-night ceremonial (see Wyman, 1970b, p. 25). The "Way to Remove Somebody's Paralysis," or "one's return-glide-way," is merely a prayer to restore a person suffering from a temporary loss of mind (Haile, 1938b, p. 645).

Coolidges who asserted that the Male, Female, and Cub branches are used to treat diseases coming from killing, dreaming of, or coming in contact with the influence of male, female, and cub bears respectively. Today the male branch seems to be performed less frequently than the female branch.

Although Father Berard in several contexts mentioned only one Cub branch, in his monograph on Sacrificial Figurines, he spoke of an informant [Salt Water Man of Lukachukai, Arizona, 1934] who referred to male and female Cub branches of Mountainway.[10] Father Berard, however, expressed some doubt as to whether Cub-way should be accepted as a distinct chantway at all. He suggested that it might be merely a subbranch of Female Mountainway or, perhaps, only an etiological reference (see above). In the myth manuscript in the Museum of Navaho Ceremonial Art in Santa Fe, New Mexico, recorded by Margot Astrov, it is said that Cub-way branches off where the Bear came and took away the baby born to him and the heroine, implying it is a branch ceremonial.

Father Berard also listed a fourth branch, the Jicarilla Apache branch, which the Navajo borrowed from their Apache cousins, but he said, "how much of this the Navahos have adopted is a matter for conjecture as I have no Navaho account of this Mountainway branch." It is possible that designating such a branch was a matter of confusion with the Jicarilla Holiness Rite from which Navajo Mountainway and Beautyway may have been derived (see pp. 29–30).

Perhaps the fact best known to outsiders about Mountainway is that a nine-night performance may include the Dark Circle of Branches phase [Fire Dance, Corral Dance] (see pp. 25–29 below). This is the performance which has been likened to a great sacred vaudeville show and which attracts non-Navajo spectators as well as hordes of Navajos. The nine-night form of Mountainway [and of Nightway as well] may not be performed before the first killing frost in the fall nor after the first thunderstorm in the spring, that is it may be given only when rattlesnakes and bears are hibernating and there is no danger from lightning. Seven of Kluckhohn and Wyman's informants insisted that no nine-night chant may be held in the summer, and that only a five-night Mountainway may be given in the frostless months (1940, p. 187). Kluckhohn and Leighton stated that in practice Nightway and Mountainway are virtually

---

[10] Haile, 1938b, pp. 641, 643, 645; 1946, introduction; 1947a, p. 48; 1950, p. 242. See also Wyman and Kluckhohn, 1938, p. 5.

limited to November and December, following the season of harvest and lamb sales. Thus, they "follow periods of intensive economic activity when cash and credit are readiest; they offer change and emotional release before settling back into the humdrum of ordinary existence" (1962, p. 228). According to Father Berard's notes a five-night Mountainway ceremonial may be devoted to the Chant with Prayersticks phase (see p. 55), and of course most any performance of Mountainway is a Chant with Sandpaintings.

From all accounts, Mountainway is performed only according to Holyway ritual, that is, its ceremonials are dominated by a pattern of behavior, theoretically directed by the Holy People, which concerns itself with the attraction of good and restoration of the patient. There is no evidence that it is or ever has been performed according to Evilway [Ghostway] ritual, that is, governed by procedures suitable for exorcising native ghosts in order to cure diseases caused by them, or for counteracting the effects of witchcraft. Reichard includes the Mountain Chant in her category of "Evil (emphasis on exorcism)" in the "classification of ceremonies" in her book on Navajo religion (1970, p. 323), but later in the same book she says, "The Night Chant, some of the Wind chants, and, possibly, the Mountain Chant, all of which have numerous subdivisions, belong to the category 'good'" (p. 328). Hence her final conclusion agrees with the facts as known today.

We know that Mountainway may be performed according to Injuryway [Angryway, Fightingway, Weaponway] subritual because the actual ceremonial described in the manuscript by Astrov in the Museum of Navaho Ceremonial Art (see footnote 15 below) was a chant governed by this subritual. This method of procedure is employed when the patient has been subjected to direct attack by the etiological factors involved — struck by lightning, bitten by a snake, mauled by a bear. Its purpose is to remove the weapon or the injury. Ceremonials governed by this subritual are called red-inside because the red portions of the rainbow-bars, or other red and blue elements, in sandpaintings and on prayersticks, are placed toward the figures in the painting or toward the body of the stick instead of in their normal outside positions. Since this subritual is used infrequently, we may assume that the majority of Mountain Chants are governed by Peacefulway subritual, for any Holyway ceremonial is to be regarded as Peacefulway unless the contrary is stated. This name implies that the patient is no longer at odds with the Holy People and that peaceful conditions have been restored, rendering him immune to further attack.

The Uses of Mountainway

*A case in the neighborhood comes to mind, in which a woman
complained of pains in her shoulder caused by carrying a sack of
pinyon nuts, which she had gathered inside of a brush corral. She
figured that these pains were sufficient evidence of . . . "bear does-
it-way," in other words that a bear was causing her shoulder trouble.
She called upon a singer of . . . the "female branch of Mountain-
Top-way," to hold a ceremonial of this chantway for her benefit.
The choice of this chantway, in this instance, was probably
prompted by the well known unconcern of the she-bear with cubs
about seeking the most convenient feeding grounds. The woman,
however, had no business doing likewise. The pains in her shoulder
reminded her of this!*

Father Berard Haile[11]

AS HAS BEEN POINTED OUT many times before, Navajo curing ceremonials are directed toward appeasing or exorcising the etiological
factors supposed to have caused the patient's troubles rather than
toward the physical symptoms of the illness itself. The etiological
factors with which Mountainway is designed to deal are animals
which live in the mountains. There are many of these, in fact animals are mentioned as factors perhaps more commonly in connection
with Mountainway than with any other chantway. First and fore-
most is the bear; indeed the ceremonial may be considered primarily
as a cure for bear disease. Other mountain creatures which are mentioned frequently in myths, songs, and prayers are porcupines,
weasels, squirrels and chipmunks of various species, badgers,
skunks of at least two species, and wild turkeys. Other beasts which

---

[11] Haile, 1938b, p. 644.

may be factors but which appear less often are mountain sheep, marmots, coyotes, frogs, toads, snakes, ants, and owls. The kinds of prayersticks cut for various supernatural beings and the invocations addressed to them give us lists of possible etiological factors. These are discussed later in the section on prayersticks. Besides the creatures mentioned above we find in these lists natural phenomena such as Thunder [lightning], Sun and Moon, and winds; mythological beings including Big Snake, Changing Bear Maiden, Snapping Vagina, Holy Woman, and Holy Young Man and Woman; and participants in the chant itself, the Meal Sprinklers and the Young Spruce, Re-whitening, and First Dancers. In his work on sacrificial figurines (Haile, 1947a, pp. 81–86) Father Berard included the Song Strung on a Line, taken from the Female Cub Branch of Mountainway, which is especially employed for children when the cause of sickness is not known. It has forty-two stanzas, each invoking a different being. Father Berard said, "Because the song mentions so many possible sources of illness, one is reasonably assured of finding the true source through this song." Besides the animals and birds specified above, the song names dog, gopher, wolf, mountain lion, blue fox, field rat, beaver, otter, jack rabbit, rattler, eagles and buzzards, crow, magpie, four kinds of hawks, three kinds of owls, and six kinds of small birds.

The primary etiological factor against which the power of Mountainway is directed is the bear. Bear sickness may be contracted through a great variety of injuries or insults to this animal. Of course hunting and killing it, skinning it or handling its hide, and eating its flesh, are the most serious misdemeanors inflicted on it and the effects of such behavior are most dramatic. Today, however, such contacts would be most unlikely. Bears are carefully avoided, although if one should attack a man he would be permitted to kill it in self-defense. Hill said in 1938, "There are few Navaho alive today who have participated in a bear hunt. Those that have are extremely reticent in recounting the details even to their own relatives."[12] In times past, however, the ritual hunting of bears was practiced in order to obtain their paws to make medicine bags for the Mountain Chant, their claws to attach to pouches made from

---

[12] In his monograph on agricultural and hunting methods of the Navajo, Hill presented a thorough discussion of bear hunting (1938, pp. 157–161) and some comparative notes on bear lore in other tribes (p. 187). Opler brought together many references to beliefs about bears among the Navajo and other Southwestern tribes in his comparison of them with Jicarilla Apache beliefs and practices (1943, pp. 61–78). See also Haile, 1947a, pp. 59–63, and Reichard, 1970, pp. 384–385.

buffalo or buckskin in the shape of a bear's paw, or to other Mountainway equipment, or their gall for one of the ingredients of a medicine for dizziness, fever, and fainting ascribed to witchcraft. Merely seeing a bear die or seeing its blood is very dangerous, especially so for a pregnant woman or her husband, for the Navajo believe that prenatal influences may affect the child later in life. This theory also applies to any of the various kinds of contact referred to below.

Although killing a bear is a remote possibility for a Navajo today, there are plenty of other kinds of contacts which are dangerous. Many of these might come about quite inadvertently but they are none the less harmful. In summer a bear often rests in the shade of a tree, and sleeping in or merely walking over such a resting place invites bear infection. Stepping on a bear's bones; handling or walking or sitting on a stone which a bear has turned over in search of ants; getting ants on one's person that a bear has rolled over or slept on; using dried branches for fuel that a bear has broken off; using wood for any purpose from a tree against which a bear has rubbed himself, especially for making a baby's cradle; drinking at a bear's watering place; and stepping on bear tracks or simply crossing his path—all these acts may lead to bear disease. Even the breath of a bear coming from a distance may affect the heart or make one weak. One is not supposed to talk about hunting bears. Dreams about bears, good or bad, may require ceremonial intervention.

If one has been directly injured by a bear, or has wrestled with a bear, a Mountain Chant performed according to Injuryway [Angryway, red-inside] subritual is called for.[13] The shock rite which occurs in Mountainway, and in ceremonials of other chantways as well, renders the patient immune to harm caused by bears because in it he is frightened into swooning [in theory at least] by an impersonator of a bear.

Like most chants, Mountainway on occasion may be recommended for almost any sickness if it has been traced to one of the chant's etiological factors. Bear disease, however, seems to be firmly associated with two groups of illnesses, arthritis and mental disturbances. Throughout the myths there are constant references to the hero's or heroine's sore, aching, swollen limbs. As the hero of Matthews' myth fled from the Utes and as the heroine of Yucca

---

[13] Ceremonials governed by Injuryway subritual are called red-inside because the red portions of the rainbow-bars, or other red and blue elements, in sandpaintings and on prayersticks are placed toward the figures in the painting or toward the body of the stick instead of in their normal outside positions.

Patch Man's story tried to escape from the relentless Bear Man, their feet, ankles, knees, and wrists became so sore and swollen that they could barely drag themselves along. They could not sleep because of the pain. Thus, Mountainway is recommended for rheumatism, swollen extremities, or arthritic pains. The only mythic passages which seem to refer to the cure of mental disease by Mountainway are in Matthews' myth and in the story dictated by Lefthanded. In the first we find: "But to him the odors of the lodge were now intolerable and he soon left the house and sat outside" (Matthews, 1887, p. 410), and, "The ceremony cured Dsilyi¹ Neyáni of all his strange feelings and notions. The lodge of his people no longer smelled unpleasant to him" (ibid., p. 417). Lefthanded said of his hero, "Now the Boy was absolutely cured of all evil, and his old evil dreams; he had new thoughts in a new body" (Wheelwright, 1951, p. 16). Nevertheless, the Mountain Chant is a preferred treatment for such manifestations of bear disease as mental uneasiness and nervousness, fainting, temporary loss of mind, delirium, violent irrationality, or insanity.

Another member of the mythological bear family, Changing Bear Maiden, may be held responsible for mental disturbances. In a study of prayersticks of Female Mountainway by Father Berard Haile, which is presented later, he describes an excerpt ceremony in which a figurine of the Bear Maiden is offered and prayersticks are cut for her "when persons lose their mind or become insane. Rattling of the teeth, or gnashing them, which may be done by indisposed persons, is ascribed to Changing Bear Maiden. A person eating bear meat and taking sick and vomiting thereafter, or if a person gets sores on this account on his legs, are indications of Changing Bear Maiden's influence."

Another brief excerpt ceremony also in the figurine complex, which is in the purview of Male Mountainway and which invokes another mythological being who may be identified with the bear, has been described in detail by Father Berard (Haile, 1947a, pp. 47–57). This rite called Straightener involves figurine and prayerstick offerings to a mythological personage known as Snapping Vagina, a female monster in the form of a beautiful woman who mutilated the genitals of men who had intercourse with her. Brief myths about her and a discussion of the etymology of the name of the ceremony may be found in Haile, 1947a (p. 100) and O'Bryan, 1956 (pp. 96–97). The Straightener ceremony is a treatment for venereal diseases, itching in the crotch region, other genitourinary troubles and disturbing sexual dreams.

Although there is no direct injunction against killing a porcupine and eating the meat, it is considered somewhat dangerous to do so, and abuse of the animal such as burning it, or the sight of a dead one may lead to porcupine disease. The chief symptoms of this ailment are stomach trouble, constipation, gall bladder trouble, internal pains, and the like, or kidney and bladder disturbances, such as anuria. Mental illness has also been mentioned by informants, especially when the influence from seeing a dead animal has been prenatal.

Weasels may be killed for their skins to be used in ceremonial paraphernalia, but this should not be done by either parent of an unborn child for fear of prenatal infection. Yucca Patch Man remarked in telling his myth that, "This disease is very dangerous and affects a person in this manner . . . it dries up a person in disease."

"It is permitted to eat pine squirrels, but again killing them for their hides or eating their flesh may cause sickness. When children frequently scratch their nose, a parent infers that some wanton act has been done to the chipmunk. Usually this is traced to killing or eating them during the period of pregnancy. Like the chipmunk the ground squirrel also makes its influence felt by a pricking sensation in the nose" (Haile, 1947a, pp. 65, 66, 70). Yucca Patch Man in discussing the cutting of prayersticks for squirrels in his myth said, "This is a terrible condition, when coughing is a disease at large."

Itching of the nose or other parts of the body, pimples, and skin diseases may be attributed to seeing a turkey killed or to eating its meat, especially when one's wife is pregnant. Deafness and eye troubles may be ascribed to the mountain sheep. Pricking of the skin or dreaming of being covered with ants might call for the cutting of their prayersticks, although holding a Red Antway ceremonial would be a more likely solution for such problems.

Impersonators of the Meal Sprinklers, the dancers of the Young Spruce Group, or the impersonator of a bear, all of whom perform in the Dark Circle of Branches, will become ill if they cut or injure young spruce or pinyon trees (Haile, 1947a, p. 63). Moreover, if one has disturbing dreams about the Meal Sprinklers, or the Rewhitening or First Dancers, or if a child has marks on its body resembling their body decorations or makes noises like their cries leading to suspicion of prenatal influence from them, their prayersticks should be cut in a Mountainway ceremonial (Yucca Patch Man).

Ceremonial Procedure
in Mountainway

MATTHEWS, IN HIS DEFINITIVE PUBLICATION on the chant (1887), presented a detailed description of the ceremonial procedure in an actual performance of Mountainway which he witnessed (MMC).[14] Moreover, there is a fairly extensive mythic account in Yucca Patch Man's legend given below in this volume (YPM), and there is a long description presumably of an actual performance of the chant conducted according to Injuryway [Angryway] subritual in a manuscript by Margot Astrov in the Museum of Navaho Ceremonial Art in Santa Fe, New Mexico (HS).[15] Besides these accounts of the entire ceremonial there are several published writings devoted solely or almost entirely to the procedure of the final night, the Corral or Fire Dance. One is an eyewitness account by Reagan (1934); another is the little volume, *The Navaho Fire Dance*, by Father Berard Haile (1946), which is a compilation of materials drawn chiefly from Matthews' monograph and Yucca Patch Man's myth; and finally there are briefer narratives in the book by the Coolidges (1930; CCM) and in a short myth published by O'Bryan (1956, pp. 121–126; OBS). There is also some cursory mention of ritual conduct in a manuscript of a myth by an unknown author which is among Father Berard's papers in the Library of the Univer-

---

[14] The capital initial designations for the published or manuscript sources used for convenience here are the same as those employed in the discussion of the mythology of Mountainway. (See list on p. 123.)

[15] This chant conducted by "Old Man Gordy," with Joe Arnold acting as interpreter for the recorder, was performed "at a remote place between Sawmill and Deerspring, Arizona," during the first half of December in 1946. It is interesting to compare the accounts of Mountainway chants with the extensive and detailed mythic description of a nine-night performance of Hailway, including a Dark Circle of Branches or Corral Dance, which was dictated by Lefthanded of Newcomb, New Mexico, in 1938, and published by Reichard in 1944.

sity of Arizona in Tucson (HM). There is no need, therefore, to do more here than give a brief summary of the ceremonial procedure in Mountainway.

The first eight days, or nights using the Navajo method of reckoning time from sundown to sundown, of a nine-night chant are taken up with the usual order of ceremonies which has been amply described in various publications.[16] Ceremonies are quasi-independent organizations of acts and procedures within the ceremonial, set off by pauses in activity following and preceding them. These are consecration of the hogan at the beginning of the first night; unraveling and short singing on the first four evenings [only one described on the fourth night in YPM]; two garment ceremonies on the second and third nights (YPM, HS), in which yucca cinctures and/or long garlands of bundles of Douglas fir or other evergreens, and/or various plants tied to long yucca thongs or otherwise put together, are wrapped or otherwise placed around the patient and cut to pieces with flints and removed by impersonators of the Slayer Twins, Monster Slayer and Born-for-Water;[17] sweat and emetic ceremonies on the first four mornings, and offering and sometimes figurine ceremonies in the forenoon. Prayerstick offerings and figurines will be discussed at greater length below. On the fifth (YPM, HM, CCM) or sixth (MMC, HS) night a shock rite may be performed, sometimes in connection with the first sandpainting, the *Home of Bear and Snake,* or with a special painting such as *Bear's Den* (see the descriptions of these paintings below for more details concerning this ceremony; pp. 69, 102). On one of these days also, a necessary preliminary to the Dark Circle of Branches is performed, the selection, dressing, and dispatching of the Meal Sprinklers or couriers who invite distant guests to the ceremonies of the final night (see Link, 1968, p. 53, for a picture of these performers). This episode is treated at length in the myths and the Meal Sprinklers' likeness may be seen in the depiction of Mountain Gods in the

[16] Kluckhohn and Wyman, 1940, pp. 76–107, Table 1; Wyman, 1973, Table 2, p. 43; 1970b, pp. 4–6 (adapted and reprinted in the Introduction to the present volume).

[17] More detailed descriptions and discussions of garment ceremonies may be found in Kluckhohn and Wyman, 1940, pp. 102–103; Wyman and Bailey, 1943, pp. 19–26; Reichard, 1970, pp. 661–666. These ceremonies, like the unraveling ceremony, symbolize release from evil and danger. "Made of knots, the garment represents tied-in power; cutting the knots signifies freeing the patient and destroying the evil" (Reichard, 1970, p. 544). "Matthews was correct in his assumption that the garment represents the bonds of disease and the cutting freedom from these bonds" (ibid., p. 665).

sandpaintings (see pp. 76, 91, 92). On the fifth, sixth, seventh, and eighth mornings, a setting-out ceremony advertises the sandpainting ceremonies to follow. On the eighth day the usual bath and body painting ceremonies occur, and the rest of the day is spent in preparing properties to be used in the acts to be performed in the Dark Circle of Branches of the final night and in assembling the materials with which to build the corral.

In two of the myths (YPM, HS) a special type of sudatory, the trench sweat or firing pit sudorific like that employed in Nightway, is described (see p. 142 for further details).

Sometimes a nine-night performance of Mountainway may be split into two five-night ceremonials and performed at different times. The ceremonial witnessed by Matthews at Hard Earth, New Mexico, in 1884, had been split in this way. He said, "The first four days' ceremonies in this case had been performed during the previous year. Such a division of the work is sometimes made, if more convenient for the patient and his friends, but usually all is done in nine consecutive days" (1887, p. 418).[18] Condensation of

---

[18] Opler, in noting that the Jicarilla Holiness Rite closely follows the pattern of the last five days of the nine-night Mountain Chant but shares almost none of the ceremonies of the first four days, suggests that the ritual pattern of the first four days of a nine-night Navajo ceremonial may be a later or a separate development which has been prefixed to a ceremonial pattern centering around the drypainting ceremonies (1943, pp. 94–95). It could also be argued that since two of the three principal ceremonies of the first four days, unraveling and the sweat-emetic, have an exorcistic flavor, while only one, the offering ceremony, is invocatory, and since all of the main ceremonies of the last days are invocatory, the first part was, therefore, derived from the fundamental Evilway ceremonials, which may be older, and the second part was attached to this already existing, simpler, and perhaps more primitive pattern of ritual behavior. Condensed, the whole forms the familiar and commonly performed five-night ceremonial. Miss Wheelwright noted that the nine-night chants are composed essentially of four days of Evilway ceremonies plus four days of Holyway ceremonies, with a public exhibition on the last night. Kluckhohn and Wyman (1940, p. 106) and Wyman (1957, p. 12) expressed the opinion that the five-night form may be the basic ceremonial which may be condensed into two nights or elaborated into a nine-night ceremonial by spacing the component ceremonies over a longer period. It is still possible, however, that the two parts could have developed separately, the one as a possibly earlier and mainly exorcistic rite, the elements of which may have been brought along by the early Athapascans in their southward migrations, and the second as a chiefly invocatory rite derived from the drypainting practices of the Pueblo Indians after the arrival of the Athapascans in the Southwest. Whether these two parts were first fitted together into a five-night ceremonial which was later expanded in time, or whether they were first attached to each other linearly in a nine-night performance which was condensed later is a moot point. Perhaps we will never know. Some further discussion of these matters may be found in Wyman and Kluckhohn, 1938, p. 10, and in Wyman and Bailey, 1943, p. 45.

all ceremonies into five nights to make a complete five-night ceremonial, as is often the case for other chantways, is not mentioned
in any of the accounts of Mountainway, but there are numerous
references in various writings to a five-night chant.[19]

The discussion of Mountain-Shootingway in Wyman, 1970b,
contains the following:[20]

> The performance popularly called a Fire Dance is a spectac-
> ular all-night exhibition of various acts by teams representing
> various chantways — each team putting on a specialty of its
> chant and culminating in the Fire Dance proper, in which
> nearly naked, clay-daubed dancers run about brandishing
> torches of cedar bark amid showers of sparks. The whole is like
> a great sacred vaudeville show — and provides the climax of
> the final night of a nine-night ceremonial. A chant that includes
> this feature must last nine nights. The performance is carried
> out in a great circle or "corral" of evergreen branches, hence
> the other popular name, Corral Dance, and the formal Navaho
> designation, Dark Circle of Branches. The Fire Dance is usual-
> ly associated with a Mountain Chant, but other ceremonials
> may have this phase, although some, such as Hailway and Bead-
> way, may forbid it even though it is described in their myths
> (Reichard, 1970, pp. 547–548).[21]

The corral is built along a great circle marked off with cornmeal
by Talking God in the myths, by the singer in an actual performance. The singing during the final night is accompanied by the
rhythmic growl of a hardwood rasp rubbed with another hardwood
stick. The end of the rasp is held against an inverted Navajo basket
which serves as a sounding board. In notes in the Museum of Navaho Ceremonial Art pertaining to a male Mountain Chant given by
one John Sherman at the Saw Mill, north of Fort Defiance, Arizona,
on November 17, 1951, it is said that two rasps and two baskets
were used, inverted over abalone shells. Father Berard remarked

---

[19] Franciscan Fathers, 1910, p. 403; Coolidge and Coolidge, 1930, p. 201; Kluckhohn
and Wyman, 1940, p. 187.

[20] Mountain-Shootingway is a phase of Shootingway in which a Fire or Corral Dance,
a feature borrowed from Mountainway, is included in a nine-night performance of
the chant (see Wyman, 1970b, p. 25 for details).

[21] In discussing the interdict against the Corral Dance in Beadway, Reichard suggested that having forgotten or lost the skill to perform certain acts in the Dark Circle of Branches the Navajo "now attribute their absence to holy decree" (1939, p. 23).

that the hollow, rasping sound, "to an extent, imitates the low growl of a bear" (1946, p. 11).

Among the eleven (MMC, CCM) to fourteen (YPM, Reagan) acts or "dances" described in the longer accounts of the final night of Mountainway, five are relatively constant features. These are Re-whitening and Arrow Swallowing performed by the two sets of First Dancers, the dance of the Ye'i group representing Nightway, and the two final acts, the dance of the Young Spruce group and the Fire Dance itself.

First Dancers is a term applied to the performers who open the public exhibitions of the final nights of both Mountainway and Nightway (see Haile, 1951, vol. 2, p. 120). The First Dancers, usually twelve in number, who open the Corral Dance of Mountainway perform a sort of fire dance called "which is re-whitened" because a bundle of downy feathers on the end of a stick which the dancer has burned off in the fire is restored, apparently by magic but actually by a trick wand, while he races around the fire (see Haile, 1950, vol. 1, p. 145). This act, which symbolizes restoration of the patient to health, is discussed at length in Father Berard's monograph on the Fire Dance (Haile, 1946, pp. 14–22). Moreover, detailed descriptions of the other acts mentioned below may be found in the same publication.

Following the act of the Re-whitening dancers another group (usually two in number although there may be as many as six or eight) enters carrying the Great Plumed Arrows (see the discussion of the sandpainting of these arrows, p. 109 below). These performers are also called First Dancers thus making two sets known by this name in Mountainway. Matthews said that the plumed arrow, "seems to be the most revered implement and the act in which it appears the most revered alili of the night. All other shows may be omitted at will, but the dance of the . . . [plumed arrows], it is said, must never be neglected," and "these arrows are the especial great mystery, the potent healing charm of this dance." The hero of the myth was shown this procedure by the Mountain Gods in their home at Wide Chokecherry (Matthews, 1887, pp. 407, 409, 414, 429, 434, 451, Figs. 54, 55). The shafts of the Great Plumed Arrows are so constructed in two parts, of hollow reed and wood, that they can be telescoped and the dancers create the illusion of swallowing them by placing their points in their mouths and telescoping their shafts (Reagan, 1934, pp. 434–435; Haile, 1946, pp. 22–27). The arrows are applied to the body of the patient either before or after the swallowing act. Father Berard said, "More than likely the intent of the arrow-swallowing performance is to show complete restoration from any arrow or other injury" (ibid., p. 27).

Nightway is represented in the Dark Circle of Branches by a team of three masked impersonators of the Ye'i, a class of supernatural beings often referred to as "gods" although the term Ye'i is untranslatable (see Wyman, 1967, pp. 5–9). These are Talking God, the leader of the Ye'i, who is also called Ye'i bichai, the "grand-uncle" or "maternal grandfather of the Ye'i" (Grandfather-of-the-gods), Humpback, and either a Female God or Water Sprinkler. Talking God not only dances but taps a basket drum while the others dance.

Just before dawn a group of dancers, usually four, "from Young Spruce Knoll" (Haile, 1946, p. 52), enter carrying spruce twigs or little trees which they apply to the patient's body. Sometimes this is the last act, closing the ceremonial just before the dawn procedures (YPM, HS, HM). In other instances, the Corral Dance culminates in the spectacular Fire Dance which gives the entire final night of Mountainway one of its popular names (MMC, CCM, OBS, Reagan).

Besides Nightway, Shootingway is another chant complex which presents one or more specialties, probably in every performance of Mountainway. Shootingway dancers wear the pointed red feather headdress characteristic of the chant with imitations of buffalo horns attached to it and carry feathered wands composed of two triangular segments of reeds.[22] Sometimes a boy and a girl attired thus dance together. Among the specialties presented by Shootingway dancers are: two or four dancers bearing blue Sun and white Moon disks, and sometimes black and yellow Wind disks, on their chests [rising] or backs [setting],[23] or carrying long Sun, Moon, and Wind wands (Wyman, 1970b, p. 44, Plates 26, 27); the Whirling Tail Feather or dancing Sun disk, a feathered disk which whirls or dances in a basket, apparently magically but actually manipulated by invisible strings (CCM, Reagan; see Wyman, 1970b, p. 32, Plate 1); a feathered Sun disk which rises magically to the top of a tall "pole which does things" which stands upright also apparently magically (MMC; Haile, 1946, pp. 34–37); the dancing feather, a tall feather again operated by invisible strings which rises and dances in a basket in time with the singing and the steps of a young

---

[22] Matthews, 1887, p. 438; Coolidge and Coolidge, 1930, illustration opposite p. 194; Wyman, 1967, pp. 3–5, Fig. 1.

[23] Reagan, 1934, Plate 8, Fig. 2; Wyman, 1970b, pp. 43–44, Plates 24, 25; MMC, CCM, Reagan.

dancer (see p. 118 below; MMC, CCM); dancers with lightnings, devices built like lazy tongs which can be opened and closed and thus shot forward simulating lightning flashes (CCM).[24] In the notes on the Mountain Chant given in 1951 by John Sherman (see above; Museum of Navaho Ceremonial Art) is this statement: "They said also, they gave the lightning dance where four men carry sticks which they shot out over the fire and over the patients." Shooting-way may present still other specialties, some of which are mentioned in Haile, 1946 (p. 33).

Besides the dancing Ye'i group, Nightway may exhibit dancers bearing feathered wands or pinyon poles which they pretend to swallow, led by a masked Male God (MMC).

Dancers representing Beautyway may present the dance of the standing arcs in which eight dancers carrying feathered, semicircular wooden arcs kneel in two rows and balance their arcs, apparently magically, on the heads of their opposite partners.[25] Navajo Windway may be represented by dancers carrying cactus.[26] Waterway, too, may present its specialty (YPM, CCM). In Navajo theory, the patient of a Mountain Chant not only benefits from the chant itself but also from every other ceremonial whose representatives present their specialties in the Dark Circle of Branches. As Reichard remarked the Dark Circle is a "kind of cross section" of the entire ceremonial system (1970, p. 330). Father Berard said, "Thus, if Shootingway has performed in the Mountainway corral, the patient is not obliged to have another Shootingway ceremonial performed over him. And so with the others who have performed there. On this basis it is less expensive to combine many ceremonials in one corral dance, than to have each one performed in succession" (1946, p. 57). Thus the Fire Dance may effect a considerable saving of time, money, and resources.

Specialties of Mountainway itself which may appear in the Corral Dance are: the magical growth of a yucca plant and the maturing of its fruit (MMC, CCM, OBS); an impersonator of a bear, covered with evergreen twigs and accompanied by one or two attendants (MMC); a man who washes his hands in a shower of melted, burning pitch, apparently magically unharmed (MMC, OBS), a stunt first

[24] CCM; Reagan, 1934, Plate 8, Fig. 4; Wyman, 1970b, p. 45, Plate 29.

[25] Matthews, 1887, pp. 437–438; Wyman and Newcomb, 1962, p. 39, Fig. 1; Wyman, 1970b, p. 46, Plate 31.

[26] Reagan, 1934, Plate 8, Fig. 3; Wyman, 1970b, pp. 44–45, Plate 28.

performed by Porcupine (CCM) or Badger (HM);[27] and a weasel
[stuffed skin] which appears from a basket of spruce twigs (MMC).

In three myths of Mountainway the Jicarilla Apaches who had
been invited to the Corral Dance of the *Prototype Ceremonial*
arrived late because they had stopped to play a hoop and pole game
and almost forgot the ceremonial. Finally they came bringing the
sticks and hoops used in the game and used these implements in
the dance which they presented (MMC), performing the trick of
swallowing the sticks (HM), or making a bird sing which was
perched in a treetop of spruce attached to the stick (CCM). This
appearance of the Jicarillas in the myths of Mountainway may be
associated with the likely assumption that Navajo Beautyway and
Mountainway were derived from the Jicarilla Holiness Rite, or
perhaps the three ceremonials came from a common source. This
idea was discussed at some length and a brief myth of the Jicarilla
Apache Holiness Rite, "The Place of Worship," was presented in
the volume on Beautyway (Wyman, 1957, pp. 145-151). Moreover,
Opler had previously discussed the relations between these Navajo
and Jicarilla ceremonials quite exhaustively, coming to the conclusion that they belong to a "Navaho-Jicarilla ritual complex,"
which may have "received its original impetus from Pueblo sources
(there are hints of a like set of associations for the Hopi) and became
particularly elaborated by the Apachean peoples because of their
stronger basic fear of bear and snake and their greater tendency to
employ animals in the etiology of disease" (1943, pp. 73-95).

There are many obvious parallels between the Jicarilla Holiness
Rite and the two Navajo ceremonials, Female Mountainway and
Beautyway. The Jicarilla myth, although brief, with its theme of
the abduction of two maidens by Bear and Snake, their rescue by
the Slayer Twins, the indisposition suffered as a result of their
adventures, and their restoration by their former masters, conforms
with the myths of the two Navajo chants and their common introduction, *The Pueblo War*. Although the cure of Bear and Snake sicknesses, diseases thought to come from some sort of improper contacts
with these animals, has been segregated into two separate ceremonials by the Navajo, Mountainway and Beautyway, their emphasis on the connections between the two provides for them, as Opler

---

[27] Father Berard said that washing the hands in hot pitch is a Male Shootingway specialty, but, attributing the prototype of this feat to Porcupine, relates it decidedly to
Mountainway (Coolidge and Coolidge, 1930, pp. 209-210; Haile, 1946, p. 33).

remarked, "the unity of ritual defense against Bear and Snake which is achieved in a single ceremony, the Holiness Rite, by the Jicarilla" (ibid., p. 81). Moreover, there are many close correspondences in ritual behavior between the Jicarilla rite and Navajo Mountainway: the similarities in the general designs and use of drypaintings and the employment of the first one of the four made in connection with a shock rite which is almost identical in the two cultures; the color-directional sequence of black, blue, yellow, white, beginning in the east; the identification of practitioner and patient by seriatim contact of body parts; the use of two musical rasps as well as the basket drum to accompany the singing; plumed wands and feathered arrows as ritual implements; the evergreen corral and the performances within it; the employment of legerdemain by the dancers to produce apparently magical effects; the association of the small spruce tree with the final procedures; these and many other parallels have been brought out by Opler in the work cited (1943), and may be found in the briefer descriptions of the Holiness Rite by Russell (1898) and E. Curtis (1907, vol. I, pp. 56–60). We should not be too surprised, however, by this parallelism because the Jicarilla and the Navajo were among the more northerly of the southern Athabascan tribes who once were closer neighbors before the western migration of the latter.

About the Ceremonial[28]

BY YUCCA PATCH MAN*

YOU SEE, when a five-night one is to be, they give me twenty-five [dollars] and tell me to conduct it for five nights. In two days it will be, one tells them.

The emetic they should prepare of these: chokecherry, serviceberry, wild currant, orange gooseberry, wild rose, cattail flag, rush [or spike rush], bearberry [or manzanita], myrtle box-leaf, buckbrush [deer-brush], blue spruce, ground juniper, needle spruce,

---

* Recorded and translated by Father Berard Haile. Edited by Leland C. Wyman.
[28] Although the following brief account of the first night's procedure, consecration of the hogan, and unraveling, adds nothing to what has been published numerous times, it is interesting to have a description of it in a Navajo singer's own words, especially those of the one who told the myth of Female Mountainway presented in this book.

limber pine, Douglas fir, you see that many are obtained for the emetic, which is pounded and boiled before they drink it.

Then they should obtain the pokers from a lightning-struck pinyon; one breaks a limb extending on the east side, also one on the west side of it. Then one breaks a south side limb from a juniper which has not been lightning-struck, likewise on the north side of the tree.

At the east side of a wavyleaf oak one breaks a limb off, and on the west side also, but these are not cut off with a knife, likewise those on the south and north sides of the tree. That many are obtained.

Bark is also torn off, Douglas fir too is brought, one tells him. A yucca leaf is also plucked from the east side of a plant, also from the west, south and north sides, then they are tied together.

Again a certain amount of Douglas fir is brought, and five yucca leaves are plucked with no definite sequence.

Then his pouch he follows [to the patient's home] and at sunset he arrives there. That so is done [he tells him].

He applies five unravelers; only the weasel unravelers are applied. As soon as he has administered the medicine, he applies the unravelers.

Unraveling Songs

(1) Holy Young Man his magic he unravels with you, zigzag lightning, which is spiral one laid upon the other and opened again, his magic he unravels with you.

Holy woman her magic she unravels with you, straight lightning . . . [etc., as in the first stanza], her magic she unravels with you.

Magic killer his magic he unravels with you, sunray . . . his magic he unravels with you.

Acquirer of Holy Things his magic he unravels with you, rainbow . . . his magic he unravels with you.

[The cords, with which the bundles to be unraveled are tied, are called zigzag and straight lightning, sunray and rainbow.]

(2) He unraveled with you . . . [etc., as in song 1].

(3) From him it has gone [etc.].

(4) Upon him it has returned, far away it has gone [etc.].

From here on, after making the unravelings, he begins the ceremonial, he puts foot liniment[29] and medicine into a bowl of water. That done he intones songs and finishes fifteen and administers the medicine. After finishing the songs he places the wavyleaf oak sticks at all cardinal point crevices, east, west, south, and north. He whitens them [the hogan beams] with cornmeal below the wavyleaf oak stick in the four places. Then he strews it around in a circle. "Nicely you will perform it in the proper way," one tells him. Then they go to sleep.

The Songs of Mountainway

IN HIS DISCUSSION of the songs of the Mountain Chant, Matthews (1887, pp. 455–467) gave a list of thirteen sets of songs which could be sung during an evening's short singing ceremony or in the corral on the final night when no special song pertaining to a particular act or procedure is in progress. Presumably, they could also be used for the final night of a five-night ceremonial without the Dark Circle of Branches. He called them "songs of sequence" because if the singer begins with one from a particular set, he may not follow immediately with songs from any of the preceding sets but must go on with songs from some of the following sets. Moreover, in any set the songs must be sung in a certain order of sequence which may not be reversed. The sets were, sixteen songs of the First Dancers, twelve of the Great Stick [Plumed Wand], twelve of Mountain Sheep, twelve of Lightning [Thunder], twelve of Holy Young Man, sixteen of Changing Bear Maiden, eight of Reared-in-the-Mountains [hero of the male myth], eight Awl songs, eight Whitening songs, seven songs of Porcupine, eight of Plants, twenty-six of the Exploding Stick, and sixteen Dawn songs. Matthews gave examples with literal and free translations of songs from eight of these sets.

Besides these "songs of sequence" there are, of course, many songs which accompany the various acts and procedures of the different ceremonies, such as the Unraveling Songs dictated by Yucca Patch Man and presented above.

---

[29] This is Father Berard's rather literal translation of the Navajo name for the cold infusion of mints and other fragrant herbs used mainly for external application, which Kluckhohn and Wyman called chant lotion (1940, p. 51). The Navajo call it foot liniment because it is applied to the patient beginning at the bare feet and proceeding upward to the top of the head.

Father Berard tried to obtain the sequence of songs for the various nights from Yucca Patch Man but said he seemed "to have had difficulty in grasping the proposition." He did, however, give a sequence of eight sets of songs for the final night which were, fifteen First Songs, fifteen Bridge songs, eighteen songs of Preparing Them, thirty-four Arrow songs, fourteen Spruce [Douglas fir] songs, sixteen songs of Raised-in-Earth, thirteen Medicine songs, seventeen Big Snake songs. He omitted the Dawn songs. The First Songs are the only ones which correspond with any of the sets given by Matthews. Perhaps this is because he was concerned with the male Mountain Chant whereas Yucca Patch Man was a singer of Female Mountainway.

Yucca Patch Man dictated the fifteen songs of the Bridge to Father Berard, who said that "further on in the text he equated them with the First Songs." Father Berard was of the opinion that the Bridge songs are also a set of "First Songs" which may be substituted for the regulation First Songs at the option of the singer. He also thought that these songs could be employed in securing the various medicinal herbs used in the ceremonial. Professor David P. McAllester of Wesleyan University has revised Father Berard's translations of these songs and his revisions of them follow here. The prose notes between the songs are comments which Father Berard made about them.

THE SONGS OF THE BRIDGE

(1) His own hand, with this he is taking it out, just with this he
is taking it out.

Now Holy Young Man himself is taking it out, just with this
he is taking it out,
Now Dark Mountain, its center, from there, he himself is
taking it out, just with this he is taking it out,
Now dark medicine, he himself is taking it out, just with this
he is taking it out,
Now sacred medicine, he himself is taking it out, just with
this he is taking it out,

His own hand, with this he is taking it out, just with this he
is taking it out.

Now Holy Woman herself is taking it out, just with this she
is taking it out,

Now Blue Mountain, its center, from there, she herself is taking it out, just with this she is taking it out,
Now blue medicine, she herself is taking it out, just with this she is taking it out,
Now sacred medicine, she herself is taking it out, just with this she is taking it out,

His own hand, with this he is taking it out, just with this he is taking it out.[30]

The second stanza changes the color scheme but retains the general theme. The next song proceeds to describe the accomplished fact.[31]

(2) His own hand, with this he brought it here, just with this he brought it here,
Now Holy Young Man himself is bringing it here, just with this he is bringing it here [etc., as in song 1].

(3) His own hand, with this he placed it in water, just with this he placed it in water [etc., as in song 1].

The second "female" stanza in each song mentions Holy Woman instead of the expected Holy Young Woman to correspond to Holy Young Man of the first stanza. This may be because Holy Young Woman is the wife of Holy Young Man, whereas the songs identify Holy Woman with the woman chased by Bear Man. This allows variety in the theme of the songs. Thus, while the three preceding songs describe the manner of procuring the medicinal herbs, with the woman chased by the Bear Man as the procurer, her journeys to the homes of various supernaturals are now introduced in the following songs to elaborate this general theme. The sequence in the theme is loosely retained, and she is described as visiting the home of Holy Young Man. Here she finds a room in the rear of his hogan, or one hogan within another. The children of Holy Young Man are playing there, and she hears their voices.

---

[30] "His own hand," "he is taking," "he calls," etc., instead of "she" because this is a repetition of the initial refrain which serves as the chorus. Of course Navajo does not differentiate the gender.

[31] This and subsequent comments concerning the songs are notes made by Father Berard Haile. Most of these notes refer to the myth, for as Matthews said, the songs "cannot be comprehended without a full knowledge of the mythology and of the symbolism to which they refer" (1887, p. 456).

(4) He calls "áye!" He put it down, "áye!"[32]

> Now Holy Young Man, at his home he put it down, he calls, "áye!" He put it down, "áye!"
> Dark Mountain, of this is his home, at the inside, in the back, he put it down, he calls "áye!" He put it down, "áye!"
> The sacred hogan, inside in the back there are voices, "áye!" He calls, "áye!" He put it down, "áye!"
> Now Holy Young Man's children are calling, "áye!" He calls, "áye!" He put it down, "áye!"

> He calls, "áye!" He put it down, "áye!"

> Now Holy Woman, at her home she put it down, she calls "áye!" She put it down, "áye!"
> Now Blue Mountain, of this is her home, at the inside, in the back, she put it down, she calls "áye!" She put it down, "áye!"
> The sacred hogan, inside in the back there are voices, "áye!" She calls, "áye!" She put it down, "áye!"
> Now Holy Woman's children are calling, "áye!" She calls, "áye!" She put it down, "áye!"

> He calls, "áye!" He put it down, "áye!"[30]

(5) The home, a sacred place, you went there, his home you went there, ꞌiyo.[33]

> Now Holy Young Man, his home you went there, his home, you went there, ꞌiyo,
> Dark Mountain, of this is his home, you went there, inside, to that place, she went there, his home, you went there, ꞌiyo,
> Now Holy Woman, her children, inside, they were sitting there, inside, they were sitting there, she found, his home, you you went there, ꞌiyo,

> The home, a sacred place, you went there, his home, you went there, ꞌiyo.

---

[32] Because "áye" with a high "á" would be an unusual vocable, Dr. McAllester suggests that this is the call itself.

[33] Since Father Berard was in the habit of omitting many vocables and introductory formulae in his much condensed renditions of songs, Dr. McAllester has supplied vocables and reconstructed introductory formulae and choruses from such phrases as Father Berard supplied, in this and in the subsequent songs.

Now Holy Woman, her home, you went there, her home, you
went there, 'iyo,
Blue Mountain, of this is her home, you went there, inside,
to that place, she went there, her home, you went there,
'iyo,
Now Holy Young Man, his children, inside, they were sitting
there, he found, her home, you went there, 'iyo,

The home, a sacred place, you went there, his home, you
went there, 'iyo.

"You went" refers to the woman of the legend who was chased
by Bear Man.

(6) In his home I desired to enter, in his home I entered,

Now Holy Young Man, in his home, I entered, in his home
I entered,
Dark Mountain, in his home of this, I entered, inside, to
that place, I entered, in his home I entered,
Rain-streamers hold them back, his sacred power holds
them back, in his home I entered,

In his home I desired to enter, in his home I entered,

Now Holy Woman, in her home, I entered, in her home
I entered,
Blue Mountain, in her home of this, I entered, inside, to that
place, I entered, in her home I entered,
Sunrays inside hold them back, her sacred power holds
them back, in her home I entered,

In his home I desired to enter, in his home I entered.[30]

The song emphasizes the respect due to a sacred place. Therefore
the supernaturals "hold back" or throw out those who disrespect
holy things.

(7) In a sacred way, in a sacred way, I came upon it, in a sacred
way I came upon it, niye,

Holy Woman, her young one, in a sacred way I came upon
it, in a sacred way I came upon it, niye,
The Earth Mountain, at that place, beyond there, it was, in
a sacred way I came upon it, in a sacred way I came upon
it, niye,

The dark mountain sheep, its young one, in a sacred way
   I came upon it, in a sacred way I came upon it, *niye*,
At Earth Rock, at that place, beyond there, it was, in a sacred
   way I came upon it, in a sacred way I came upon it, *niye*,

In a sacred way, in a sacred way I came upon it, in a sacred
   way I came upon it, *niye*.

She had reached the rim of a mountain, looked across the country,
and had seen the mountain sheep, hence, "I came upon it." [Dr.
McAllester suggests that the mountain sheep may be identified
with the Holy Woman in this song, just as Father Berard suggests
that she is identified with the she-bear in the next song. Thus,
the woman of the legend could speak of coming upon mountain
sheep's young one in the same terms as she speaks of Holy Woman's
young one.]

(8) She, in a sacred way, lovingly she lifts it up, she lifts it
   up, *niye*,

Holy Woman, her young one, lovingly she lifts it up, her
   young one, she lifts it up, *niye*,
Dark Mountain, truly, its center, at that place, lovingly she
   lifts it up, her young one, she lifts it up, *niye*,
Her dark young one, lovingly she lifts it up, her young one,
   she lifts it up, *niye*,
Dark all over, lovingly she lifts it up, her young one, she
   lifts it up, *niye*,

She, in a sacred way, lovingly she lifts it up, she lifts it
   up, *niye*.

The dark mountain sheep, her young one, lovingly she lifts
   it up, her young one, she lifts it up, *niye*,
Blue Mountain, truly, its center, at that place, lovingly she
   lifts it up, her young one, she lifts it up, *niye*,
Her blue young one, lovingly she lifts it up, her young one,
   she lifts it up, *niye*,
Blue all over, lovingly she lifts it up, her young one, she
   lifts it up, *niye*,

She, in a sacred way, lovingly she lifts it up, she lifts it
   up, *niye*.

At the Sacred Canyon the woman chased by Bear Man sat down at its rim and saw the she-bear dancing with her cubs, as told in the legend. The she-bear, in these songs, is identified with the Holy Woman, and the context seems to imply that the female mountain sheep is meant in the second stanza.

(9) With me it is shaking, with me it is shaking.

> Holy Woman, the mountain, with me it is shaking, with me it is shaking,
> The mountain, on top of it, with me it is shaking, with me it is shaking,

> With me it is shaking, with me it is shaking,

> The dark mountain sheep, the rock, with me it is shaking, with me it is shaking,
> The canyon, across it, with me it is shaking, with me it is shaking,

> With me it is shaking, with me it is shaking.

The sight of the she-bear with her cubs frightened her, and the trembling of the mountain made her dizzy. The informant said this incident happened to her four times. The song may employ the imperfective or the perfective, "it is shaking," or "it shook."

(10) *'Aineya*, I came to it, I came to it, I came to it,

> The East, below it, to that place, to one who hinders me, indeed you came, I came to it, I came to it,
> The White Mountain, below it, at that place, to one who hinders me, indeed you came, I came to it, I came to it,
> The Yellow-bill Tail, my offering he hinders, indeed you came, I came to it, I came to it,

> The South, below it, to that place, to one who hinders me, indeed you came, I came to it, I came to it,
> The Blue Mountain, below it [etc., as in the first stanza],
> The Big Hawk Tail, blue, my offering he hinders [etc., as in the first stanza],

> The West, below it, to that place, to one who hinders me, indeed you came, I came to it, I came to it,
> The Yellow Mountain, below it [etc., as in the first stanza],
> The Red Tail, my offering he hinders [etc., as in the first stanza],

The North, below it [etc., as in the first stanza],
The Dark Mountain [etc.],
The Magpie Tail, my offering he hinders [etc.],

I came to it, I came to it, I came to it.

The heroine visited the mountain homes at the cardinal points, in the homes made of white, blue, yellow, and dark mountains, but could not enter them because the various birds spread and shook their tails to prevent her passage. The Yellow-bill is the eagle, the Red Tail is here identified with the red-shafted flicker. Other informants seem to think of the red-shouldered hawk when they mention Red Tail.

(11) With him they stand in a row, with him they stand in a row,

Now Dark Mountains they stand in a row, with him they stand in a row,
Holy Young Man, with him they stand in a row, with him they stand in a row,
His offering for you, with him they stand in a row, with him they stand in a row,

With him they stand in a row, with him they stand in a row,

Now Blue Mountains, they stand in a row, with her they stand in a row,
Holy Woman, with her they stand in a row, with her they stand in a row,
Her offering for you, with her they stand in a row, with her they stand in a row,

With him they stand in a row, with him they stand in a row.[30]

The heroine gets the impression that the mountains are set in a row.

(12) When I ascend it looks at me, when I ascend it looks at me,

Mountain, into the skies rising up, when I ascend it looks at me,
Holy Woman's young one it is that looks at me, when I ascend it looks at me,
Rocks, at their highest point it looks at me, rocks at their highest point it looks at me, when I ascend it looks at me,

Rocks, into the skies rising up, when I ascend it looks at me,
Dark Mountain Sheep's young one it is that looks at me,
    when I ascend it looks at me,
Water, at its highest point, it looks at me, water, at its highest
    point it looks at me, when I ascend it looks at me,

Water, into the skies rising up, when I ascend it looks at me,
The Water Monster's young one it is that looks at me, when
    I ascend it looks at me,
Clouds, at their highest point it looks at me, clouds at their
    highest point it looks at me, when I ascend it looks at me,

Clouds, into the skies rising up, when I ascend it looks at me,
Now White Thunder's young one it is that looks at me, when
    I ascend it looks at me,
The Mountain, at its highest point it looks at me, the Moun-
    tain, at its highest point it looks at me, when I ascend it
    looks at me,

When I ascend it looks at me, when I ascend it looks at me.

As the heroine sat on the summit of the mountain she saw the cub
bear on a mountain, a young mountain sheep on top of a cliff, the
young of a Water Monster on the water surface, and the young of
White Thunder on top of a cloud. These young ones look at her.

(13) Far away the mountains are rounded, far away the mountains
    are rounded,
Now Holy Woman, her young one, she thought of it, far away
    the stones are rounded, far away the stones are rounded,
The Dark Mountain Sheep, her young one, she thought of
    it, far away the water is rounded, far away the water is
    rounded,
The Water Monster, her young one, she thought of it, far
    away the water is rounded, far away the clouds are rounded,
Now the White Thunder, its young one, she thought of it,
    far away the clouds are rounded, far away the mountains
    are rounded.

The heroine looked towards the Hogback and beheld a fine range
of mountains. She wondered how this view had escaped her before.
"They certainly are a nice range of mountains, or rounded ones,"
she thought. This gave the theme for this song. She cried as she
recalled her sister.

(14) Among them, when I visit, they play stick dice; among them, when I visit, they play stick dice,

Holy Young Man, he plays stick dice,
Now dark medicine, when I come to him for it, he plays stick dice,

Among them, when I visit, they play stick dice,

Now Holy Woman, she plays stick dice,
Now blue medicine, when I come to her for it, she plays stick dice,

Among them, when I visit, they play stick dice; among them when I visit, they play stick dice.

Again the scene varies. She came to a place called Frogs-playing-stick-dice. This was a small knoll from which lightnings darted out. As they invited her in she began to sing this song. At the cardinal points she noticed rock mica which provided light while they gambled at stick dice. While gambling, the frogs were yelling "up" or "down" with the fortunes of the game. She spent the night there but was unable to distinguish her surroundings well because they had employed some witchery on her eyes to blind her. She felt around for the doorway but was unable to find her way out. After the sun was well up, she heard some person enter and overheard them tell this person that someone entered here and "went blind on us." The stranger, however, remarked, "You cannot leave the person in this shape, make some medicine for her!" The stranger happened to be Holy Young Man. The frogs put medicine in a bowl of water and foot liniment and sang the following song.

(15) 'E-ne-yana, eat it, eat it, eat it, eat it, eat it, neyowo,

Now Holy Young Man, eat it, eat it, eat it, eat it, neyowo,
Mountain top berries, eat them, eat them, eat them, eat them, neyowo,
Now dark medicine, eat it, eat it, eat it, eat it, neyowo,
Now sacred medicine, eat it, eat it, eat it, eat it, neyowo,
Now old age, going on into it, eat it; now in the way of blessing, eat it, eat it, eat it, eat it, neyowo.[34]

---

[34] "Old age, going on into it," and "in the way of blessing," are Dr. McAllester's renderings of two Navajo terms, sa'ąh naagháí and bik'eh hózhóón, often pronounced together, which serve as the climax or benediction of many, if not most, prayers and songs. Father Berard often translated these as "long life-happiness." For a fuller discussion of the meanings of these terms see Wyman, 1970a, pp. 28–30.

Now Holy Woman, eat it, eat it, eat it, eat it, *neyowo*,
Water top berries, eat them, eat them, eat them, eat them,
    neyowo,
Medicine which turns over, eat it, eat it, eat it, eat it, *neyowo*,
Blue medicine, eat it, eat it, eat it, eat it, *neyowo*,
Now sacred medicine, eat it, eat it, eat it, eat it, *neyowo*,
Now old age, going on into it, eat it; now in the way of
    blessing, eat it, eat it, eat it, eat it, *neyowo*,

Eat it, eat it, eat it, eat it, eat it, *neyowo*.

Prayersticks

The word 'prayerstick' is essential to a discussion of any South-western religion. . . . The seriousness with which invocatory prayersticks are regarded is attested by the prominent place given their description in the chant myths. Certain parts of the ritual may be left out of the story, but in the major myths no detail is spared concerning the prayersticks; time and again fear is expressed lest the offerings prove unacceptable. One man said, "They are just like a written invitation" — they differ in that the recipient is compelled to accept the invitation if properly proffered. . . . The care with which all offerings are made is paralleled by that with which they are deposited — a demonstration of ritualistic etiquette. Offerings must be found by the deity to whom they are appropriate where he would look for them. Chanters give assistants explicit directions about the place and method of deposit.

Gladys A. Reichard[35]

OFFERING CEREMONIES, in which invocatory prayersticks are cut, decorated, and deposited in spots supposed to be easily accessible to the supernatural beings whose aid is being invoked, are an important part of the first four days of a nine-night Mountainway ceremonial. Most of the prayersticks are offered to various animals, creatures of the mountains, thought to be etiological factors responsible for human discomfort or disease. Father Berard has said that,

---

[35] Reichard, 1970, pp. 301, 302, 307. Detailed discussions of prayersticks and their accompanying prayers may be found in: Matthews, 1887, pp. 451–455; 1902, pp. 36–40; Franciscan Fathers, 1910, pp. 394–398; Kluckhohn and Wyman, 1940, pp. 28–31, 67–68, 88–89; Haile, 1947a; 1947b, pp. 46–53, 140–156, 158–159, 169–171, 182–184; Reichard, 1944; 1970, Chap. 18, pp. 301–313; Wyman, 1970a, pp. 26–28, Fig. 6.

"the offender has not so much injured or abused the animal form, as he has the human or supernatural form of the animal in question. Because of his actions or omissions, therefore, this supernatural being, not his animal garment, is 'exercising a hold' on the transgressor. In native conception this supernatural always reminds the transgressor through sickness or indisposition of some kind" (Haile, 1947a, p. 4). The disease is not a punishment but "a sharp reminder that the supernatural must have his coveted sacrifice" before he will release his hold on the patient.

We have five quite detailed lists of Mountainway prayersticks, three of them including descriptions of their decoration and directions for depositing them. Although Matthews witnessed only one offering ceremony and did not specify the nature of the six wood and reed prayersticks made in it, twelve kinds were mentioned in the myth as the hero learned about them from various supernaturals in his *Journey for Knowledge and Power*. These are discussed further in a section on "Sacrifices" containing descriptions with some directions for their deposit which Matthews obtained from Navajo informants (1887, pp. 453–455). Since from one to four of each kind are made when they are used, the list contains thirty-one sticks. Twenty-eight Mountainway prayersticks of twenty kinds are described in the work on Navajo sacrificial figurines by Father Berard Haile (1947a, pp. 47–70). He obtained the information from Salt Water [clan] Man of Lukachukai, Arizona, in the spring of 1934. In the myth told by Yucca Patch Man presented below, thirty prayersticks of twenty varieties are mentioned as the heroine learned about them during her *Journeys*. Moreover, Father Berard appended a "Study of Prayers and Sticks" to his translation of the myth which will be presented here. In it he described some fifty prayersticks of twenty-nine kinds and gave the directions for depositing them, as well as including the Navajo texts and translations of the prayers accompanying each kind as dictated by Yucca Patch Man. Finally, among Father Berard's papers in the Library of the University of Arizona in Tucson there is a list of no less than ninety-one prayersticks for Female Mountainway comprising some forty-two types, together with the introductory invocations of the prayers used in offering them. There are no data with this list to indicate its source, but a handwritten note at the end is signed "Leopold."

Besides the four offering ceremonies on four successive days in a nine-night Mountain Chant or in the five-night performance when the ceremonial has been split into two parts, Father Berard spoke of "five-night stick cutting ceremonials of this branch" in his "Study," indicating that Mountainway is subject to the Chant with Prayersticks phase, a variety of Holyway ceremonials in which invocatory offerings are emphasized. Moreover, prayersticks are cut in the one-night excerpts from Mountainway, in which cornmeal dough or carved wooden figurines of etiological factors, usually animals or birds, are sometimes offered together with the sticks (Haile, 1947a, pp. 47–70). Father Berard said that the entire bear and other mountain animal group of excerpts is chiefly concerned with stick-cutting rather than with figurine reproductions (ibid., p. 98). The latter may be considered to be features added to the older prayerstick ceremony. Such excerpt ceremonies provide an inexpensive way of determining if a suspected etiological factor is at work or which one is operative from a suspected group. If some relief is obtained, then the more elaborate Mountainway Chant may be performed for the patient.

Four to six prayersticks are selected from the repertoire of offerings for Mountainway to be made in each of the four ceremonies in a nine or five-night chant. Thus, as many as twenty-six kinds may be offered in a single ceremonial. For example, in the *Prototype Ceremonial* of Yucca Patch Man's myth they were five for chipmunk (see footnote 37) on the first day; five for weasels on the second day; two for bear, two for turkey, and two for mountain sheep on the third day; one each for Holy Young Man and Holy Young Woman, one for striped rock squirrel, and one for chipmunk on the fourth day. In the ceremonial described in the manuscript by Astrov in the Museum of Navaho Ceremonial Art (HS; see p. 22 and footnote 15 above), prayersticks were cut for five kinds of squirrels on the first day; two for "where a bear dies," two for "where a bear sleeps at night," and two Windway prayersticks on the second day; one for Changing Bear Maiden, two for "little birds" [swallows], two for coyote, along with two cornmeal dough figurines of coyote, two of swallows, one of blackbird, and one of bluebird on the third day;[36] four plain, short prayersticks [kind not stated] on the fourth day.

The language of the prayers accompanying the offerings, which the patient repeats sentence by sentence after the singer while he holds the offerings [litany], is on the whole conciliatory, expressing the patient's desires to be restored to health. Examples are given in the "Study" below.

-----

[36] This is the figurine ceremony performed by special request only when a person believes he has troubles stemming from the influence of Changing Bear Maiden.

Forty-three kinds of prayersticks are given in the five lists mentioned above [excluding six groups concerned with place names and nine which cannot be interpreted in "Leopold's" list]. The number cut for a given supernatural being in a ceremonial varies from one to four, but usually it is one [thirty-nine examples] or two [fifty-two examples], a male and female pair. Cutting four sticks for a single being is mentioned in only ten instances. Of the forty-three kinds of supernatural beings or circumstances receiving prayerstick offerings, seven occur in all five lists: chipmunk, white and black pine squirrels,[37] weasel, bear [lying in a den], porcupine, skunk. Four others are in all but Matthews' list, striped rock squirrel, ground squirrel, turkey, badger; and Big Snake is in all but that of Haile, 1947a. Mountain sheep, various ants, toad, and three of the sticks concerned with bear's activities, bear's resting place, stone turned by bear, wood handled by bear, are found in the "Study" and in "Leopold's" list, while the first three are also in Yucca Patch Man's myth and the last three are also in Haile, 1947a. Thus, these eighteen kinds of prayersticks, nearly half of the entire repertoire, may be considered the offerings for the chief supernatural factors of Mountainway.

While prayersticks cut for the Meal Sprinklers, the Re-whitening Dancers, the First Dancers, marmot, Sun and Moon, and Changing Bear Maiden, are described in the "Study," the first four are also in "Leopold's" list, Sun and Moon in Yucca Patch Man's myth, and the last in Matthews. Charred wood, a symbol of bear, and Young spruce prayersticks are found in Haile, 1947a, and in "Leopold's" list, while a stick for Holy Woman is in Matthews and the myth.

Prayersticks for the following supernatural beings are unique, occurring in only one list apiece: Thunder, snakes and water creatures, and Holy Young Woman in Matthews; gopher, magpie, bear's watering place, and Snapping Vagina in Haile, 1947a; Holy Young Man in Yucca Patch Man's myth; coyote, owl, swallows, and wind

---

[37] To equate the Navajo names for squirrels, chipmunks, ground squirrels, rock squirrels, etc., with the numerous biological species of these creatures which occur in the southwestern United States would require a major field study by an ethnobiologist, and this has not been done. There are descriptions of no less than twenty-nine such species in Vernon Bailey's monograph on *Mammals of New Mexico* (North American Fauna No. 53, Washington, D.C., 1931). Pending such a study, therefore, common names have been assigned to Navajo names as follows: *hazéí tsoh* (*'álíl 'aghání*)—striped rock squirrel; *hazéí* or *hazéí ts'ósii* (*dighin yósíní*)—chipmunk; *dlozítgai*—white pine squirrel; *dlozishzhiin*—black pine squirrel; *tsindit'inii*—ground squirrel.

in the "Study"; turtle, raccoon, and wood rat in "Leopold's" list. Moreover, in this last list six sets of prayersticks are mentioned which seem to be concerned with geographical places or features, such as Slim Water Canyon [Mancos River], Wide Chokecherry, and Black Mountain, and the names of nine sets could not be interpreted.

It is not surprising that the lists of prayersticks in the "Study" which follows here and in Yucca Patch Man's myth are similar, since the same singer was the source of the information in both. The myth, however, mentions prayersticks for two supernatural beings who are not in the "Study," Holy Woman and Holy Young Man, while the "Study" has nine which are not in the myth—the Meal Sprinklers and the Re-whitening and First Dancers, the three pertaining to bear's activities, coyote, owl, and wind.

A STUDY OF PRAYERS AND STICKS OF FEMALE MOUNTAINWAY

BY FATHER BERARD HAILE*
(with prayers by Yucca Patch Man)

THE LEGEND RECORDS how certain prayersticks were to be obtained for use in the ceremonial. As a general rule, all prayersticks of this branch are made of box elder [with the pith removed][38] three fingers in length, with these exceptions: the stick of marmot is the length of a small span, the outstretched thumb and index finger. The stick of Changing Bear Maiden is the length of a big span, the thumb and middle finger span. The stick of toad is made of reed, that of Big Snake is made of giant-reed.

The sticks are moistened or sized with chokecherry juice. A ball of feathers is rolled in pollen and plugs the bottom of the stick, wild tobacco is inserted and the tip is stoppered with moistened pollen. The stick is then colored in the prescribed color. It is then laid upon a cloth and the following articles are laid with it: jewels, turkey down, eagle down, bluebird wing feathers, cotton cord, turkey beard. Three jewels are required which are usually small chips. For a male patient, turquoise is placed first, for a female patient, white shell. Any other jewel may accompany these, white shell, abalone shell, jet, but three are required for each stick. As a rule six sticks are selected for each cutting on four consecutive days.

The following prayers are prompted by the singer and then repeated verbatim by the patient, who holds the sticks in his hand

---

* Recorded and translated by Father Berard Haile. Edited by Leland C. Wyman.

[38] All statements enclosed in brackets are explanatory notes provided by the editor (Leland C. Wyman).

during prayers [litany]. The commas fairly well indicate the pauses made by the singer [to allow the patient to repeat the phrase]. The prayers accompanying the sacrificial offering of these sticks are identical, excepting that the invocation of the respective supernatural varies [the initial phrases of each prayer]. There are usually two, a male and a female stick. The prayers for the female supernatural repeat the same words, excepting of course that "young woman chief" is said, and "behind me" alternates with "before me," being mentioned first in the female parts [of the prayer].

> Magic which kills, chief for the mountain, young man chief, I have made your offering, I have prepared your smoke,
> My feet restore for me, my legs restore for me, my body restore for me, my mind restore for me, my voice restore for me.
> Your magic [spell] you will remove out of me, you have removed your magic out of me,
> By which it did it to me, that you have taken out of me, you have taken it away from me, you have taken it out away from me, you have taken it far away from me,
> This very day it will be moved from me, it will move down above me, it will move far away from me, this very day I shall recover,
> This very day I shall get well again, just as I was before, in that same condition I shall go about, always in good health I shall go about, immune to attack I shall go about,
> With a cool body I shall go about, with a light body I shall go about,
> Full of energy I shall go about, in the proper manner you will perform over me,
> With a breeze going through my feet I shall go about, with a breeze going through my legs I shall go about, with a breeze going through my body I shall go about, with a breeze going through my mind I shall go about, with a breeze going through my voice I shall go about, with a breeze going through my headplume I shall go about,
> I am long life — happiness as I shall go about,
> Before me it is blessed as I shall go about, behind me it is blessed as I shall go about, it has become blessed again, it has become blessed again.

> Magic which kills, chief for the mountain, young woman chief [etc.; the rest of this prayer is the same as above except that "behind me" comes before "before me"].

These two prayers are addressed to striped rock squirrel, called "magic which kills," because its influence will kill, injure, or bewitch the patient. The cause is invoked to destroy the effect of the witchery, hence, striped rock squirrel will remove his magic from the interior of the patient, "out of me."

> Who acquires holy things, chief for the mountain, young man chief [etc., as above].

> Who acquires holy things, chief for the mountain, young woman chief [etc., as above].

These two prayers are addressed to chipmunk, whose invocation is equivalent to "he will wish many holy things to a person," consequently they are acquired through him.

> Around tree who runs, chief for the mountain, young man chief [etc.], and . . . young woman chief [etc.; addressed to white pine squirrel].

> Who runs up the mountain, chief for the mountain, young man chief [etc.], and . . . young woman chief [etc.; addressed to black pine squirrel].

> Traveler on stone peaks, chief for the mountain, young man chief [etc.], and . . . young woman chief [etc.; addressed to ground squirrel].

Male and female sticks are here counted as one, hence, in this set for the first day there are five. The white stick of striped rock squirrel with seven black stripes on each side [FBH—yellow with two black lines][39] is deposited inside of [or near] a log. The yellow stick of chipmunk [MMC—white with two pairs of red and blue longitudinal stripes, and yellow with many black and yellow longitudinal stripes; FBH—with three black stripes] is deposited under any tree [FBH—in rock ledges]. The blue one of white pine squirrel [FBH—blue with a red spot on the back near the top and a white plume (the tail) near the bottom] is deposited under a pine, the

---

[39] Differences from Father Berard's descriptions found in other lists of prayersticks are given enclosed in brackets. The lists are identified by the following symbols: MMC—Matthews, 1887, pp. 453–455; FBH—Haile, 1947a, pp. 47–70; YPM—Yucca Patch Man's myth (presented herein). Although it is not mentioned in the descriptions, it should be understood that there are red and blue bands around both ends of all sticks and that some have a pair of red and blue bands in the center as well.

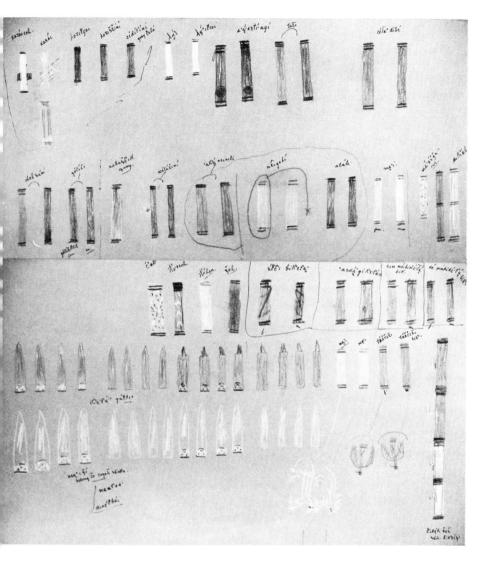

FIG. 2. Mountainway prayersticks; painting by Yucca Patch Man in the Haile Collection (see note 49). Left to right: top row — striped rock squirrel (1), chipmunk (1), white pine squirrel (1), black pine squirrel (1), ground squirrel (1), weasel (1), yellow weasel (1), den (bear; 2), turkey (2), mountain sheep (2); second row — porcupine (2), skunk (2), badger (1), black ant (2), Meal Sprinklers (2), Re-whitening Dancers (2), First Dancers (2), coyote (2), owl (1), marmot (2); third row — toad (1), Big Snake (1), Moon (1), Sun (1), Wind (2), sitting place (bear's; 2), wood turned over (by bear; 2), stone turned over (by bear; 2); fourth row — talking prayersticks (16), coyote (2), swallows (2), Changing Bear Maiden (1); bottom row — talking prayersticks ("belong to coyote"; 16). See pp. 46–56 for details.

brown one of the black pine squirrel [MMC—blue; FBH—with the red spot] is deposited under a spruce tree. The gray stick of ground squirrel [FBH—blue] is deposited at the rim of a cliff [FBH—at a rock ledge].[40]

> At the extreme end of valley white weasel, chief for the mountain, young man chief [etc.].
>
> At the extreme end of meadow yellow weasel, chief for the mountain, young woman chief [etc.].
>
> Who lies in a den, chief for the mountain, young man chief [etc.], and . . . young woman chief [etc.; addressed to bear].
>
> Mountain toward who runs with spread wings, chief for the mountain, young man chief [etc.].
>
> On mountain sticks who runs with spread wings, chief for the mountain, young woman chief [etc.; addressed to turkey].

These may be sufficient for one cutting, or they may be requested for one cutting with the following six sticks [mountain sheep, porcupine, skunk]. The white stick of the male weasel is deposited in any white spot in valley or mountain. The yellow stick of the female weasel is deposited in a meadow [YPM—four sticks, white, yellow, blue, black]. The den [bear] sticks, black male, blue female [MMC, FBH—three red and blue bands at ends and center] should be deposited at a den in the mountains [FBH—at the base of a young pinyon or spruce]. At the lower end of the male [black] stick a blue spiral circle is drawn, on the female a similar black circle, to represent the bear den. The turkey sticks, black male, blue female [FBH—blue, red, yellow, white bands at ends and middle] are deposited at the top of any hill.

> On the mountain top who sounds, chief for the mountain, young man chief [etc.], and . . . young woman chief [etc.; addressed to mountain sheep].
>
> Who walks through the mountain, chief for the mountain, young man chief [etc.].

---

[40] Yucca Patch Man provided Father Berard with colored drawings of the prayer-sticks described in this "Study." They are reproduced in Fig. 2.

Who walks through the rock, chief for the mountain, young woman chief [etc.; addressed to porcupine].

At the rock pile, big skunk, chief for the mountain, young man chief [etc.].

At the rock pile, spotted skunk, chief for the mountain, young woman chief [etc.].

The black and blue stick of mountain sheep is deposited at the rim of a cliff. The black and blue porcupine sticks [MMC, FBH — with white dots representing quills] are deposited at any tree gnawed by a porcupine [MMC — bury under pinyon tree; FBH — at any young pinyon or spruce]. The big [male] skunk and spotted [female] skunk sticks are spotted with white marks on black and blue grounds [MMC — with longitudinal white stripes or rows of white spots; FBH — white lozenge on front and back of big skunk stick, white spots on black spotted skunk stick]. The tips of the sticks, when deposited at any small rock pile, should point away from the hogan.

Under earth traveler, chief for the mountain, young man chief [etc.], and . . . young woman chief [etc.; addressed to badger].

Big black ant, chief for the mountain, young man chief [etc.].

Listening ant [female], chief for the mountain, young woman chief [etc.].

The badger and ant sticks seem to form a set of their own. There is only one gray stick [FBH — yellow sprinkled with white and black] for the badger, but the same stick is addressed "young man and woman." It is deposited "somewhat at his burrow," or a little distance away from it. The two black ant sticks should be deposited "near any kind of log."

Who travels with zigzag lightning, chief for the mountain, young man chief [etc.].

Who travels with straight lightning, chief for the mountain, young woman chief [etc.].

The sticks of the Meal Sprinklers may be added to the preceding badger set, or to the following set [Re-whitening and First Dancers], depending upon the decision of holding the Dark Circle of Branches. The two sticks are colored black and blue. They are deposited "alongside of a straight road." Zigzag and straight lightning is drawn on the calves of the legs of these runners, possibly to symbolize the speed expected of them. Their name has reference to this, although we may conceive that originally they employed lightnings in their journeys.

The following sticks of the Re-whitening Dancers, of the First Dancers, and of coyote may be cut only when a Dark Circle of Branches has been requested. In this event they may substitute for any other sticks. If one dreams of any of these three, they may be requested. Or, if they are suspected of being the cause of "likeness to them," they may be requested. Usually this is evidenced in a child by some marks on its body, imitation of their cries or bark, and the like, which may be traced to prenatal influence.

> Who travels with sunray, chief for the mountain, young man chief [etc.].
> Who travels with rainbow, chief for the mountain, young woman chief [etc.].
>
> Who travels with flash lightning, chief for the mountain, young man chief [etc.].
> Who travels with rainray, chief for the mountain, young woman chief [etc.].
>
> Who was raised within dawn, chief for the mountain, young man chief [etc.].
> Who was raised with dawn, chief for the mountain, young woman chief [etc.; addressed to coyote].

The invocation of the Re-whitening Dancers has prime reference to the leaping motion with which they proceed, they leap with sunray and rainbow. The informant did not mention this of the First Dancers who swallow the arrows. Both Re-whitening and First Dancers are males, but they are addressed as male and female in prayer. The two sticks of the Re-whitening Dancers are colored yellow and white respectively and should be deposited "in the center of a bare spot about the size of the Dark Circle of Branches." The First Dancer sticks, black and blue, should be deposited in "a smooth, round place in valley or mountain." The coyote sticks, white and yellow, are deposited "at footprints of a coyote." In the exhibit, the Re-whitening and First Dancers did not use women. Today women are not permitted in the hogan while the First Dancers are dressing, excepting if women have their own exhibit or know some of the songs.

> Who knows all things on earth, chief for the mountain, young
> man chief [etc.], and . . . young woman chief [etc.; address-
> ed to owl].

The stick of Owl Man may also be substituted for others, if the patient so requests. The stick has a yellow base spotted with small dots of various colors. It is deposited "at a distance from a tree."

> Mountain echo, chief for the mountain, young man chief [etc.].
> Rock echo, chief for the mountain, young woman chief [etc.].

This animal has a "small tail, gray and black legs," perhaps the marmot. Its sticks are black and white, with red and blue bands also added on the center as well as at the tip and butt. They are deposited "on top of a hill."

The following sticks apply to the bear, or to the use of stones or wood turned over by a bear, and to sleeping in or walking over a bear's resting place.

> Who turns the stone, chief for the mountain, young man
> chief [etc.] and . . . young woman chief [etc.].
> Who turns wood, chief for the mountain, young man chief
> [etc.], and . . . young woman chief [etc.].
> At sitting place, chief for the mountain, young man chief
> [etc.], and . . . young woman chief [etc.].

The deposits of these sticks should be made near a stone or tree turned or moved by a bear [FBH—near its tracks], or in gutters or depressions near a tree where a bear has squatted or slept [FBH— or in any depression under a tree or in any hollow place; FBH— they have red and blue bands around the ends and center].

> Who jars the mountain interior with it, chief for the moun-
> tain, young man chief [etc.].
> Who jars the rock interior with it, chief for the mountain,
> young woman chief [etc.; addressed to wind].

The two sticks for wind are deposited "near a place struck by the wind."

> Who shines out with abalone, chief for the mountain, young
> man chief [etc.; addressed to Sun].
> Which shines out with a perfect disc, chief for the mountain,
> young woman chief [etc.; addressed to Moon].

The Sun and Moon are never separated. Reference is made here to the sticks themselves, the Sun's being called "an abalone which shines out of an abalone basket," the Moon's a "perfect white shell bowl which shines out of a white shell basket." Both sticks are deposited "together on a high hill towards the east."

> Who roars within mountain, chief for the mountain, young man chief [etc.].
> Who roars within rock, chief for the mountain, young woman chief [etc.; addressed to Big Snake].
>
> Toad, chief for the mountain, young man chief [etc.], and . . . young woman chief [etc.].

The legend associates Big Snake with the toad. [MMC—four sticks for Big Snake, black, blue, yellow, and white, each with four deer tracks of contrast color; YPM—Big Snake's prayerstick is made of giant reed with four fawn's feet on it, Toad's is of common reed painted white with black, blue, yellow, and red spots.] The two terms used in the invocation to Toad are evidently foreign words. Big Snake's prayerstick is deposited "near a crooked tree root" [MMC—buried in the snake-like heap of earth thrown up by a mole], that of Toad "at a lake or pool of water."

My notes on the purposes of the forty-four odd prayersticks of this [female] branch are not as complete as I desired. However, the bear "stick of the den" is requested for swelling in the joints and limbs, which seems to correspond to the general trend of the legend and to the cure in the firepit [trench sweat]. The "stick of one lying in the den" need not be considered as the sole feature of this branch but it is central in the sense that concomitant prayersticks radiate from it. Thus, pimples and skin diseases are ascribed to the turkey. But these diseases are equated with "witchery caused by the turkey," due, perhaps, to the general ignorance of the cause of skin diseases. In a similar manner, deafness and eye troubles are ascribed to the mountain sheep, and the stick of the mountain sheep is made for a cure of these maladies. Pricking of the skin, and a fancy or dream of being covered with ants, point to the ants and their stick as a remedy. The legend, too, makes mention of meeting the Snake and Toad at the spring, and that these supernaturals shot their arrows into various parts of the woman's body. While provisions for these are made in the prayerstick complex, no provisions seem to be made for White Thunder whose darts struck close to her.

The set of bear sticks for offenses by the use of stones or wood turned over by the bear, or the use or trespass of a bear's resting place do not appear to have a warrant in any particular chapter of the legend, yet they are included as available for five-night stick-cutting ceremonials of this branch. Incidentally, I may mention that these three sticks may be reproduced in the so-called figurine complex, and are then separated from the chant, that is to say, the one-night ceremony consists chiefly in reproducing these sticks and depositing them in the prescribed manner. More than likely, the figurine complex offers a more economic method of meeting ritual offenses than is offered by the elaborate apparatus of this branch.

The legend offers an incomplete account of Changing Bear Maiden, but its introduction into this legend accounts for one of the singular features of this branch, the sweatbath in the firepit to offset the rheumatic pains caused by the heroine's flight from Bear Man. One member of the bear family, as it were, offers a remedy against the pranks of the chief of the tribe, just as other members do [for example the Bear Woman]. This branch, therefore, offers four sticks for the Changing Bear Maiden, two for the coyote again, the white one to represent White Coyote whom she took for her husband, the yellow stick to represent yellow coyote which in turn represents herself. The two sticks of the blue and black swifts or swallows are added to symbolize that they cut up the coyote as told in the legend.

> Who rumbles [like the wind] toward the mountain, chief for the mountain, young man chief [etc.; east].
> Who rumbles toward rock, chief for the mountain, young woman chief [etc.; west].
> Who rumbles toward water, chief for the mountain, young man chief [etc.; south].
> Who rumbles toward clouds, chief for the mountain, young woman chief [etc.; north].
> Who moves out with a dawn corn, chief for the mountain, young man chief [etc.; coyote].
> Who moves out with evening twilight cord, chief for the mountain, young woman chief [etc.; coyote's wife].
> Who moves out with horizontal skyblue, chief for the mountain, young man chief [etc.; blue swallow].
> Who moves out with darkness, chief for the mountain, young woman chief [etc.; black swallow].

Each of the four sticks of Changing Bear Maiden is plugged at the bottom with the usual feather ball, tobacco is inserted into each, then the white one is stoppered with moistened pollen. They are as long as the big span, and the red and blue bands around the sticks represent "her garments" [MMC—all black, with three pairs of red and blue bands]. It appears, too, that a figurine of the Bear Maiden is made of "ground and roasted sweet corn." This is set in the center of a basket, with the prayerstick for the east lying east of the figurine. In the west end of the basket, four sets of talking prayersticks are laid, the white ones representing male, the yellow ones female talking prayersticks (Fig. 2; see Wyman, 1970a, pp. 26–28, Fig. 6). As soon as the prayer of the east prayerstick is finished, it is carried in another basket to the east where it is deposited in a cave or in "a curved bluff" [MMC—buried under a young pinyon]. This is done also with the other sticks for the west, south, and north. Apparently, too, the coyote figurine is made of sweet corn, the coyote white stick is placed east, the white talking prayerstick west of the figurine. The yellow stick of Changing Bear Maiden is laid west, then the figurine, then the yellow talking prayerstick. Thus, five baskets are required for the five persons who recite these prayers with the patient, and one basket in which the sticks are arranged. This latter basket only becomes the property of the singer.

The talking prayerstick seems to be "going in the lead or chief one" of the set, but no prayer was given for it. Both coyote and swallow sticks are accompanied by talking prayersticks, but no deposit places were mentioned. Presumably, they should be placed near the deposit of the Changing Bear Maiden sticks, but these are carried to the cardinal points. It would seem proper then to deposit the coyote and swallow sticks near the east Bear Maiden stick. This, at least, is my assumption.

These sticks are requested when persons lose their mind or become insane. Rattling of the teeth, or gnashing them, which may be done by indisposed persons, is ascribed to Changing Bear Maiden. A person eating bear meat and taking sick and vomiting thereafter, or if a person gets sores on this account on his legs, are indications of Changing Bear Maiden's influence. Hence, the sticks belong to this branch [of Mountainway] and may be cut by special request only.

The Sandpaintings
of Mountainway

The Navajos developed "sand painting" into a high art. This must have taken many years to develop, but it perhaps had its beginning when a Pueblo-trained priest initiated his sister's son into the art of bringing spirits to the ceremony by drawing their symbols.

Ruth M. Underhill[41]

FOUR OF THE SANDPAINTINGS of Mountainway have long had the distinction of having been the first Navajo drypaintings to be published. Two of these, the *Home of Bear and Snake* and the *Long Bodies* (see Figs. 4 and 21), were put before the reading public as line drawings in 1885, and the four appeared in color in Washington Matthews' great monograph of 1887.[42] A few years later the sandpaintings of Nightway were similarly introduced to white America by Stevenson (1891). Many years ago Matthews said:

> These pictures, the medicine men aver, are transmitted from teacher to pupil in each order and for each ceremony unaltered from year to year and from generation to generation. That such is strictly the case I cannot believe. There are no standard pictures on hand anywhere. No permanent design for reference is ever in existence, and there is, so far as I can learn, no final authority in the tribe to settle any disputes that may arise. Few of these great ceremonies can be performed in the summer months. Most of the figures are therefore carried over from winter to winter in the memories of fallible men. But this much I do credit, that any innovations which may creep into their work are unintentional and that if changes occur they are wrought very slowly (1887, pp. 445–446).

---

[41] Underhill, 1956, p. 51.
[42] Matthews, 1885, Plates XXXII, XXXIII; 1887, Plates XV, XVI, XVII, XVIII.

Slowly indeed, for in spite of Matthews' disbelief, comparison of the designs he witnessed in 1884 with similar ones made in recent years shows that they are remarkably alike, in fact practically identical.[43] Thus, we have a record of extraordinary stability in this art throughout a period of nearly nine decades. Almost a century is surely a sufficient period for establishing the reliability of the "memories of fallible men" among the members of the Navajo singer's profession.[44]

To describe the technique, materials, nature, purpose, and use of Navajo drypaintings in the face of the many descriptions of these which have been published since Matthews' time is seemingly the acme of redundancy.[45] To spare the reader who is not familiar with Navajo ceremonial practice the annoyance of having to search for enlightenment in other publications, however, a brief résumé of these matters is given here. Others may disregard this section.

A song ceremonial performed according to Holyway ritual, a pattern of behavior which emphasizes restoration of the patient being treated and the attraction of good, is made up of about a dozen procedures designed to invoke supernatural beings who can counteract the harm done by them or by their earthly cognates. The most spectacular among these procedures is the sandpainting ceremony. Pictures of the protagonist of the myth which sanctions and explains the ceremonial being given and/or the Holy People he encounters in his mythical adventures who are the agents of his instruction [accompanied by numerous subsidiary symbols] are made by strewing dry pigments from between the thumb and flexed forefinger on a background of tan-colored sand smoothed out with a weaving batten. The pigments are red, yellow, and white sandstone and charcoal pulverized on a grinding stone, and a few mixtures of these basic colors, charcoal and white sand for a bluish color, red and black for brown, red and white for pink. Although the term sandpainting has been used ever since Matthews first spoke of sand pictures, drypainting is a more accurate term because charcoal is

---

[43] For instance compare Fig. 4 with Matthews' Plate XV, Fig. 21 with his Plate XVI, Fig. 8 with Plate XVII, and Fig. 29 with Plate XVIII.

[44] See Wyman, 1970b, p. 40.

[45] For instance see Matthews, 1887, 1902; Newcomb and Reichard, 1937, pp. 18–24; Reichard, 1939, pp. 14–25; Kluckhohn and Wyman, 1940, pp. 45, 61–62, 69, 83, 93–100; Kluckhohn and Leighton, 1962, pp. 213–215, 218–219; Wyman, 1952; 1959; 1962, pp. 275–278; 1973, pp. 206–208; 1970a, p. 65; 1970b, pp. 5–7; 1971, pp. 13–25; Foster, 1964. The nomenclature for the elements and symbols of drypaintings used in the discussion presented here will be mainly that established by Reichard, by Kluckhohn and Wyman, and by Wyman.

not sand, and sacred pictures for Blessingway rites are made with cornmeal, plant pollens, powdered flower petals, and charcoal, often strewn on a buckskin or a cloth substitute for the skin. Any man who knows how may work on them under the direction of the singer, who seldom participates except to lay down some fundamental lines. Women do not take part for fear of injury from the potent influences invoked, although they may grind the pigments. When the Holy People showed the protagonists of the myths how to reproduce their sacred pictures, which they kept rolled up on clouds, they forbade their reproduction in permanent form lest they be soiled or damaged. The finished picture may be a foot or less in diameter, or one which occupies most of the floor of the family's hogan which has been emptied and swept for the ceremonial. Sometimes a painting twenty feet across is made in a hogan especially erected for one of the great winter chants. The average sandpainting is about six feet in diameter and, depending on its complexity, may be completed by from four to six men in three to five hours guided only by their memory or that of the singer. No one, not even the Navajo, knows how many different drypainting designs are known today. A Navajo count would be very different from ours since they regard paintings which look very different to us as the same if they depict the same supernatural beings, whereas a slight change such as making a snake's tongue red instead of yellow, would be an important difference to them while it might not be noticed by us. Perhaps five or six hundred designs, different to our eyes, have been recorded by white collectors and by the few Navajos who have dared to defy the supernatural injunctions. Possibly, around a thousand designs, which we would distinguish, are known, but this figure is conjecture. A Navajo estimate, of course, would be much smaller. All Holyway chants, most or perhaps all Evilway chants, and the Blessingway rites are known or are alleged to have employed drypaintings.[46] The number pertaining to a given ceremonial, from which the singer may select the one made in a

[46] In contrast to Holyway ritual which is concerned with the attraction of good, Evilway (or Ghostway) ritual is characterized by procedures designed to exorcise ghosts and the evil or disease caused by them, and, hopefully, to counteract the effects of witchcraft. The Blessingway rites are not specifically concerned with curing disease as are the chantways but are carried out to avert misfortune and to bring good luck and blessings upon man's possessions and activities. Thus they are used for many purposes, the blessing of a new house, consecrating ceremonial paraphernalia, aiding childbirth, recognizing a girl's adolescence, blessing a marriage, and many others (see Wyman, 1970a; 1970b, pp. 2–3). At least one Blessingway song is included in every chant to counteract possible errors which might make the ceremonial ineffectual.

two-night performance or the four different ones made on successive days in a five or nine-night chant, varies from scarcely more than the required four for such chants as Hand-tremblingway or Eagleway to about a hundred for Shootingway, although here the Navajo count might be closer to fifty.[47]

Just before dawn on the day a sandpainting is to be made, a setting-out ceremony is performed in which wooden bundle-prayersticks, decorated with painted symbols and feathers, are stuck upright in a mound of earth before the hogan door to notify human and supernatural beings of the event. Upon completion of the painting in the late forenoon or early afternoon, the bundle-prayersticks are brought in and set upright around it. Cornmeal is sprinkled on it by singer and patient, and sometime during the singing, the latter, stripped to a G-string if a man, wearing a single skirt if a woman, sits on some figure in the painting. While singing the singer applies his palms moistened with herb medicine to various parts of the painted figures' bodies and then applies the adhering sand to corresponding parts of the patient's body. This identifies the patient with the Holy People represented who have been attracted to the scene to look at their portraits, and makes him strong like them and immune to further harm. The patient also absorbs their powers from the sands, exchanging evil for good. After similarly applying the bundle-prayersticks and parts of his own body to the patient, the singer erases the sandpainting, and the now infectious sand is carried out and deposited north of the hogan where it can do no harm. Since this process of identification makes the patient a Holy Person himself for a time, his acquired power could harm others; therefore, he has to observe four days of ceremonial restrictions obeying precise rules of behavior.

For one who is familiar with the symbolism of drypaintings and with the ceremonial myths, the sand pictures can serve as illustrations or at least reminders of the cardinal episodes of the stories. Few, however, are frankly narrative as we understand narration. Most of them show the Holy People in pairs or in quartets, or in larger multiples to increase their power, standing around on rainbow-bars, their means of transportation, or on black foundation bars, representing usually the earth, as if waiting for something to happen. To a Navajo the pictures are full of motion symbolically

---

[47] The selection depends first of course upon the singer's knowledge of the designs, and then upon his or the patient's wishes, the etiological factors thought to have caused the disease being treated, the ability of the sponsor to pay for more or less elaboration, or some such determinant.

indicated. The direction of the calves of a figure's legs, of his pouch, or his head feather, indicate the direction of his movement. These Holy People may always have human forms or they may be anthropomorphized animals, plants, natural phenomena, or even material objects. The pairs are called male and female although actually representing distinctions of power. Animals and plants may also be drawn in more or less naturalistic forms, and there are standard abstractions for natural phenomena, heavenly bodies, and mythological creatures. Place is eminently important to a Navajo and a locality symbol, the center in radial compositions or the foundation bar in a linear arrangement, is a conspicuous feature. Sequences of colors have directional, sexual, and other ritual meanings. Finally the entire picture is or should be surrounded by a border open to the east. This guardian, usually the red and blue Rainbow deity or garland, protects the space within it, while the eastern opening, often additionally guarded by a pair of small symbols, permits the entrance of good and the expulsion of evil into the outside world. Since these normally invisible powers made visible in the symbols of sand are extremely dangerous if mishandled, the drypainting designs are now frozen for safety's sake within traditional limits of ritual prescription. The innumerable combinations of an actually limited number of symbols, however, are evidence of ingenious creativity some time in the past. Most of this lateral variability within the confines of sanctioned style must have taken place before the end of the nineteenth century when Matthews made our first records, for as mentioned above there has been remarkable stability since that time.[48]

Reproductions of Mountainway Sandpaintings

BESIDES THE FOUR PUBLISHED by Matthews in 1887, ninety-two colored reproductions of Mountainway sandpaintings were found in ten different collections, all but a few crayon drawings painted in watercolor. Of these, twenty-six are duplicates of paintings in the same or in other collections. Seven of these copies were made as improvements over crude original sketches in the same collection, while nineteen of them were copies of paintings in other collections made by the same artist or by artists other than those who made the original reproduction. Seven Mountainway sandpaintings in the Arizona State Museum in Tucson are such copies: one of a painting in the Haile Collection; three of paintings collected

---

[48] For a detailed discussion of the symbolism, artistry, and psychology of Navajo sandpainting see Wyman, 1959.

by Laura A. Armer now in the Museum of Navaho Ceremonial Art in Santa Fe, New Mexico, made by Margaret Schevill Link formerly of Tucson; and three copies of paintings in the Wetherill Collection made by Clyde A. Colville of Kayenta, Arizona (see Wyman, 1952, p. 15). In the Museum of Navaho Ceremonial Art, there are copies of the four subjects in the Haile Collection and another of a painting which has disappeared from that collection, so it and a copy of it in the Arizona State Museum (see above) are the only witnesses to the particular design represented. There are also copies of the five Mountainway paintings in the Wetherill Collection, made by Clyde A. Colville, and a copy of a painting in the Huckel Collection. The single Mountainway sandpainting found in the Bush Collection of Religion and Culture at Columbia University, New York City, and one in the Reichard Collection in the Museum of Northern Arizona are apparently copies made by Franc J. Newcomb of her painting, *Great Plumed Arrows*, in the Museum of Navaho Ceremonial Art, although there is no evidence as to which of the three was the first one she made.

Table 1 shows the distribution in collections of the sixty-six paintings left after eliminating the duplicates, the recorders or collectors of those made by Navajos, the Navajo singers who made or directed the making of the original sandpaintings, their homes or the location of collecting the paintings, the dates of collecting, the number of reproductions, publication data, and the number published.[49]

---

[49] Following are the collections represented, each followed by the recorders or collectors of the paintings in them in parenthesis: John Frederick Huckel Collection, in the Taylor Museum, Colorado Springs (Sam Day, Jr., Saint Michaels, Arizona, or his brother Charlie, Chinle, Arizona; see Wyman, 1971); Wetherill Collection, now in the Museum of Northern Arizona, Flagstaff (Louisa Wade Wetherill, Kayenta, Arizona; see Wyman, 1952); Haile Collection, in the Museum of Northern Arizona (Father Berard Haile, Saint Michaels, Arizona); Museum of Navaho Ceremonial Art (MNCA), Santa Fe, New Mexico (Laura Adams Armer, Fortuna, California; Franc Johnson Newcomb, Albuquerque, New Mexico; Kenneth E. Foster, Santa Fe; Young Deer, no data, probably a Navajo); Oakes Collection, in MNCA (Maud Oakes, Big Sur, California); Museum of New Mexico (MNM), Santa Fe (Bertha P. Dutton, Santa Fe); Newcomb Collection, Albuquerque, New Mexico (Franc Johnson Newcomb; since her collection was in storage at the time of this study only the four paintings listed could be examined but in 1951 she said that she had twenty-seven Mountainway paintings; doubtless many of these are duplicates of her paintings in MNCA); Gladys A. Reichard Collection, in the Museum of Northern Arizona (Franc J. Newcomb). Singers' names are English renderings or transliterations of their Navajo nicknames or Anglo names by which they were known to the recorders.

Table 1
Reproductions of Mountainway Sandpaintings

Collection	Singer	Locality	Recorder, Collector	Date	No.
Huckel°	Speech Man	Canyon de Chelly, Ariz.	Sam Day, Jr.	1902	9
		(Published: 2-E.S. Curtis, 1907**; 1-N. Curtis, 1907; 7-Wyman, 1971)			
Wetherill	Sam Chief	Oljeto, Utah	Wetherill	1910 – 18	5
			(Published: 5-Wyman, 1952)		
Haile	Yucca Patch Man	Fort Defiance Coal Mine, Ariz.	Haile	1935	5†
	The Crawler	Black Mt., Ariz.	Armer	1926	3
		(Published: 1-Berry, 1929)			
	Busy Singer	Black Mt., Ariz.	Armer	1929	5
	unknown	Black Mt., Ariz.	Armer	1929	1
	Tall Navajo's Son	Huerfano region, N.M.	Newcomb	1926	2
Museum of Navaho Ceremonial Art	Lefthanded	Newcomb, N.M.	Newcomb	1928	2
	unknown	Newcomb, N.M.	Newcomb	1929	1
	Gray Chief	Newcomb, N.M.††	Newcomb	ca. 1935	6
	Woman Singer	Canyon de Chelly, Ariz.	Newcomb	ca. 1935	1
	Salt Water Man	Chuska Mts., N.M.	Newcomb	1936	1
	Female Shootingway Singer	Sweetwater, Ariz.	Newcomb	1938	2
	Little Man	White Cone, Ariz.	Newcomb	1938	1
	Wilito Wilson	Mariano Lake, N.M.	Oakes(?)	1940's	1
	Jack Lee Frazier	Red Rock, Ariz.	Foster	1956	1
	Young Deer	unknown	unknown	unknown	6
Oakes	Willie Little	Mariano Lake, N.M.	Oakes	1946	4
Museum of New Mexico	Sam Tilden	Canyon de Chelly, Ariz.	Dutton	1940	4
	Gray Chief	Newcomb, N.M.††	Newcomb	1938	1
Newcomb	Red Singer	unknown	Newcomb	1938	1
	Tall Navajo's Son	Huerfano region N.M.	Newcomb	unknown	1
	unknown	unknown	Newcomb	unknown	1
			(Published: 1-Newcomb, 1949)		
Reichard	Gray Chief	Newcomb, N.M.††	Newcomb	ca. 1935	2

° *See footnote 49 for details concerning the collections and recorders or collectors.*

°° *See footnotes 51, 52, 53, 54, for detailed citations.*

† *One of these paintings has been lost and is known only from copies in the Museum of Navaho Ceremonial Art and the Arizona State Museum.*

†† *Gray Chief, who was "the biggest Mountain Chant singer" (Newcomb – notes), lived on the Washington Pass road between Crystal and Naschitti, New Mexico.*

Among the sixty-six reproductions listed are two small designs not used in the sandpainting ceremony, one a drypainting for a Blessingway rite (see p. 118 and Fig. 34), and the other a small sandpainting for the sweat-emetic ceremony. Among the remaining sixty-four designs, or sixty-eight including the four collected by Matthews, there are many which differ from one another only in trivial ways even to us—certainly not in ways which would be considered significant by a Navajo—such as different symbols used for the small paired guardians of the eastern opening, differences in the details of the costume of People or in the objects carried in their hands, or differences in the nature of the encircling guardian. Only eight categories of main theme symbols, or nine if one which is unique is included, are represented among the sixty-eight paintings. Moreover, there are only twelve types of designs made up of these symbols, or perhaps eighteen or twenty at the most, which would be distinguished by the Navajo, although we might discern up to about thirty-three designs which we would consider different. These main theme symbols and design types are presented in Table 2.

Table 2
MAIN THEME SYMBOLS AND DESIGNS
OF MOUNTAINWAY SANDPAINTINGS

Home of Bear and Snake		5	(2)*
People of The Myth		33	(12)
radial	14	(6)	
linear	9	(5)	
with long hair	6	(1)	
with packs	4		
The Long Bodies		8	(3)
Whirling Rainbow People		2	
Bears		3	(5)
Bear's Den (Shock Rite)		3	(1)
Porcupines		6	
Great Plumed Arrows		7	(3)
Big Snakes		1	

* *Number of reproductions of sandpaintings having the symbol or design. Numerals in parentheses are the number of copies of the same design in various collections.*

At least eighteen and possibly twenty-seven of the sixty-eight paintings have the advantage, or possibly disadvantage in one instance [Sam Chief], of having been made directly by Navajo informants. The paintings in the Huckel, Wetherill, and Museum of New Mexico Collections were made by Indians; those in the Haile Collection possibly were; and the five paintings by Young Deer in the Museum of Navaho Ceremonial Art probably were [the alleged artist's name could be a translation of a Navajo name and his crude sketches look like native work]. Of course, records made by Navajos themselves are more valuable than those which have been reproduced by non-Navajo recorders. In one instance, however, that of Sam Chief's paintings in the Wetherill Collection, the pictures suffered from his apparent delight in experimenting with the colored crayons provided by Mrs. Wetherill and possibly his reluctance to reproduce sandpaintings too accurately for fear of both supernatural and human reprisals (see Wyman, 1952, pp. 14–15, 114–115). Two of his three paintings, with bears as main themes, are fairly orthodox and so is one of his radial compositions with People as main themes (ibid., Figs. 14, 15, 18), but the other two pictures contain decidedly unusual features (ibid., Figs. 16, 17). All five Mountainway paintings made by Sam Chief have been described, discussed, and illustrated in the monograph on the Wetherill Collection (Wyman, 1952, pp. 48–56, Figs. 14–18).

Twenty-one of the sixty-eight designs have been published, seven in color,[50] one as a line drawing with slight color,[51] twelve in black and white half-tones or line drawings,[52] and one in sepia.[53] Moreover, four of the designs have been reprinted one or more times, all in black and white, in other publications.[54] Robert Thom, an artist, copied a portion of the sandpainting of the *Long Bodies* (Matthews, 1887, Plate XVI) in his oil painting to show a sandpainting ceremony as it was in the late nineteenth century for *A History of Medicine in Pictures*, published by Parke, Davis & Company in 1957. It shows a singer administering medicine in an abalone shell cup to a female patient seated on the sandpainting.

---

[50] Matthews, 1887, Plates XV–XVIII; E. S. Curtis, 1907, vol. 1, opp. p. 78; Newcomb, 1949, frontispiece; Wyman, 1971, cover.

[51] N. Curtis, 1907, opp. p. 366.

[52] Berry, 1929a, p. 16; Wyman, 1952, Figs. 14–18; 1971, Figs. 15–20.

[53] E. S. Curtis, 1907, vol. 1, Plate 39.

[54] Matthews, 1885, Plates XXXII, XXXIII; *El Palacio*, vol. 14, pp. 175–183, 1923; vol. 38, pp. 72–73, 1935; Berry, 1929b, Fig. 3; Armer, 1953, p. 8.

Thom's painting was reproduced in half-tone in Wyman, 1971, Fig. 3. Details concerning the publication of paintings from the Huckel Collection, including four of the Mountainway sandpaintings may be found in this monograph (pp. 29, 31).

Statements in the notes of the collectors of thirty-four of the sixty-eight sandpaintings indicate the branch of Mountainway, male or female, for which they were used, and presumptive evidence in the notes suggests the branch for thirteen others. According to these data, twenty-nine of the paintings are for the female branch and eighteen are for the male branch. The difference is not great enough to allow the conclusion that the female branch is the more common or preferred form of Mountainway, and moreover the figures would depend upon the specialties of the informants. Likewise, there is no definite correspondence between the nature of the main theme symbols or the design types and the two branches.

Three types of composition are used in sandpaintings: *radial* in which the main theme symbols are cardinally oriented in a Greek cross with subsidiary symbols in the quadrants around a locality center; *linear* in which the symbols are in a row or rows; and *extended center* in which an enlarged central symbol occupies most of the design. The composition of most Mountainway sandpaintings is about equally divided between radial and linear, with twenty-eight and thirty examples, and two which could be interpreted either way; eight other paintings have an extended center composition. Moreover, there are distinct correlations between some main theme symbols and compositions. All paintings of the *Home of Bear and Snake, Whirling Rainbow People,* and *Bears* are radial; those of *Long Bodies* and *People of the Myth with Packs* are linear and so is the single painting of *Big Snakes;* the paintings of *Bear's Den* for the shock rite and all but one of the paintings of *Porcupines* are extended center. The other paintings of *People of the Myth* have about the same number of radial and linear compositions, sixteen and thirteen, while the paintings of the *Great Plumed Arrows* show a mixture of compositions, two being definitely radial, three linear, and two with a combination of radial and linear arrangements.

Color, Sex, and Directional Symbolism

LACKING SUCH DISTINCTIONS as a difference in the shape of the head for the two sexes which occurs in the drypaintings of some chantways [Nightway, Navajo Windway, Red Antway], round for males and square for females, clues for associating color with sex or relative power are meagre in the sandpaintings of Mountainway. The notes accompanying the paintings in collections are likewise reticent in this respect. The few indications which we have, notes with paintings in the Haile Collection and with the depiction of porcupines by Young Deer, the pairing of the porcupines in the painting by Female Shootingway Singer (Fig. 28), the shape of the bear tracks in the pictures of *Bear's Den* by Speech Man, reveal that black and yellow are male colors, blue and white are female. Black and blue and yellow and white are bisexual pairs. This is like the situation in the sandpaintings of Navajo Windway (see Wyman, 1962, p. 286) but unlike that in Shootingway or Red Antway (Wyman, 1973, p. 213; 1970b, p. 12). In paintings by Mrs. Armer's informant, Busy Singer, those by Sam Tilden, and one in the Newcomb Collection by Red Singer, judging by the crooked or straight lightning marks on the arms and legs of the figures, black and blue are male colors, white and yellow are female. This is like the color symbolism of sex in Shootingway sandpaintings. Such a discrepancy is not surprising for Reichard pointed out long ago that color patterns and sequences for sex and direction are not fixed, even within a single chantway (1970, Chapter 13, p. 214 ff.).

In fifty Mountainway sandpaintings in which the usual four colors presumably have directional significance, three sequences predominate. In twenty-four radial or extended center compositions where direction is unmistakable, the east, south, west, north [sunwise] sequence is white, blue, yellow, black in ten, and black, blue, yellow, white [east and north have exchanged colors] in fourteen. The one linear painting of *Big Snakes* by Young Deer (Fig. 33) also shows this succession from south to north. These are the two commonest directional sequences. The second with black in the east represents protection from danger coming from that quarter and often is used in paintings of dangerous creatures, beings, or events (see Reichard, 1970, pp. 221–223; Wyman, 1962, p. 286; 1970b, p. 13). Eight of the paintings having black in the east contain dangerous elements, bears, snakes, or Whirling Rainbow People. The three paintings used for the shock rite in the Huckel Collection are in this group, and this procedure is associated with the bear as a dangerous participant (see Wyman, 1973, pp. 56–58). The other seven are radial paintings of *People of the Myth* which do not present any obvious associations with special dangers. Six other radial paintings of *People* have the first sequence with white in the east, an arrangement of lower potency, and so do all but one of the paintings of the *Home of Bear and Snake* (Figs. 3–5), including the one by Yucca Patch Man, who used another sequence for his other Mountainway sandpaintings. Apparently this sequence is firmly associated with this design which is puzzling considering that the protagonist's visit to the home of these fearsome creatures would have been fraught with danger. The one exception is the somewhat problematical picture made by Young Deer (Fig. 6) who did employ the danger sequence mentioned above.

The third predominating sequence, yellow, blue, white, black, reading from south to north, which is the direction usually said by informants to be the sunwise path, occurs in seventeen linear compositions. The reason for this sequence, or for a north to south reading of black, white, blue, yellow, in the absence of statements from informants, is not clear. Reichard did not include it in her extensive discussion of the symbolism of color combinations. Eleven of the fifteen linear paintings of *People of the Myth* having four figures show this sequence, including all four of *People with Packs* (Figs. 19, 20), and so do six of the eight paintings of the *Long Bodies* (Figs. 21, 23)—two more instances of definite associations of a directional color sequence with designs. One of the exceptions for the design of the *Long Bodies* was the one by Yucca Patch Man (Fig. 22) who used a south to north series of blue, yellow, white, black for all but one of his four paintings [the *Home of Bear and Snake*]. The other was the one by Wilito Wilson who used white, yellow, blue, black. Both of these are unexplained. The four other linear paintings of *People* with different sequences include two by Yucca Patch Man, just mentioned, and one by Lefthanded; but in the latter, two pairs of male beings, blue and black in the south and yellow and white in the north, approach the game animals in the center of the picture (see Fig. 16), so here we have an instance of pairing for some reason.

Single examples of each of four other unexplained sequences are as follows: black, blue, white, yellow in a radial painting of *People* by Mrs. Newcomb's informant, Red Singer; white, yellow, black, blue in a radial design by Sam Chief (Wyman, 1952, No. 19, p. 49); black, white, blue, yellow [south to north] in a linear painting of *Great Plumed Arrows* by Newcomb's informant, Little Man; white, yellow, blue, black, in the painting of *Porcupines* by Female Shootingway Singer, which is obviously an instance of sex pairing. The other three examples could well be recording-artist deviations (Wyman, 1962, p. 284).

In summary, of the three predominating sunwise directional color sequences in Mountainway sandpaintings, white, blue, yellow, black, the sequence of lower potency, occurs in the majority of paintings of the *Home of Bear and Snake,* and in about half of the radial paintings of *People of the Myth;* black, blue, yellow, white, the danger sequence, occurs in the other half of radial paintings of People, and in the paintings of *Whirling Rainbow People, Bear's Den* [shock rite], *Bears* (1), and *Big Snakes* (1); the south to north linear sequence of yellow, blue, white, black, occurs in the majority of linear paintings of *People of the Myth* and of the *Long Bodies.* Individual singers are quite consistent in their use of given sequences.

Symbols and Designs in Mountainway Sandpaintings

Not even the toughest-minded observer could make much sense of Navaho, Zuni, or Spanish American culture without becoming actively concerned with beauty and ugliness, enjoyment and avoidance. These and other elementary aesthetic-appreciative categories appear indispensable to a meaningful description of their life-ways.

Ethel M. Albert[55]

IN THE FOLLOWING DISCUSSIONS of the main theme symbols and design types of Mountainway sandpaintings, the provenience of individual paintings which may be described is indicated by the name of the Navajo author of the painting. Details concerning him, concerning the recorder or collector, the collection, and so on, may be found in footnote 49 and Table 1. The symbols and designs are listed in Table 2. Unless otherwise denoted, statements enclosed in quotation marks are taken from the field notes of the recorder or collector, presumably supplied by the Navajo author of the painting.

HOME OF BEAR AND SNAKE

ALL BUT ONE [Young Deer] of the five versions of the *Home of Bear and Snake* which have been recorded were said to be the first sandpainting made in a performance of Mountainway. In the chant described by Matthews (1887), this painting was made between one and three o'clock in the afternoon of the fifth day of the nine-night ceremonial and used after seven o'clock in the evening for

---

[55] 1966, introduction to chapter 9 in: *People of Rimrock, A Study of Values in Five Cultures,* Evon Z. Vogt and Ethel Albert, eds., p. 267.

a shock rite (Matthews, 1887, pp. 422–424; Wyman, 1973, pp. 45, 56–58) followed by a restoration rite (Wyman and Bailey, 1944, pp. 332–337). These are optional ceremonies which normally may be added to a ceremonial at extra expense if requested by the patient. More will be said about them in the discussion of the sandpaintings of *Bear's Den* below. The somewhat deviant painting by Young Deer was said to "be used at any time that is convenient, usually the second night, if the patient requests it," presumably for a shock rite.

This design commemorates the visit of the hero or heroine to the home of the bears and/or the snakes.

> 'Off in this direction,' whispered Niltci, pointing to the northeast, 'is a place called . . . (Where Yellow Streak Runs Down). Let us go thither.' Here they entered a house of one room, made of black water. The door was of wind. It was the home of . . . (Long Frog), of . . . (Water Snake), of . . . (Arrow Snake), and of other serpents and animals of the water. It was called . . . (They Came Together), because here the prophet . . . visited the home of the snakes and learned something of their mysteries. The ceremonies sacred to these animals belong to another dance, that of the . . . (chant of terrestrial beauty); but in the mysteries learned in . . . the two ceremonies are one. Here he was instructed how to make and to sacrifice four kethawns. To symbolize this visit . . . and this union of the two ceremonies, the first sand picture is made (Matthews, 1887, p. 409).

> . . . the Bear and Snake had made a circular house half white and half black on a mountain nearby, and the Bear sat on the white side smoking a white shell pipe, the Snake at the black side to the north smoking a turquoise pipe (Wheelwright, 1951, p. 4).

In the myth dictated by Yucca Patch Man, there are detailed instructions for making this sandpainting (p. 228). It is one of the two published by Matthews as a line drawing in 1885 (Plate XXXII) and in color in 1887 (Plate XV). The chief differences between the five recorded versions are in the varieties of snakes which are depicted. In the one by Yucca Patch Man (Fig. 3) all the snakes are slender and crooked. They have only deer track markings [chevrons] on their bodies, and there are red spots on their heads symbolizing

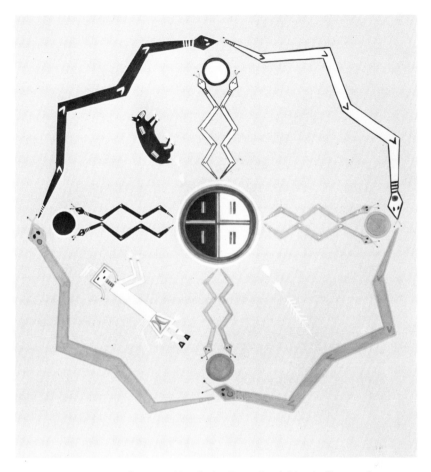

FIG. 3.   *Home of Bear and Snake,* by Yucca Patch Man (collection data for all the illustrations of sandpaintings may be found by referring to the Navajo author's name in Table 1). White snakes and mountain at east. Copy by Margaret Schevill Link in the Arizona State Museum.

their dangerous venom. Moreover, the pairs at the cardinal points are not crossed and there is a mountain [circle] of the same color as the snakes [directional; white, blue, yellow, black] above each pair. The four crooked snake guardians extend along the quadrants of the design. In the painting published by Matthews and in one of the two by Gray Chief which is almost identical to it (Fig. 4), all snakes are straight. In these and in the other one by Gray Chief, the snakes' body markings include both deer tracks and phases of the

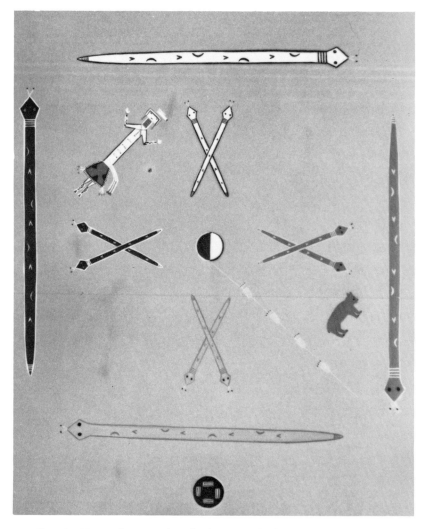

FIG. 4. *Home of Bear and Snake,* by Gray Chief. White snakes at east.

moon [curves]. The pairs at the cardinal points are crossed, and the four guardian snakes are along the cardinal sides of the picture. Moreover, west of each picture outside of the snake guardian is a black mountain with four short rainbow-bars on it. In practice this is a little mound made in relief. In Matthews' myth this mountain is the home of the porcupines (1887, p. 408). A trail of yellow corn-meal leads from the mountain to the center of the painting, and there are four bear tracks on it in the southwest quadrant. In Yucca Patch Man's version there are two tracks on opposite sides of the

FIG. 5.   *Home of Bear and Snake,* by Gray Chief. White snakes at east.

center. In one of the two versions by Gray Chief the snakes are all straight Big Snakes, mythological creatures which cannot be equated with any known natural species (Fig. 5). They are represented as short, thick serpents often swollen in the middle and either straight or crooked (Wyman, 1957, p. 167).

The black and white center of the sandpaintings represents the house [caves] of the Bear and the Snake. In Young Deer's version this was said to be the La Plata Mountains of southwestern Colorado, the black and white halves representing darkness and daylight, with four trees growing from the center.

In the sandpainting by Yucca Patch Man and the two by Gray Chief, the white human figure in the northeast quadrant [northwest in Yucca Patch Man] and the blue bear in the southwest [black, in northeast in Yucca Patch Man] represent Older Sister, the heroine of the myth, and her relentless pursuer, Bear Man. These are paintings for the female branch of Mountainway and these two beings are the chief actors in the myth of that branch. Matthews said that the white Person in the sandpainting which he published represented the Wind who accompanied the Navajo hero of the myth to the home of the snakes and that he believed that the bear was a symbol of the hero himself (1887, p. 447). The myth which Matthews recorded is presumably a story of the male branch and he related the sandpaintings which he recorded to it. There is no assurance, however, that the actual performances of Mountainway which he witnessed and from which he derived his copies of the paintings were of the same branch as that of the myth which he collected. In fact the close similarity between his version of the *Home of Bear and Snake* and one by Gray Chief said to be for the female branch suggests either that both were for Female Mountainway or that the same design may be used for either branch.

The *Home of Bear and Snake* by Young Deer differs considerably from the other four versions (Fig. 6). In fact the set of five paintings made by him are more or less deviant from most other Mountainway sandpaintings. His pair of porcupines and the two linear paintings of pairs of People show some differences, perhaps insignificant ones, in design and details, but his painting of *Big Snakes* is unique. Nothing is known about this informant. The paintings are said to be for Male Mountainway but there is no other evidence that this branch is the determinant for the differences. In his *Home of Bear and Snake* there are no pairs of snakes in cardinal positions, no Person and no bear. The guardians are crooked, horned and feathered, Big Snakes, with red spots of venom on their heads and dens [squares] on their bodies, as well as the other markings mentioned above. They lie along the quadrants of the design and there is a pair of bear tracks inside each one. Moreover, in the sunwise color sequence black is in the east and white is in the north, instead of the reverse as in the other versions of this design. Employing this danger sequence is congruous with the use of this painting for the terrifying shock rite, and it is also found in the shock rite sandpaintings of *Bear's Den*. Perhaps the use of the milder sequence with

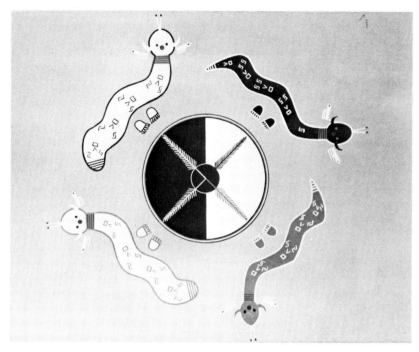

FIG. 6.   *Home of Bear and Snake*, by Young Deer.
Top of painting east. Copy by Miriam Hurford.

white in the east for the other versions of the *Home of Bear and Snake* indicates that these normally dangerous beings really meant no harm to the heroine of Female Mountainway but were simply concerned with her instruction.

PEOPLE OF THE MYTH

PEOPLE, THAT IS BEINGS IN HUMAN FORM, are the main theme symbols in forty-four sandpaintings which have been recorded. These include depictions of People in both radial and linear compositions, the *Long Bodies, Whirling Rainbow People,* and the two figures in one of the shock rite paintings (Wyman, 1971, Fig. 18). For the following discussion of People in general, three of these paintings have been eliminated because they contain decidedly unorthodox or uncertain features, leaving forty-one.[56]

---

[56] In the two paintings of pairs of People by Young Deer, their headdresses and the objects carried in their hands are unlike those of any other Mountainway sandpaintings. The painting of *People with Long Hair* by Jack Lee Frazier not only displays a weasel headdress characteristic of Beautyway and peculiar arm strings, but the notes with it are equivocal as to its chant affiliation.

The identity of the People was not always clearly stated by the informants but most of them no doubt represent the Mountain Gods or Goddesses [in the paintings by Busy Singer the figures are said to be feminine], called Reared-in-the-Mountains, to resemble whom the hero was molded, painted, and dressed by Butterfly Woman in Matthews' myth (1887, p. 406; Wyman, 1971, p. 60), and the Meal Sprinklers [couriers], painted and costumed in actual practice of the ceremonial (Matthews, 1887, pp. 424–425; Haile, 1946, pp. 1–4). The People in some paintings of the female branch are said to be the heroine of the myth (Gray Chief, Woman Singer; Fig. 8). In others they are called dancers in the Dark Circle of Branches [Corral Dance, Fire Dance] in a ceremonial (Salt Water Man, Fig. 11; Lefthanded, Fig. 16; Tall Navajo's Son, Figs. 9, 17; unknown – Armer).

Usually no sex distinctions are made among the People in a single sandpainting, leaving us to assume that they are all the same. Differentiation of sex by the shape of the head does not occur, but in a few paintings two of the four figures in a set have crooked lightning on their arms and legs while the other two have straight lightning, a difference which ordinarily indicates male and female beings (Busy Singer, Sam Tilden, Red Singer; Figs. 14, 15). Moreover, Father Berard's notes designate the figures from south to north in the linear design which he called "Holy Young Man's sandpainting" as Holy Boy, Holy Young Woman, Holy Young Man, Holy Girl (Yucca Patch Man; Fig. 13). In single instances People in paintings are called "gods of the cultivated plants" (Matthews, 1887, pp. 404, 447–450), "mountain medicine boys" or "tracking bear boys," and "spirits of the mountain girls" (Sam Chief; Wyman, 1952, pp. 49, 52), or "Bear Gods" (The Crawler).

Besides the usual earrings and necklaces of turquoise and coral, arm strings, decorated skirts with tassels, sashes and embroidered pouches, People in Mountainway sandpaintings exhibit certain characteristic features, some of which they share with the People of other chants. In twenty-six of the forty-one paintings they wear tall feather and weasel-skin headdresses which differ from the weasel headdress of Beautyway (Wyman, 1957, p. 176) in that they do not include the pointed red feather hat which is also characteristic of Shootingway (Wyman, 1970b, p. 13).[57] Instead the center

---

[57] The Long Bodies in the painting, said to be by Wilito Wilson, wear a typical Beautyway headdress with the red hat so this may be one exception, but the collection data with the painting are uncertain.

consists of five tall erect feathers, white or variegated, with bent and drooping streamers, usually short and variegated, at the sides of the head (Figs. 7, 13–15, 20–23; see Matthews, 1887, p. 450). These are strips of weasel skin or "strips of reeds ending in prairie dog fur" (Gray Chief). In one Beautyway sandpainting Big Thunder wears a headdress like this (Wyman, 1957, Plate XV). In only two paintings the headdresses are the tall erect feathers alone (The Crawler—*People with Long Hair*, Fig. 18; Busy Singer—*People with Packs*, Fig. 19). In seven sandpaintings, five of dancers (Salt Water Man, Tall Navajo's Son, Lefthanded, unknown—Armer) and two of *Whirling Rainbow People* (Tall Navajo's Son, Gray Chief), the tall feather and weasel headdress is made more intricate by the addition of a pair of bison horns (Figs. 9–11, 16, 17, 24). Some of these are very elaborate, "gorgeous headdresses of weasel pelt, buffalo horns, cane strips, and medicine bundles" (Tall Navajo's Son, Fig. 17). They remind us of the bison headdresses of Shootingway and Mountain-Shootingway, but these consist of the familiar red feather hat with bison horns attached to it (Wyman, 1970b, pp. 26, 27, 44, Plates 24–26). Finally, in five paintings the People wear the simple standard head plume seen in the majority of the sand-paintings of many chants (Matthews, 1887, Plate VII; the two by Sam Chief). In two of these the figures depict the heroine of the myth of female Mountainway (Gray Chief, Woman Singer; Fig. 8).

In thirty-five of the forty-one paintings the People have square heads, round heads in only six (Matthews, Gray Chief, Woman Singer, and the three by The Crawler). Obviously, as mentioned above, the differentiation of sex by the shape of the head which Matthews made known long ago does not occur in Mountainway sandpaintings. As Reichard said, "The choice is probably different in every chant," and "the head shape must be learned for each painting" (1970, pp. 176–177). Her suggestion, however, that square-headed figures represent earth people or their interme-diaries and that "round heads stand for deity itself," that is, round and square represent dominant and secondary power, does not hold here because among the few round-headed figures are the heroine of the myth in two paintings (Gray Chief, Woman Singer). An unusual feature is that in the painting by Woman Singer and in two by The Crawler the head of the Rainbow guardian is round like those of the main theme figures.

In twenty-nine sandpaintings the faces of People are white repre-senting either face painting (Matthews, 1887, p. 406), or a white mask. The Long Bodies in Lefthanded's painting of them have "masks of white mist, held on by strips of pollen and rainbow" (Fig. 21). White faces are also characteristic of Beautyway sandpaintings, and of those of Waterway and Beadway (Wyman, 1957, pp. 165–166, 184). The square female faces in Red Antway paintings are white and so are those of some of the figures in Mountain-Shootingway, Nightway, Plumeway, Upward-reachingway, and Blessingway drypaintings. In six paintings Peoples' faces are pink (Speech Man — Wyman, 1971, Fig. 17; unknown — Armer), representing masks of weasel skin (Woman Singer, Fig. 8) or prairie dog hide (Salt Water Man, Fig. 11). Whirling Rainbow People also wear pink masks of weasel skin (Lefthanded, Tall Navajo's Son; Fig. 24). In six other paintings faces are brown representing natural skin color. This is true of all of Matthews' designs having People and of the dancers in four other paintings (Lefthanded, Tall Navajo's Son, unknown — Newcomb).

The People in twenty-one sandpaintings wear an otter or beaver skin collar with a whistle attached to it (Fig. 7) and in five paintings they have the collar but without a whistle (Fig. 20). This property, sometimes also worn by People in Beautyway paintings, is an important item in a Shootingway singer's bundle and may be worn by figures in Shootingway and Mountain-Shootingway sandpaintings (Wyman, 1972).[58] Among the fifteen designs in which the otter skin collar and whistle does not appear are five showing dancers, five with the Long Bodies, and the two with Whirling Rainbow People.

About half of the paintings containing People show them wearing clothing adorned with beads and porcupine quill embroidery stolen from the Utes (see pp. 146, 148; Matthews, 1887, p. 397; Wheelwright, 1951, pp. 12–13).[59] These decorations are represented by groups, usually five in number, of spots or of parallel vertical marks of all colors, distributed evenly along the bodies of the figures (Figs. 13–15, 19, 20). Among the twenty designs not showing this feature are the eight pictures of Long Bodies where the multiple skirts would naturally hide such ornaments, five paintings of dancers, the three by The Crawler, the two by Sam Chief,

---

[58] The fur collar serves as a badge of recognition for singer and patient and the attached whistle is used to signal, summon, and attract the supernatural Holy People. The collar may be made of either otter or beaver skin, but a Shootingway singer must possess at least a small strip of otter skin.

[59] In the sandpaintings of Beadway, Scavenger, the hero of the myth, wears beads obtained by trickery, in this case from the Pueblo people.

and the Whirling Rainbow People whose bodies are composed of the rainbow colors (Fig. 24).

Since in actual chant practice the Meal Sprinklers are painted and adorned so as to resemble the hero of the myth of Male Mountainway [after he had been made to look like the Mountain Gods, Reared-in-the-Mountains, who are depicted in the sandpaintings], it is strange that the plume bundles representing wings [attached to the upper arms of these couriers] to give them speed are shown only in the three paintings by The Crawler (Matthews, 1887, pp. 406, 425, Fig. 52; Haile, 1946, p. 2). Here they are depicted as eagle plume feathers attached by tie strings to the middle of the upper arms (Figs. 12, 18). In thirteen other paintings, however, there are two white lines across the upper arms of the People which may very well be substitutes for showing the plumes themselves (Figs. 7, 15). In thirty-seven paintings, on the other hand, the blackening of the forearms and lower legs with charcoal from burned plants, a regular part of the decoration of the Meal Sprinklers, is depicted and the white lightning marks drawn on them are shown (Matthews and Haile, ibid.). In thirty instances these lightning marks are zig-zag on all the People in the painting, but in the other seven they are zigzag on two of the four figures and straight on the other two, a distinction which ordinarily indicates male and female beings (Busy Singer, Fig. 15; Sam Tilden, Fig. 14; Red Singer, Fig. 7). This adornment symbolizes "lightning on the surface of the black rain clouds" (Matthews, 1887, p. 448), and gives the couriers the speed of lightning (Haile, 1946, p. 2). In a painting of the *Long Bodies* (Lefthanded, Fig. 21) the blackening with charcoal from the logs burned in the Fire Dance and the lightning symbols show that "the Mountain Goddesses are not afraid of the fire and will not be burned by it." "This fire really belongs to the Mountain People as it was the mountain area which produced the trees used for the ceremony."

The four objects, one or more of which are held in the hands or are attached by strings to the wrists of People, in the majority of Mountainway sandpaintings are: a hide rattle like that used in Shootingway and other chants (see Kluckhohn and Wyman, 1940, pp. 40–43; Wyman, 1972), a magic travel basket, bundles of twigs or branches of spruce, and Sun's tobacco pouch. The basket, a colored circle usually crossed by rainbow or other stripes, has four eagle plumes attached at four sides in a swastika-like arrangement. This "whirling basket was used by the heroine as a means of moving swiftly; she stepped into it and was transported wherever she wished" (Gray Chief). It is a "magic basket in which to fly from place to place" (Woman Singer). The basket is shown in twenty-nine paintings, in the left hand in twenty of them. The rattles appear in thirty-two paintings, held in the right hand in all but one. Spruce twigs or boughs are carried in twenty-seven paintings, in the left hand in sixteen, in the right in nine, and in both hands in two. The Sun's tobacco pouch is in eleven paintings, attached to the right wrist in eight, the left in three. A common arrangement is with the rattle and tobacco pouch on the right, the basket and spruce on the left (nine examples). In eight paintings chokecherry branches are carried instead of spruce. This mountain plant, a favorite food of the bear, appears in all four sandpaintings of *People with Packs* (see Wyman, 1971, p. 60, Fig. 16), and in two or perhaps three of the *Long Bodies* (Matthews, 1887, p. 450; Lefthanded, Fig. 21; Yucca Patch Man, Fig. 22). It reminds us of Wide Chokecherry, the home of the Mountain Gods, Reared-in-the-Mountains, who live in a chokecherry house (Matthews, 1887, p. 409). In The Crawler's three paintings, two of the People in each of the four quartets carry an ear of corn in the left hand, a rattle in the right, while the other two carry a basket and spruce twigs [or chokecherries ?]. The first pair may be the males (Figs. 12, 18). Other objects found in only one or two paintings are a "charm" or "plume stick" [prayerstick] (Matthews, 1887, pp. 448, 450, Plates VI, VII); medicine bag of "prairie dog skin," plumed wand, and a pair of eagle feathers (Sam Chief; Wyman, 1952, pp. 49, 52, Figs. 14, 16); fir trees (Woman Singer, Fig. 8); "medicine herbs and tree branches" (Salt Water Man, Fig. 11); yellow cane flute (*Long Bodies*—Newcomb).

Red, the color of danger, war, sorcery, flesh, and blood, is also the color of fire. Black God, the Navajo fire god, the being in control of fire and fire making, always wears a red kilt when he is depicted in sandpaintings, such as those of Nightway. Red, therefore, is an appropriate hue to be associated with a ceremonial which includes a Fire Dance among its ceremonies. Mrs. Newcomb said that red skirts are associated with this dance and are sometimes worn by figures in Beautyway sandpaintings because this chant presented a fire dance in its prototype (Wyman, 1957, p. 166, Plates VII, XI). Red dance kilts, therefore, should certainly be prominent in Mountainway sandpaintings for one of its most distinctive features in the final Fire Dance. The multiple skirts worn by the Long Bodies are invariably red, and thirteen other recorded sandpaintings show red skirts. One of these is Matthews' radial design of Mountain People whose skirts were said to be "of red sunlight, adorned with sunbeams" (1887, p. 448, Plate XVII). There are also a few references in recorder's field notes to "the red dancing kilt that belongs only to those ceremonies which end in a fire dance" (Salt Water Man) or to the "red [fire] kilts" worn by the male dancers in the picture (Tall Navajo's Son).

People usually stand on individual short rainbow-bar foundations (in twenty-seven paintings), which represent protection and/or their means of travel. In radial compositions pairs or quartets of People are on longer rainbow-bars (Figs. 12, 18). In the paintings by Yucca Patch Man the People stand on triangular cloud symbols (Figs. 13, 22). In fifteen of twenty-two linear compositions, besides the individual foundations there are long foundation bars for the entire set of figures. In two paintings of *Long Bodies* (Newcomb) there are no individual bases, only the one long bar. Such foundation bars are usually black and spotted at intervals with groups of dots, short dashes, or crosses of various colors. They are said to represent the earth full of many colored seeds. In one painting by Busy Singer the bar is blue with stars [?] on it (Fig. 15). In Yucca Patch Man's two paintings of the Holy People the black foundation bar is incorporated in the west side of the body of the encircling Rainbow guardian (Fig. 13). In all the other designs having the bar it is separate and above the guardian (Figs. 14, 15).

The symmetrical shape of the tall feather and weasel-skin head-dress worn by People in most Mountainway sandpaintings does not give us a clue to the direction of their movement as does the standard head plume streaming out behind, but the bulge of the calf of their legs naturally being in the rear and their decorated pouches hanging behind them serve as guides. These clues, and the standard head plume in the five paintings having it, show that in all radial compositions the People are marching sunwise around the center, that is from east to south and so on to the north. The one discrepancy is in Matthews' radial design where the head plume and the calves and pouch indicate opposite directions, an obviously impossible situation and therefore an error in recording. In the linear compositions the movement is from south to north in all except Yucca Patch Man's two paintings of Holy People where it is from north to south (Fig. 13), in one by Lefthanded in which two pairs of People approach the animals in the center of the picture (Fig. 16), and in two paintings of the *Long Bodies* (Matthews, 1887, Plate XVI; Yucca Patch Man, Fig. 22) where the calves of the legs show that the figures are standing still. South to north is usually taken as the sunwise direction in linear designs.

People of the Myth — radial

SANDPAINTINGS WITH *People of the Myth* in radial arrangement exist in sixteen reproductions, including the two of *People with Long Hair* described below. In seven of these, People possessing the general characteristics discussed above proceed around a circular center which represents a pool, lake, or spring (Fig. 7). This body of water is blue in two reproductions (unknown — Armer, Gray Chief) and black in five (Matthews, 1887, Plate XVII; Speech Man, in Wyman, 1971, Fig. 17; Sam Chief, in Wyman, 1952, Fig. 14; Red Singer; Gray Chief — "a spring with tiny sunflowers around it"). Matthews said the one he recorded was the picture the hero

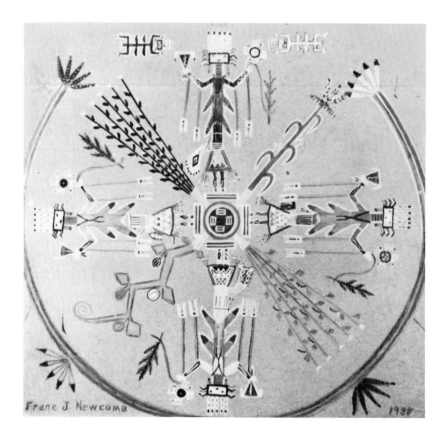

FIG. 7. *People of the Myth — radial*, by Red Singer. In this and in subsequent paintings having an encircling guardian the opening in it is at the east.

saw in the home of the bears in the Carrizo Mountains: "and they drew from one corner of the cave a great sheet of cloud, which they unrolled, and on it were painted the forms of the yays of the culti-vated plants" (1887, p. 404). Speech Man called the central water "the moisture of the mountain." The two radial designs of People by Sam Chief, one quite orthodox, the other containing several fantastic features such as the bears' houses with service-berries in them, have been adequately illustrated and described in Wyman, 1952 (pp. 49–52, Figs. 14, 16).

In Woman Singer's painting, figures of the heroine of the myth of Female Mountainway, masked in weasel skin [pink], appear around a black center with a fire [red cross] in it (Fig. 8). This represents the corral or Dark Circle of Branches. The inner white outline, "de-notes where the initiates are and each successive circle denotes each type of spectator until the outer black circle which is the trees surrounding the corral. Four fir trees project from the center," and

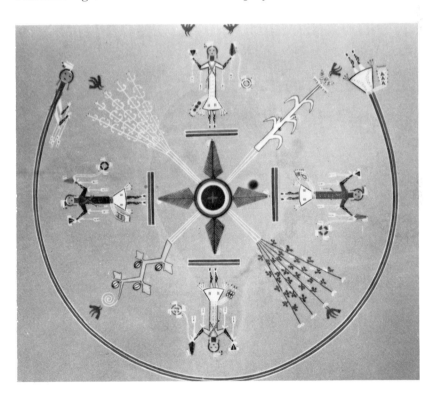

FIG. 8.   *People of the Myth—radial* (the heroine of the myth), by Woman Singer.

FIG. 9.   *People of the Myth — radial* (dancers), by Tall Navajo's Son.

the figures carry a little fir or spruce tree in their left hands. The last group of dancers who enter the corral at dawn "carry little spruce trees in their hands" (O'Bryan, 1956, p. 125). They press these to the body of the patient, "sanctifying him" (Haile, 1946, p. 52).[60] These dancers from Young Spruce Knoll commemorate the episode in the myth where White-Circle-of-Teeth-Woman saves the heroine from Bear Man by wrapping her in a spruce [fir] garment, which is "what he [Bear Man] really fears" (Yucca Patch Man). The belief that the bear fears spruce thus forms the basis of a procedure in the combat against him as an etiological factor. The Rainbow guardian has a head like those of the People with a pink masked face, one

---

[60] At dawn four men carrying spruce trees enter, walk around the fire four times singing, and then press the trees to the patient in ceremonial order, one after the other. The patient then arises, walks around the fire four times followed by the singer with a basket of water which he sprinkles in the patient's footsteps. Then the patient leaves the ceremonial hogan, walks up a hill, and says a pollen prayer to the rising sun (myth by Hastin Sei, recorded by Margot Astrov).

of the rare examples of a round-headed Rainbow deity (see The Crawler's paintings below).

Four pairs of dancers wearing bison headdresses and carrying "mountain herbs" [chokecherry?] in each hand also dance around a black corral "on a mountain" in a painting by Tall Navajo's Son (Fig. 9). White and yellow outlines are the pollen which is used to demarcate and bless the circle before the Dark Circle of Branches, shown outside of them, is erected. The fire, a red cross, is in the center and zigzag and straight trails lead in four directions to the dancers' rainbow foundation bars. There is a bear [black, blue, yellow, white] between each pair of dancers, "because they are holding the ceremony in their domain." The Rainbow guardian also wears a bison headdress, a red "fire kilt," and has a brown face like the dancers.

In still another sandpainting the center speckled with all colors is "the mountain top where the fire will be built" (unknown— Newcomb; Fig. 10). Trails, two zigzag and two straight, lead from it

FIG. 10. *People of the Myth—radial* (dancers), by unknown (Newcomb, 1929).

to the four mountains around the center, "which bound the Navajo territory, as a token that everyone in Navajo country will be invited." In practice the mountains are built up in relief and green twigs are erected in their tops, making an arrangement that resembles a Dark Circle of Branches. The four dancers wear bison headdresses, Mountain Medicine People are in the quadrants, and the guardian is a rainbow rope or garland with black cloud symbol ends. The paired guardians of the east are also mountains, a black one and a white one, each with a pair of bear tracks on it. "A fire ceremony is never held in the fall until someone has seen the footprints of a bear in the hoar frost or snow."

A painting by Salt Water Man has the most complex center of all Mountainway radial designs (Fig. 11). The red fire cross in the middle is surrounded by white heat with an outline of black ashes. Outside of this is the yellow pollen outline with which the singer marked off and blessed the circle for the corral. The blue and red

Fig. 11. *People of the Myth—radial* (dancers), by Salt Water Man.

outlines show where the spectators will sit and the black outline around them is the corral itself. Outside of this are twenty-four tents to house the visitors, in four groups of six each, interrupted at the four sides by the "tall painted headdresses that will be worn by dancers." Zigzag and straight trails lead from the center to the rainbow-bars on which are four pairs of dancers, wearing bison headdresses, pink masks of prairie dog hide, and carrying medicine herbs [chokecherry?] and branches for the singer to use in the ceremonial. "These things belong to the Mountain Gods and to the Bear who control all mountain magic." A white trail leads from the center to the white southeast mountain in the encircling guardian and thence to the other three mountains, blue, yellow, black, completing the guardian. This path indicates a trip "to ask permission of the bear to hold this fire ceremony on the mountain slopes, and to invite all relatives and friends to come to it." On the trail between the mountains are three sets of four white porcupine tracks with black claws. At the head of this trail in the northeast corner is a black porcupine, "first cousin to the bear, and like the bear, never killed by the Navajo." The paired eastern guards are black bears. This "mountain trail sandpainting" is somewhat like The Crawler's radial painting of *People with Long Hair* described below, with its guardian of mountains, porcupine tracks, and the black porcupine at the northeast (Fig. 18).

Mrs. Armer recorded two other sandpaintings made by The Crawler, each showing four quartets of People around a center with four-tiered clouds projecting from it. In one the center is black water and in the other it has segments of the four directional colors (Fig. 12). In the latter there are chokecherries in all the quadrants, instead of the usual four kinds of plants. The Rainbow guardian in both has a round head with face and headdress like those of the People, one of the very few examples of a round-headed Rainbow diety.

People of the Myth — linear

EXCEPT FOR THE TWO PAINTINGS of People by Young Deer, the linear compositions showing People of the Myth contain four figures apiece. Young Deer's designs show a pair of People, in one case said to be a male and female pair of dancers "who face each other in the dance," carrying a wand with two triangular feathered segments in each hand, and in the other a pair of Holy Young Men holding a great plumed arrow in the right hand and a sack of white

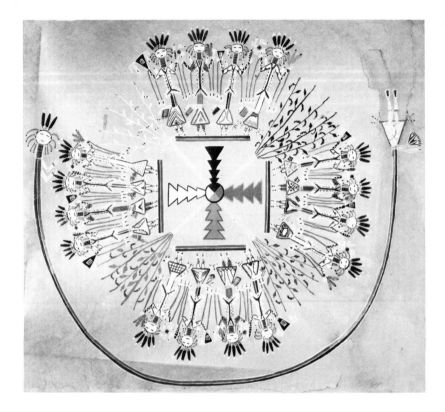

FIG. 12. *People of the Myth — radial*, by The Crawler. Copy by Margaret Schevill Link in the Arizona State Museum.

cornmeal in the left. The possible identity and the chief characteristics of the People in the other seven sandpaintings have been discussed above (Speech Man, Yucca Patch Man, Busy Singer, unknown — Armer, Sam Tilden). Each of two pairs of these paintings is from a set of four made by a given singer. The two designs in each pair are almost identical except for the paired guardians of the eastern entrance, bears or bats (Yucca Patch Man, Fig. 13), Big Flies or bats (Sam Tilden, Fig. 14). In one pair (Yucca Patch Man) the People guarded by bears have a basket in the left hand, those guarded by bats have three spruce twigs. Otherwise the members of each of the two pairs are alike. Neither informant made any statement about the use of these similar paintings. Two other pairs of paintings from sets of four made by Speech Man and by Busy Singer have People resembling each other, except for their long hair in

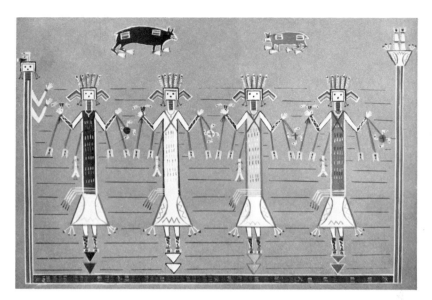

FIG. 13. *People of the Myth — linear,* by Yucca
Patch Man. Copy by Franc J. Newcomb.

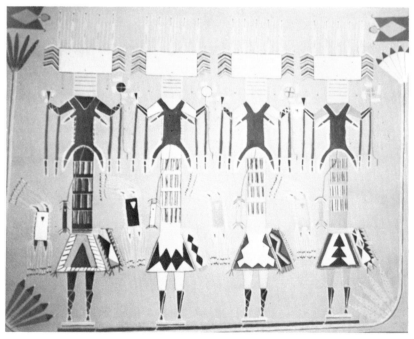

FIG. 14. *People of the Myth — linear,* by Sam Tilden.

one painting of each pair and again the paired guardians are different, Big Flies or bats (see Wyman, 1971, Fig. 15; Fig. 15). Is it possible that Yucca Patch Man and Sam Tilden omitted the long hair
from their paintings for some reason, such as a desire to avoid supernatural anger for having made too exact copies of sandpaintings
in permanent form?

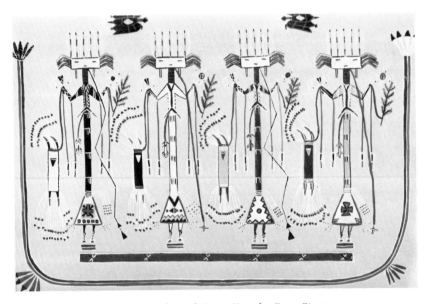

FIG. 15.   *People with Long Hair*, by Busy Singer.

People with Long Hair

FOUR LINEAR SANDPAINTINGS show four People who in most re-
spects are like the *People of the Myth* in the other linear compositions, except that they have long strands of hair hanging down from
their heads. These include the somewhat questionable design by
Jack Lee Frazier (see footnote 56). Their long hair is like the "rain
hair" of the Rain or Storm People of the Hail Chant and Water
Chant (see Wheelwright, 1946, pp. 181, 184, 188, 194, 196).[61] The
fourth supernatural home visited by the hero of Matthews' myth in
his *Journey for Knowledge and Power*, after his escape from the
Utes, was the house of the Butterfly (1887, p. 406). Here he bathed,
painted his face white and his forearms and legs black, and was

---

[61] The "Coyote Girls" in some of the sandpaintings of Coyoteway have long black
streamers hanging down from their heads which may represent long hair (see Wheelwright, 1956, Plates XVII, XVIII).

dressed and adorned with a beaver skin collar with a whistle attached to it and plumed sticks on his arms to represent wings, so that he resembled the Mountain Gods called Reared-in-the-Mountains. The Meal Sprinklers or couriers sent out to summon guests to a Fire Dance are similarly costumed to this day (Haile, 1946, pp. 2–4). "When the painting was done . . . [Butterfly Woman] took hold of his hair and pulled it downward and stretched it until it grew in profusion down to his ankles."

The Peoples' long hair in the paintings by Busy Singer and Speech Man is zigzag on two of the four figures and straight on the other two, reminding us of the zigzag and straight lightnings usually indicating male and female beings (Fig. 15; Wyman, 1971, Fig. 15). Moreover, in Speech Man's design both arms of the figures are on their right sides towards the direction they are moving. In the other two paintings all the Peoples' hair is zigzag.

In Lefthanded's painting, made "for the last day when animals [some use birds also] are blessed and there are prayers for their generous reproduction," two pairs of male dancers with zigzag long hair, wearing weasel-skin and bison horn headdresses, approach the game animals in the center of the design (Fig. 16). The pairs of

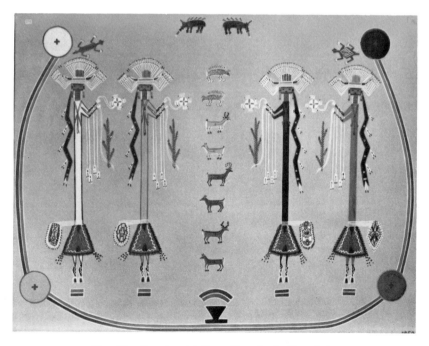

FIG. 16.   *People with Long Hair*, by Lefthanded.

dancers move in from the south and from the north, with their hands holding "pollen baskets and cedar boughs toward the animals." The animals, in a west to east vertical line above a curved rainbow-bar and a black cloud symbol, are in pairs, the male above the female and facing in the opposite direction. From west to east they are blue deer, blue mountain sheep, yellow antelope, and blue squirrels. These game animals "are probably the ones that were hunted to furnish food for the first Mountain Chant." If these were numerous, then the Navajo had plenty of food. There is an otter and a turtle, "representing water," above the heads of the north and south figures, and a pair of black bears guard the eastern entrance. "The whole ceremony is dedicated to the bear." The encircling guardian in this painting is unusual, consisting of the four sacred mountains, black, blue, yellow, and white, connected with each other by strands of rainbow rope. On top of each mountain is a red cross of fire.

A radial composition by Tall Navajo's Son is one of two recorded radial designs showing People with Long Hair. Like Lefthanded's linear painting just described, it includes game animals, "showing that they will be included in the blessing rite to produce fertility" (Fig. 17). This was said to be "the largest and most comprehensive painting" used in Mountainway. In it four pairs of dancers are "coming from the four directions." One member of each pair has straight long hair and carries a basket, with both arms on the left side, the other has zigzag hair and carries a spruce bough. All wear bison headdresses. The center presents the corral with a fire in it where the dancers will perform. Around it are four stacks of harvested corn, and zigzag or straight lightning paths connect the center with the Peoples' rainbow-bar foundations. Black corn and squash and blue beans and tobacco are in the quadrants. Circling around the dancers are thirteen animals, five kinds in pairs with the male preceding the female. Sunwise from the southeast they are a brown otter, white and yellow prairie dogs [?], pairs of yellow antelopes, blue deer, blue mountain sheep, and blue squirrels, a brown turtle, and a white squirrel. Black bears, with a pair of short rainbow-bars between them, guard the east. The encircling guardian, as in Lefthanded's painting, includes the four mountains but here they are of all colors. The southwest and northwest mountains are connected by a rainbow rope or trail while they are connected with the southeast and northeast mountains by "rainbow ladders" of all colors. "The couriers travel on these paths to invite all friendly tribes to the ceremony." If not the largest, this is certainly one of the handsomest Mountainway sandpaintings.

FIG. 17. *People with Long Hair,* by Tall Navajo's Son.

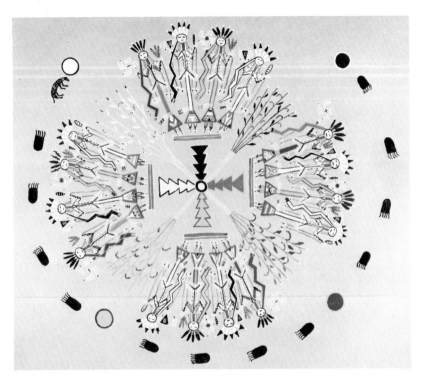

FIG. 18.   *People with Long Hair*, by The Crawler. Copy
by Margaret Schevill Link in the Arizona State Museum.

The other radial design showing People with Long Hair is one of
The Crawler's three radial compositions. It depicts four quartets
of People ["Bear Gods"], all with zigzag long hair, around a white
center with four-tiered clouds on it (Fig. 18). Chokecherries are in
the quadrants. This painting also has an encircling guardian which
includes the four mountains, black, blue, yellow, white. Three sets
of four black porcupine tracks complete the guardian between the
mountains and a black porcupine "is about to enter the white mountain of the north. He is a bigger chief than the bear. Navajos may kill
but not eat him and must not eat pinyon nuts that he has gathered."

People with Packs

ANOTHER FOUR LINEAR COMPOSITIONS show four People which
again are like other People of the Myth, except that they have
"mountains" of contrast colors on their backs with chokecherries

growing on them and carry chokecherry branches instead of spruce (Figs. 19, 20; Wyman, 1971, Fig. 16). The fifteenth place visited by the hero of Matthews' myth in his *Journey for Knowledge and Power* was Wide Chokecherry, "where, in a house of cherries with a door of lightning, there lived four gods named . . . [Reared-in-the-Mountains]. The Navajo was surprised to find that not only had they the same name as he had, but that they looked just like him and had clothes exactly the same as his" (1887, p. 409). Here he learned the dance of the Great Plumed Arrows, how to swallow and withdraw them. The sandpainting of these beings "packing the mountains" indicates that they lived below the Chokecherry Mountain.

In two of these paintings the figures' arms are both on their right sides in the direction of their movement (Speech Man; Busy Singer, Fig. 19). In the two slightly different versions by Gray Chief, the figures' arms are in standard positions, they wear red skirts, their chokecherry boughs are attached to their right wrists by long cords, and the plants growing on their mountain packs look more like feathers than they do like chokecherries (Fig. 20). Another unusual

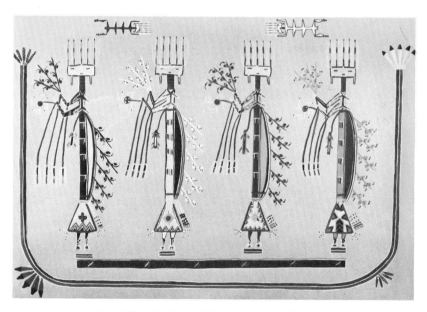

FIG. 19. *People with Packs*, by Busy Singer.

feature is that below each figure, on the west side of the painting, there is a mountain with the body of the Rainbow guardian coiled once around it. Rainbow garland or deity guardians coiled around the four mountains in this manner are found in four sandpaintings of the Long Bodies (Speech Man, Wyman, 1971, cover; Yucca Patch Man, Fig. 22; unknown — Newcomb). It is interesting that the small paired guardians of the east are different in all four paintings of *People with Packs:* bats, Big Flies, weasels, bluebirds.

THE LONG BODIES

THE LONG BODIES were Mountain Goddesses who lived at Leaf Mountain in the House of Dew. They were so tall that, "When they rose, as the strangers entered, the plumes on their heads seemed to touch the heavens" (Matthews, 1887, pp. 410, 450). "They are so tall that wisps of clouds may be seen crossing the tall eagle feathers in their headdresses; they grant the Indians permission to hold the fire dance on the mountains and to gather healing

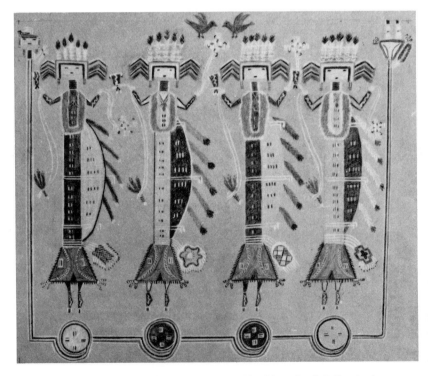

FIG. 20. *People with Packs*, by Gray Chief (Reichard Collection).

FIG. 21. *The Long Bodies,* by Lefthanded.

herbs and wood for the many fires that will be lighted for this ceremony" (Lefthanded). They are so tall "that no one garment can be
made long enough to cover such giant forms" (Matthews) so they
are shown wearing four or five red skirts, one above the other (Figs.
21, 22, 23; Matthews, 1885, Plate XXXIII; 1887, Plate XVI; E. S.
Curtis, 1907, vol. 1, Plate 39; Newcomb, 1949, frontispiece; Wyman,
1971, cover). In four paintings four such skirts cover the figures'
bodies and kilts completely (Lefthanded, Fig. 21; Matthews; Wilito
Wilson; Newcomb, 1949) and in another five red skirts are shown
(Yucca Patch Man, Fig. 22). In other paintings the figures wear the
special red skirts above and in addition to an ordinary decorated
skirt,[62] four of them in two instances (Speech Man; unknown—
Newcomb) and three in another (Sam Tilden, Fig. 23—the only
sandpainting with fewer than four). These multiple skirts are made
of red buckskin representing "fire that climbs four times as high as
usual," "the height of the leaping flames on the night of the fire
ceremony" (Newcomb, 1949, pp. 7–8; 1956, pp. 17–18), or they are
fashioned from "rosy clouds" (Speech Man). Newcomb called them
"blankets of fire." They are bordered with brown "elk hair" or

---

[62] "The beaded Ute skirt worn by dancers in the Mountain Chant" (Speech Man).

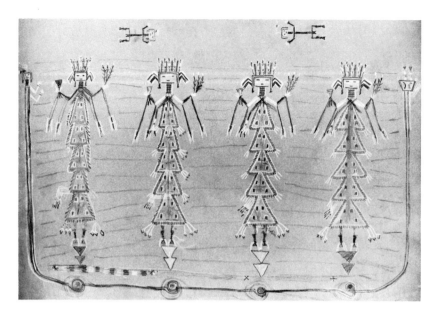

FIG. 22. *The Long Bodies*, by Yucca Patch Man (original sketch).

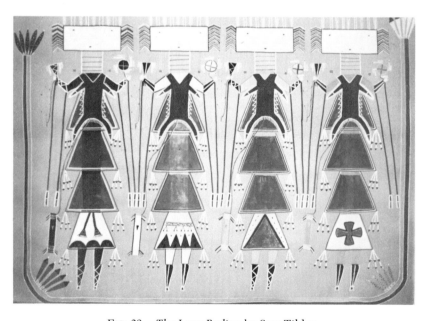

FIG. 23. *The Long Bodies*, by Sam Tilden.

fur and are embroidered with "sunbeams" [two short rainbow-bars on each skirt]. A peculiarity of Sam Tilden's painting is that the otter skin collar is so large it almost hides the uppermost red skirt and the attached whistle is also outsized. In practice the slim straight bodies of these beings are made first in appropriate directional colors as if naked and the red kilts are then superimposed on them. The exposed arms, chest, and thighs, and in two designs (Speech Man; Newcomb, 1949) a bit of the body left uncovered just above the ordinary beaded skirt show the colors of which the entire bodies are made in the first place.

The Long Bodies stand on short rainbow-bars or double cloud symbols above a separate black foundation bar in two paintings (Speech Man; Yucca Patch Man, Fig. 22), or directly on the bar with no intervening symbol in two others (Newcomb), or have no special foundation. In four paintings the encircling rainbow garland guardian [Rainbow deity in one] is looped once around each of four red mountains. In two there is a mountain below each of the four figures of the Long Bodies (Speech Man; Yucca Patch Man, Fig. 22) and in the other two the mountains are at the quadrantal ends and corners of the garland (unknown and Newcomb, 1949). The mountains are "first built about ten inches high and then covered with red sand to indicate that the vegetation on their slopes is potential fire material; the rainbow rope is laid so that the gods are able to pull it straight without causing it to knot" (Newcomb).

WHIRLING RAINBOW PEOPLE

BENT, CURVED, OR WHIRLING RAINBOW PEOPLE are pictured in sandpaintings for Male Shootingway, Beautyway, Nightway, Male Plumeway, and Navajo Windway, as well as in Mountainway paintings. They have been discussed and illustrated, and a possible prehistoric Pueblo origin suggested, in Wyman, 1957 (p. 177, Plate XI), and 1962 (pp. 304–305, Figs. 43, 44). The Whirling Rainbow People of Mountainway, like those of Nightway and Navajo Windway, are the most curvaceous of all such beings, their elongated bodies completely encircling the center of the sandpainting and their own lower extremities (Fig. 24). In the two recorded designs the Rainbow People whirl around a blue center outlined with rainbow colors representing a mountain of rainbows (Tall Navajo's Son, Fig. 24), or a fire [red cross] on rainbow mountain surrounded by rainbow outlines and twenty-eight tents similar to the central device in Salt Water Man's painting of dancers described above (Gray Chief; see Fig. 11). They wear the weasel headdresses with bison horns, pink masks of weasel hide, red "fire" dance kilts, and carry spruce boughs. The encircling guardian contains four evenly spaced mountains of all colors, made in relief, connected in the west by a rainbow "trail" and by "rainbow ladders" or "mist" of all colors on the south and north, like the guardian in Tall Navajo's Son's radial painting of *People with Long Hair* (Fig. 17). The paired guards of the east are black bears, with a pair of short rainbow-bars between them in one painting (Gray Chief).

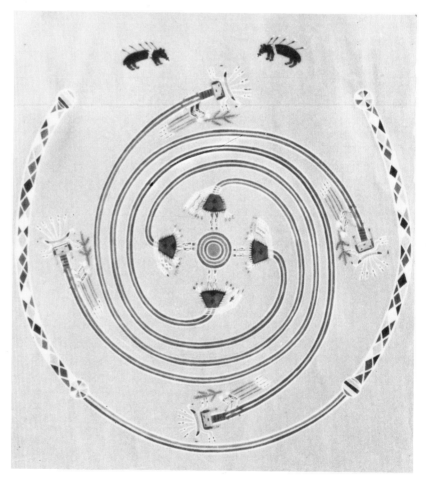

Fig. 24. *Whirling Rainbow People,* by Tall Navajo's Son (Newcomb Collection).

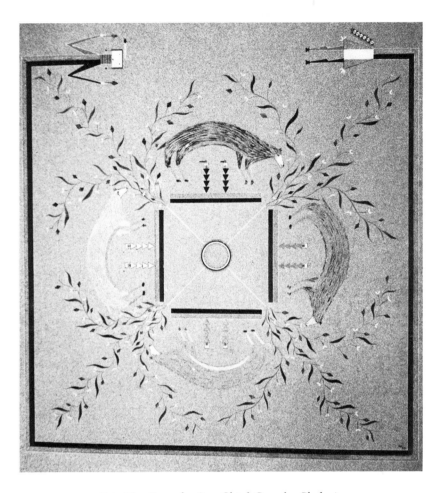

FIG. 25. *Bears*, by Sam Chief. Copy by Clyde A.
Colville in the Museum of Navaho Ceremonial Art.

"The bears have noses of cloud symbols and five red-shafted flicker
feathers along their backs" (Gray Chief).

BEARS

THE PROMINENCE OF THE BEAR in all aspects of the theory and
practice of Mountainway has been discussed above. It is remarkable, therefore, that except for the shock rite paintings bears appear
as main theme symbols only in the three rather fanciful creations
made by Sam Chief (Fig. 25). To be sure, bears are seen as subsidiary figures in sandpaintings that have other main theme symbols,

and quite frequently they serve as small paired guardians of the east, but as main themes they occur only in the Bear's Den designs used for the shock rite and in Sam Chief's offerings. Wyman (1952, p. 56) suggested that the emphasis in the latter may have been associated with the fact that in four of Sam Chief's five Mountainway sandpaintings the red side of rainbows and rainbow-bars is inside, indicating that the set is adapted for use in a chant performed according to Injuryway [Angryway; red inside] subritual, that is, one with exorcistic emphasis. This subritual is appropriate if the patient has been or is thought to have been subjected to direct attack by the etiological factors involved, in this case a bear. It aids the patient in his struggles to free himself of the supernatural weapon or injury.[63] Sam Chief's paintings of bears show them plentifully supplied with service-berries, said to be one of their favorite foods. These paintings have been sufficiently described and illustrated by Wyman (1952, pp. 49–56, Figs. 15, 17, 18).

BEAR'S DEN – SHOCK RITE SANDPAINTINGS

THE SHOCK RITE is an accessory ceremony which may be added to most any ceremonial if the patient or family requests it and is willing to pay extra for it. It is used as a test to determine if the treatment being used is the correct one. A sandpainting is made, surrounded by a low bank of earth, or merely a circular ridge of sand and earth, open to the east, about two feet in diameter to enclose a space which is sprinkled with cornmeal. Spruce tree tops are stuck up around it to form a sort of bower in which the patient sits. A person dressed as a bear, covered with branches of spruce, springs out from behind a blanket curtain or a dark corner of the

---

[63] "If the patient has been bitten by a snake, attacked by a bear, hurled aside by the wind or thunder, the evidence is clear that injury has been inflicted by these factors. Evidence even, as in the case of a direct attack by a bear or a thunderstroke, that the . . . 'weapon,' or . . . 'its arrow,' may be lodged in the patient's interior. There is evidence, in any event, of the anger of the holy ones. The first objective, therefore, of a ceremonial conducted in the holy way ritual must be to remove this weapon or dart as a sign of anger, a sort of exorcism, after which the process of rendering the patient holy or impassible to similar attacks may be begun and completed by the ceremonial. The general trend and purpose of the ritual is hereby indicated in native terminology. Those chantways which speak of . . . 'weapon or injury-way ceremonial,' evidently have the weapon in mind, which the holy one, or supernatural, has used to inflict the injury. Chantways which prefer to call such ceremonials . . . 'angry-way,' emphasize the anger more than the weapon used, but are agreed upon the etiological factors at work" (Haile, 1938b, p. 648). "In a legend of Mountain Top Way, Female Branch, recorded by Father Berard, the term . . . [bear fighting or attack side] is substituted for Fighting Way and identified with Angry Way" (Wyman and Kluckhohn, 1938, p. 9).

hogan as if to terrify the patient. This is done four times. If the patient faints or has a fit or seizure, it shows that the correct ceremonial has been chosen as a cure, and he is then resuscitated by a restoration rite (Wyman and Bailey, 1944, pp. 332–337). Descriptions of the shock rite have been published by Matthews (1887, p. 423) and Wyman (1973, pp. 45, 56–58, Figs. 20–25). Matthews's account was especially dramatic: "At a certain part of the song the chanter was seen to make a slight signal with his drumstick, a rapid stroke to the rear, when instantly a mass of animate evergreens—a moving tree, it seemed—sprang out from the space behind the singers and rushed towards the patient. A terrifying yell from the spectators greeted the apparition, when the man in green, acting as if frightened by the noise, retreated as quickly as he came, and in a moment nothing could be seen in the space behind the singers but the shifting shadows cast by the fire. He was so thoroughly covered with spruce twigs that nothing of his form save his toes could be distinguished when he rushed out in the full glare of the fire. This scene was repeated three times at due intervals."

Special sandpaintings are used for this rite, different ones for different ceremonials. In Shootingway they are special paintings of Big Snake or Coiled [Endless] Snake (Wyman, 1970b, pp. 17, 22, Plate 37). The use of the *Home of Bear and Snake* as a shock rite sandpainting in Mountainway has been discussed previously. In the Huckel Collection three of the extended center designs by Speech Man are shock rite paintings. One of these was published in color by E. S. Curtis (1907, vol. 1, p. 78) and a copy of it and the other two are in Wyman, 1971 (Figs. 18, 19, 20). One of these called *Changing Bear Maiden* shows a circular black cave in the mountains surrounded by spruce trees on or in which are two People with the general accoutrements of Mountainway People described above. Around them are four pairs of bear tracks; a white trail with four black bear tracks on it leads into the cave from the east. This sandpainting was said to commemorate the visit of the hero of the myth to the home of the Changing Bear Maidens, fierce creatures who could change from human to bear form at will (Matthews, 1887, p. 407). They taught the hero how to make four prayersticks. The People in the sandpainting could represent two of these maidens, but since they have no distinguishing characteristics they could be Mountain Gods, dancers impersonating them, or even the hero himself. The story of Changing Bear Maiden is more intimately associated with the fundamental Evilway chant, Upward-reachingway, than it is with Mountainway, in spite of the bear theme (see pp. 137 and 177–182 below). In fact it really belongs to Evilway ritual

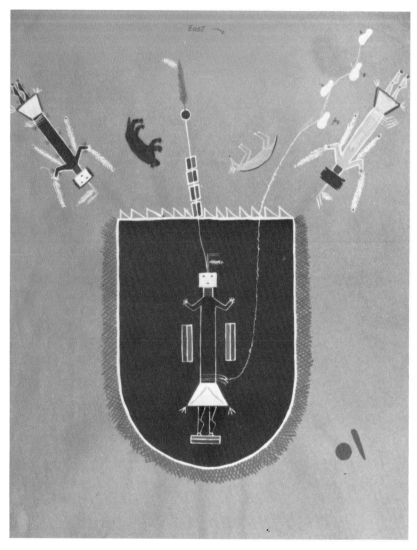

FIG. 26. *Bear's Sitting Place* (Upward-reachingway),
by Late Cane's Son (Haile Collection).

(see Wyman, 1962, pp. 33, 57; 1973, pp. 99–102, Table 9). A related sandpainting used for a shock rite in Upward-reachingway will be described below.

The sandpainting of *Bear's Den* also pictures a black mountain cave with bear tracks in it and leading to it. Inside it is a large black bear. In nearly every Mountainway myth there is an account of a visit of the hero or heroine to the home of the bears and this design commemorates it. "The bear in the picture may represent the hero himself because in the sacred stories of the Navajo the bear is called Reared-in-the-Mountains, the name claimed by the hero just following his visit" (Speech Man).

Finally there is the sandpainting of *Bear's Squatting Place* [sandpainting when rest was taken in a bear's sitting place]. "In summer the bear often chooses the shade of a spruce or other tree for a resting place. Knowingly a person should not walk over these resting places," or sickness may result from this act (Haile, 1947a, p. 62). This painting contains two bears, black and blue. Rainbow trails with four bear tracks on each one lead to their mouths. "The rainbow bands issuing from the bears' mouths are their voices raised in fearful clamor" (Speech Man). West of the two bears is a black circular bear's den crossed and encircled by rainbows, with four pairs of bear tracks around it. The small spots close to the black and yellow tracks are the pebbles around the fire in the den, mentioned in the myth (Matthews, 1887, p. 404).

Sandpainting when rest was taken in a (bear's) sitting place of Reflected-Sunred-Dwarf-Boy

A SANDPAINTING EMPLOYED for the shock rite in the Evilway ceremonial, Upward-reachingway, made by Late Cane's Son of Saunders, Arizona, has such obvious relations to the *Bear's Den* and *Bear's Squatting Place* paintings of Mountainway that it is appropriate to include it here (Fig. 26). Moreover, it illustrates the story of Changing Bear Maiden mentioned above. It was collected by Father Berard Haile in 1908 and is now in the Haile Collection in the Museum of Northern Arizona. It will be described in Father Berard's words taken from his notes.

The center represents the Dwarf Boy who travels by means of reflected sunred as shown by blue and red bars at his feet and sides. He holds nothing in his hands. The figure is enclosed in a [black] bear den circle, with the east side left open.

There is a border of soil around the den and spruce boughs are planted in this border. A zigzag lightning border in white closes the entrance. Four reflected sunred bars only allow entrance into the den. In front of these there is a [black] dugout in which a young pinyon is planted and a live feather is tied to its tip. On the north side is the [black] figure of Changing Bear Maiden, in her bear form. On the opposite south side is the [blue] figure of the Coyote who became her husband. Four footplace prints of white corn lead along the south side into the den upon the sash of the figure. The patient enters on these footprints and seats himself on the skirt of the figure, resting his feet on the two reflected sunred bars and faces east or toward the head of the figure. This practically completes the drawing. Late Cane's Son, however, added two figures at the time [1908]. In the northeast corner the black figure represents the Man-who-time-and-again-runs-out-like-a-bear, because, like the bear, he is clothed in spruce. In the southeast corner the [blue] figure of The-one-who-swoons [patient] is drawn. [Being a Navajo he has a brown face.] He is shown walking towards the footplace prints, as the out-turned calves indicate. He holds plumes in his hands and has arm fringes tied to his arms. The concept is that the person suffering from dizziness will walk upon the figure represented in the den. The personator of the bear, the north black figure, will enter as a bear and frighten the patient seated on the central figure. If the patient should show fright and become unconscious the test clearly shows that the bear and her ceremonial, the Ghostway or Moving-up rite, is bothering the patient. The blue basket and basket tap, depicted in the southwest corner, are not part of the painting, but symbolize the noise made while the bear impersonator enters to test the patient. The concept is based upon the legend which records that eleven brothers had a sister who married a Coyote. He in turn taught her how to conceal her vitals and go unharmed even if pierced with arrows. In time she loses her coyote husband, accuses her brothers of the deed and slays them all, excepting the youngest. He is safe by the ruse which induced his brothers to bury him under the fireplace, here represented in black. His sister, however, finds him and when she tries to pursue him, her brother is informed of her hidespot in which she had concealed her vitals. When he shoots them he also kills her and then restores his brothers to

life. Hence by imitiative magic the same process can be repeated today upon patients suffering with evil dreams of the
dead, or who fancy that they have seen ghosts in the shape of
fiery balls.

PORCUPINES

THE OTHER MOUNTAIN ANIMAL which is conspicuous in the songs,
prayers, and sandpaintings of Mountainway and like the bear is an
important etiological factor whose home is visited by the hero or
heroine in nearly every myth, is the porcupine. "In general, too,
there is no objection to eating porcupine meat, but killing and
eating may be the cause of indisposition, and abuse of the animal is
not in accord with good usage. The sight of a dead animal may affect
the child in embryo" (Haile, 1947a, p. 64). There are three different
porcupine designs among the recorded sandpaintings of Mountainway. One is simply a large animal protected by rainbow-bars
in front and rear, and under nose and feet and belly, and by a long
curved rainbow-bar over the back (Fig. 27). This was said to be
made in a different color, black, blue, yellow, or white, on four successive days, in a ceremonial to treat kidney, bladder, or stomach

FIG. 27. *Porcupine*, by Willie Little.

trouble (Willie Little). A linear design by Female Shootingway Singer has two pairs of porcupines, white and yellow, and blue and black, the members of each pair facing each other (Fig. 28). Mrs. Newcomb said: "The story which goes with it tells how the Navajos were very poor and ignorant of food stuffs. In midwinter when their food supplies were exhausted and they were in danger from starvation, the porcupine saved them by showing them how to use the inner bark of the fir and pine trees. In this picture the porcupines are shown carrying twigs of these trees to the fire ceremony, probably to be blessed." In Matthews' myth the porcupines offered the hero food which consisted of the inner bark of different kinds of trees (1887, p. 408). The other porcupine sandpainting, an extended center composition by Young Deer, shows a pair of large animals, a black male and a blue female, with an encircling guardian of two rainbow ropes, open at both the east and the west [like two porcupines as in Fig. 27 facing each other]. These beasts are made in solid colors with their quills shown as short white lines on them. This painting was also said to be employed when stomach trouble is thought to be due to harm done to a porcupine.

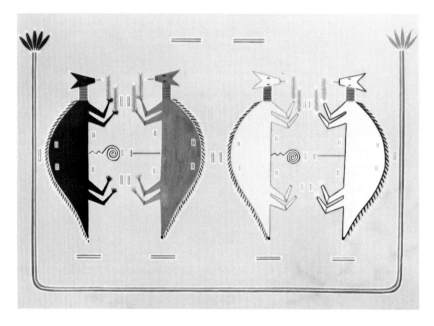

FIG. 28.   *Porcupines*, by Female Shootingway Singer.

GREAT PLUMED ARROWS

PERHAPS THE MOST IMPORTANT ACT, possibly even an essential
feature of the performance in the Dark Circle of Branches or Corral
on the final night of a Mountain Chant, is the arrow swallowing
stunt carried out by the second set of First Dancers. It seems fitting,
therefore, in view of the importance of the *Great Plumed Arrows,*
that the last sandpainting of a set of four made during a Mountain
Chant is often a picture of these implements. This is the case in the
sets of four collected or recorded by Matthews, Yucca Patch Man,
Sam Tilden, and Gray Chief. In Mrs. Newcomb's notes we find:
"These eight arrows seem to make a painting that gathers and
transmits all of the energy, the force, and the strength of all the
paintings that have been used during the previous days, to make
sure the patient has received all the energy and strength that is
necessary for complete healing."

There are six such pictures among the recorded sandpaintings of
Mountainway. The chief difference between them is in the number
and arrangement of the arrows. Two paintings have eight arrows,
two have twelve, and two have sixteen. In those with eight arrows,
four of them lie parallel to one another, pointing alternately east
and west, while the other four are in a square around them pointing
sunwise, thus forming a sort of encircling guardian (Fig. 29). In one
painting these guardian arrows are a little longer than the main
theme arrows in the center (Matthews), while in the other all the
arrows are about the same length (Gray Chief).[64] In the designs
with twelve arrows, four of them are in the center as above but there
are two sets of four arranged in two concentric squares around
them, the ones in the outer square being longer than those in the
inner square and those in both squares considerably longer than
the arrows in the center (Fig. 30). One of these designs is the only
one of the *Great Plumed Arrows* having an encircling guardian
other than the arrows themselves, a rainbow rope or "sunbeam"
(Yucca Patch Man),[65] but the other shows arrows only (Speech
Man). "There is no rainbow or other guardian around these arrows

---

[64] There are copies of this painting made by Mrs. Newcomb in the Bush Collection
of Religion and Culture, at Columbia University, New York City, and in the Gladys
A. Reichard Collection in the Museum of Northern Arizona.

[65] In a copy of this painting by M. Bridgeman in the Museum of Navaho Ceremonial
Art the rainbow rope guardian was changed into a rainbow garland by adding the
usual bunches of five feathers to the quadrantal ends and corners (Fig. 30).

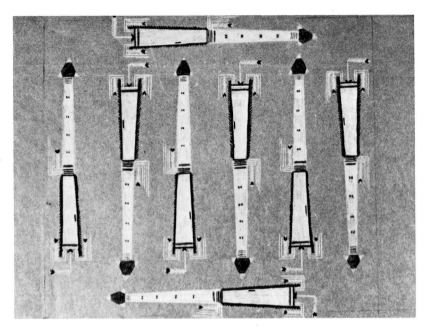

FIG. 29. *Great Plumed Arrows*, by Gray Chief (Reichard Collection).

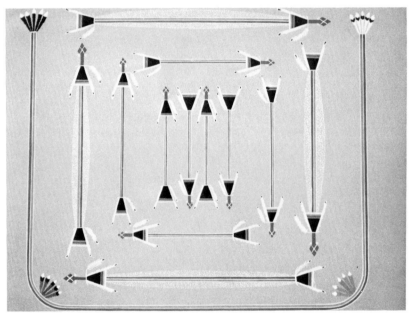

FIG. 30. *Great Plumed Arrows*, by Yucca Patch Man. Copy
by M. Bridgeman in the Museum of Navaho Ceremonial Art.

as their flight must not be limited" (Newcomb). Finally, in the two paintings with sixteen arrows all of them are arranged in concentric squares of increasing length and all pointing sunwise (Busy Singer, Fig. 31; Sam Tilden). These two are the only *Great Plumed Arrow* sandpaintings that have a center and small paired guardians of the east. The center is a black or blue circular "lake with yellow pollen around it" (Armer), and the paired guards are Sun and Moon with feather rays.

Of course the arrows in the different paintings have slight differences in the finer details of the fletching, markings on them, and so on. They have red points, of "red agate, indicating its death dealing power, and the white tips indicate they have been dipped in the fire" (Gray Chief).

Little Man's painting of arrows, "the long sticks," is very different from the other arrow sandpaintings (Fig. 32). It shows four long spearlike arrows with red points, in linear formation, with two curved appendages at four places along their length, and a bird perched on top of each one. Mrs. Newcomb's description reads: "This is the painting which blesses the arrows used for the rite of arrow-swallowing. The long sticks are made of fir with yucca strips tied in four places. The tops have small bird feathers inserted. The points are red showing that they belong to the fire ceremony. The birds are the yellow-headed blackbird, the bluebird, the pine [purple?] martin [another blue bird], and the wild canary [yellow warbler]."

BIG SNAKES

THE SANDPAINTING OF *Big Snakes* by Young Deer (Fig. 33) is unique among recorded Mountainway designs, but these mythological creatures are prominent main themes in the sandpaintings of several other ceremonials, especially in those of Mountainway's sister chant, Beautyway, and those of Navajo Windway and of Shootingway.[66] If it were not for the bear tracks and small mountains, we might suspect that this painting had been misassigned to this chant, but these are typical Mountainway features. Moreover, Big Snakes do appear in the *Home of Bear and Snake* (Figs. 5, 6), and in several of the myths Big Snake is visited in the *Journey for Knowledge and Power* and Coiled [Endless] Snake is encountered

---

[66] Big Snakes are main theme symbols in sandpaintings of Beautyway, Navajo Windway, Shootingway, Big Starway, Beadway, and Upward-reachingway, and may serve as guards in the drypaintings of some other ceremonials. See Wyman, 1957, pp. 167–169, Fig. 1, Plates I, II; 1962, pp. 297–298, Figs. 24, 25; 1970b, p. 22, Table 4.

FIG. 31. *Great Plumed Arrows,* by Busy Singer.

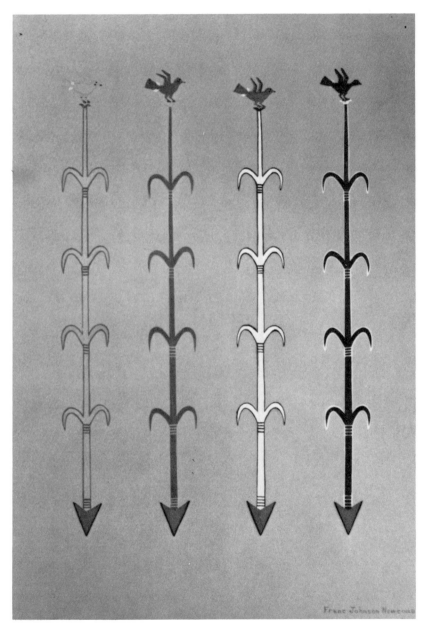

FIG. 32. *Great Plumed Arrows* ("the long sticks"), by Little Man.

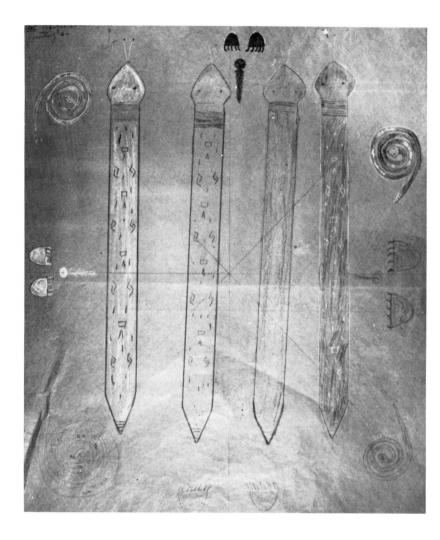

FIG. 33.   *Big Snakes,* by Young Deer.

(Matthews, 1887, p. 405). In Beautyway, of course, the main theme of the myth is the pursuit of Younger Sister by Big Snake Man, while her Older Sister is being chased by Bear Man.

In Young Deer's painting there are four straight Big Snakes in linear arrangment, their thick bodies bearing four markings representing snakes' homes and deer tracks. At each cardinal point around the Big Snakes is a pair of bear tracks, and just inside each pair a mountain, that is, a small mound of colored sand with a sprig of pinyon pine standing on it. In each quadrantal corner there is a coiled snake. These may be considered the guards of the Big Snakes.

Quadrantal Figures

THE FOUR SACRED DOMESTICATED PLANTS, corn, beans, squash, and tobacco, which occupy the quadrants of the majority of radial compositions of most chantways, are also present in seven of the thirteen radial designs of *People of the Myth* of Mountainway which have quadrantal symbols.[67] In two paintings there is a corn plant in each quadrant; in two others there are chokecherries, a mountain fruit favored by bears (Figs. 12, 18); in another there are plants with human heads, Mountain Medicine People (Fig. 10); and finally in one painting the bear himself appears in each quadrantal position (Fig. 9). In nine of the thirteen designs the sunwise directional color sequence of the quadrantal figures is the same as that of the main theme symbols. In the other four it is different.

Locality Centers

THE CENTRAL SYMBOL of a radial composition denotes the locality of the action depicted or symbolized in the sandpainting. In the paintings of the *Home of Bear and Snake*, the black and white circular center is the cave home itself. In fourteen of twenty-one other Mountainway sandpaintings having central motifs, the central circle, black in eight, blue in three, and different colors in the others, represents some body of water, a pool, lake, or spring, sometimes surrounded by yellow pollen and protected by four short rainbow-bars on it. Sometimes in practice this watery center is actually a cup of water sunk flush with the surface of the painting and sprinkled with powdered charcoal to make a flat, black surface (Matthews, 1887, pp. 446, 447). Such a symbol of water is frequently the center of radial sandpaintings in most other chantways.

The other seven sandpaintings, five of dancers in the Dark Circle of Branches or corral on the final night of the ceremonial and two of *Whirling Rainbow People*, have a center which represents the corral itself where the dancers will perform, with a fire [red cross] in it, or

---

[67] The unconventional paintings by Sam Chief are not included in the thirteen mentioned here. He used service-berries as quadrantal plants in his Mountainway designs, including those of bears, for their fruit is said to be one of the bears' favorite snacks.

a mountain on which it will be built. The symbolism of some of these centers is quite complex and has been described in detail above. In sandpaintings for Mountain-Shootingway, the center is also likely to represent the corral of the Fire Dance (see Wyman, 1970b, pp. 26, 27, Plates 24, 40).

Guardians

THE ENCIRCLING GUARDIANS, in thirty-six of the forty-six Mountainway sandpaintings that have them, are one or the other of the two commonest form of the rainbow motif. In twelve paintings the guardians are the Rainbow supernatural ["Goddess"], which is the one most frequently employed in the sandpaintings of nearly all chantways. In twenty-four, however, they are the feathered rainbow garland. The predominance of this form of rainbow is, therefore, a Mountainway characteristic. The Rainbow supernatural nearly always has a square head and white face but in some sandpaintings it has a head like those of the main theme figures in shape, color, and form of headdress. This is often true of the sandpaintings of other chantways. The rainbow garland has bunches of five feathers at its ends and angles, white, blue, red, and black—usually said to be eagle feathers at the southeast end, bluebird or "blue hawk" at the southwest corner, red-shafted flicker at the northwest corner, and magpie at the northeast end. In six designs the long body of the Rainbow deity or the garland is looped around four mountains, little heaps of sand covered with the directional colors representing the sacred mountains of the cardinal points. Four of these designs are the *Long Bodies* (Fig. 22) and two are Gray Chief's *People with Packs* (Fig. 20). Although not unique this is a distinctive Mountainway feature.

In six other sandpaintings there are also mountains in the encircling guardian. In three of these [two of *Whirling Rainbows*, one of *People with Long Hair* in a radial composition; Figs. 24, 17], the mountains are connected on the west side by a rainbow rope or "trail" and by lozenge-checkered "rainbow ladders" or "mist" of all colors on the south and north. In another painting the mountains are connected by plain rainbow ropes (Fig. 16) and in two others there are three sets of four porcupine tracks between the mountains, white on a white trail in one and black in the other (Figs. 11, 18).

Finally, two sandpaintings are guarded by plain rainbow ropes [or "sunbeam"], one with black cloud ends (Fig. 10), another [*Porcupines*] by two curved rainbow ropes with openings at east and west, and another [*Bears* by Sam Chief] by a plain black band. Of course, in the sandpaintings of the *Home of Bear and Snake* the four snakes that surround the central symbols serve to guard them so no other encircling guardian is necessary.

Paired Guardians of The East

SMALL PAIRED GUARDIANS of the eastern entrance, an optional feature, are present in thirty-five of the forty-six sandpaintings that have an encircling guardian. Among these, five symbols predominate, curiously enough in six instances each, Big Flies, bats, bluebirds, bears, and Sun and Moon. In Navajo mythology Big Fly, a white faced insect, is the omniscient and ubiquitous mentor and monitor of human and supernatural beings alike (see Wyman and Bailey, 1964, pp. 51, 137–142, Plate II). Pairs of this creature are the most popular eastern guards in the sandpaintings of other chantways. In Mountainway paintings they are a white and a black [south, north] Big Fly in three examples and two black ones in three others. In all but one of these the Big Flies wear the tall feather headdress characteristic of Mountainway and Beautyway sandpainting costumes. Bats as eastern guards are all found in linear designs of *People of the Myth.* Bluebirds are more common in radial designs of People [four of six examples]. Pairs of black bears in five paintings and a blue and a black bear [south, north] in one, often have noses and sometimes feet of clouds, white dots over their shoulders, and red-shafted flicker feathers along their backs. These represent a red glow for, "As he ran away, his fur looked red in the sunlight; this red is sometimes indicated in sandpaintings of Bear even today" (Reichard, 1970, p. 200). In two paintings there are two short rainbow-bars between the bears. Bears as paired guards are not confined to Mountainway sandpaintings but in those of other chantways a bear is more commonly one of a pair of two different symbols. In the Sun and Moon couple the Sun's rays are red-shafted flicker feathers and the Moon's rays are white eagle feathers.

In two sandpaintings the eastern guards are weasels, a white and a yellow one [south, north], another animal closely associated with Mountainway. In two other paintings, they are a simple pair of short rainbow-bars (Fig. 9), and finally, in one painting, the guards are a black and a white mountain, each with two bear [?] tracks on it (Fig. 10). None of the symbols employed as paired guardians of the eastern entrance are exclusively the property of

Mountainway, although pairs of bears, preeminently *the* animal of the Mountain Chant, could be considered the characteristic guards for this chantway.

Small Sandpaintings

A SMALL *Feather* [*dancing feathers*] sandpainting by Female Shootingway singer has a circular white center which is a raised mound covered with white cornmeal with four short rainbow-bars on it (Fig. 34). The mound is outlined with yellow pollen. It represents the basket in which the feathers will dance. Around it are four white eagle feathers with black tips. The quill of each one is thrust into a prehistoric stone bead. In practice real eagle feathers are laid on top of the ones drawn in sand. "These are to be blessed in a short Blessing rite." In each quadrant there is a pair of talking prayersticks, "of the eagle ceremony," two black and blue pairs and two yellow and white pairs. These "give a spirit to the feathers so they will understand and respond to the chant." This seems to be a drypainting for a Blessingway rite preliminary to the dancing feather act which is a Shootingway specialty presented in the Dark Circle of Branches (Matthews, 1887, p. 443; Haile, 1946, p. 33). In this act a tall feather placed in a basket is made to rise and dance, seemingly by magic but actually operated by invisible strings, in time to the chanting of the singer while a young dancer accompanies it.

A small sandpainting [*Sweat-emetic sandpainting*] by Young Deer was said to be made "before five o'clock each morning before the fire is made," presumably marking the place for the patient to kneel and vomit in the sweat-emetic ceremony (see Wyman, 1962, p. 313; 1973, p. 231; 1970b, pp. 14, 18). In it are five curved rainbow-bars, one in the center around a white coil [possibly a snake or the place for the emetic basket or the patient's sand basin which receives the vomit], and one in each quadrantal corner. Around these at the cardinal points are four pairs of bear tracks.

Summary of Symbolism

THE SANDPAINTINGS OF MOUNTAINWAY display relatively few main theme symbols and design types as compared with those of Shootingway, Navajo Windway, Plumeway, and Beautyway for instance, but they show about the same number as those of Nightway, Red Antway, Hailway, and Big Starway. A fairly large proportion of these features, however, are either confined to the

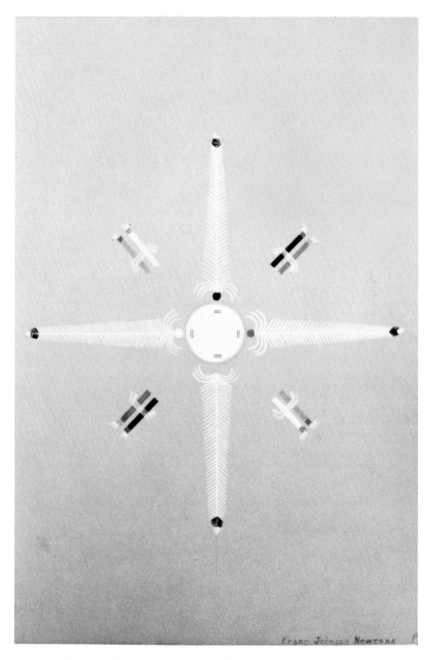

FIG. 34. *Feather sandpainting (dancing feathers)*, by Female
Shootingway Singer. Small drypainting for Blessingway rite.

chantway or are shared with the designs of comparatively few other ceremonials. Four of the main theme symbols or designs are peculiar to Mountainway, the *Home of Bear and Snake, People with Packs*, the *Long Bodies*, and *Bear's Den* [for the shock rite]. Moreover, the *Great Plumed Arrows* is a design belonging exclusively to Mountainway, although arrows are found in the sandpaintings of some other chants. Bears and porcupines as main theme figures also seem to be a peculiar Mountainway feature, although these animals do appear in subsidiary positions in the paintings of a few other ceremonials. *People with Long Hair* are shared only with Hailway, Waterway, and Coyoteway. In fact the only main theme symbols which are shared with numerous other chantways are Whirling Rainbow People and Big Snakes, and the latter occur in only one Mountainway design in a somewhat deviant series of paintings. Of course, the designation of certain human figures as *People of the Myth* of Mountainway or Mountain Gods or Goddesses, or as dancers in the Dark Circle of Branches, is also distinctive. They may be recognized as such by certain items of their costumes, but most of these accessories are also worn by the People of a few other chantways, especially Beautyway, although some may be peculiar to the Mountain Chant.

Several items of dress are characteristic of the People of Mountainway: white painted or masked faces, or pink masks of weasel or prairie dog hide in six instances; tall feather and weasel-skin headdresses or the bison headdresses worn by dancers and Whirling Rainbow People; an otter or beaver skin collar with attached whistle; beaded and embroidered clothing; red "fire" dance kilts; "wings" or symbolic indications of them on the upper arms; charcoal blackened forearms and lower legs with white lightning marks on them; and chokecherries carried in the hands in eight paintings. The distribution of these accessories among the various sandpainting designs, and the sharing of some of them with other chantways, has been discussed above. The ones which are peculiar to Mountainway are the weasel and bison headdresses which differ from those of Beautyway and Shootingway because they are not built around a pointed red feather hat, the "wings," and the blackened extremities. To be sure, the arms and legs of People in the sandpaintings of other chantways are painted and have lightning marks on them but they are decorated with the four directional colors appropriate for the positions of the individual Persons; they are not all black with white lightning as in Mountainway paintings. The characteristic face and body painting and items of costume are shared alike by the Holy People of Mountainway, whether described in the myths or depicted in the sandpaintings, and by the Meal Sprinklers in actual present day ceremonials.

The majority of the People have square heads regardless of sex and they move sunwise in radial compositions, towards the north in linear arrangments. They often carry a hide rattle and Sun's tobacco pouch in the right hand and a magic travel basket and a bunch of spruce twigs in the left. A profusion of mountain or game animals with the People in a few paintings reminds us of the designs of Plumeway: bears and porcupines from the mountains; deer, antelope, mountain sheep, squirrels, and prairie dogs, all food animals; otter and turtle or frog from the water.

Chokecherries in all four quadrants and porcupine tracks in the encircling guardian are special Mountainway features, and the four cardinal mountains in the guardian, Big Flies wearing tall feather headdresses and bears as paired eastern guards, and the Fire Dance corral in the center of radial pictures of dancers, although not exclusive are, nevertheless, quite characteristic of this chant.

Three directional sunwise color sequences predominate: the common one of white [east], blue [south], yellow [west], black [north]; the danger sequence with black in the east and white in the north; and a south to north sequence in linear compositions of yellow, blue, white, black. Black and yellow are male colors, blue and white are female in some designs, and black and blue, and yellow and white are bisexual pairs. In other paintings black and blue are male, while white and yellow are female.

In most instances where the sequence of the four designs employed in a given ceremonial was mentioned by the informant, the order was *Home of Bear and Snake, People of the Myth, Long Bodies, Great Plumed Arrows*. The *Home* and the *Arrows*, as the first and last sandpaintings made in a chant, were especially constant. The *Long Bodies* was given as the second or third but usually the third. In two series of four which did not include the *Home of Bear and Snake*, linear sandpaintings of *People of the Myth* were said to be the first two made. In two other cases, *People with Long Hair* and *Game Animals* were said to be paintings made on the last day.

The Mythology
of Mountainway

During the night he journeyed by the stars,
During the day he journeyed with Utu of heaven, . . .
He ascends the . . . mountains,
He descends the . . . mountains, . . .
Awed by the dread of the great mountains,
He wandered about in the dust;
Five mountains, six mountains, seven mountains he crossed. . . .

> Enmerkar and the Lord of Aratta:
> A Sumerian Epic Tale of Iraq and Iran[68]

SUSPENSE FILLED TALES OF FLIGHT AND PURSUIT, of "wandering in the dust" among the mountains surrounding the four corners of Utah, Colorado, Arizona, and New Mexico, are the myths of Mountainway. Only one of the eight available for this analysis was first recorded in Navajo and then translated. This was the one recorded by Father Berard Haile from the dictation of Yucca Patch Man (YPM). The transcription of the native text fills 116 double-spaced typewritten pages. Four of the others have been published and a shortened form of still another (LH) is in print, while two exist only in manuscript. Of the published myths one is Matthews' classic work, the first extensive Navajo myth to be presented to the reading

---

[68] Samuel Noah Kramer, 1952, p. 17.

public. Three manuscripts are of some length (HM, LH, HS), Lefthanded's story being a substantial manuscript of forty-three pages. The other three published tales are quite brief, only five to seven printed pages (OBA, CCM, OBS).

In the following list an approximate English rendering of the Navajo author's nickname is followed by the initial designation used in the discussions in parenthesis, his home locality, and other pertinent data.

Yucca Patch Man (YPM), Fort Defiance Coal Mine, Arizona; recorded and translated by Father Bernard Haile, O.F.M., 1935; 116 double-spaced typewritten pages; female branch.

Author (HM), locality, recorder, and date unknown; 19 page manuscript (found among Father Berard's papers, Special Collections, University of Arizona Library, Tucson); female branch.

Lefthanded (LH), Newcomb, New Mexico; interpreter Edmund Tract, Navajo living in San Ildefonso Pueblo; recorded by Arthur J. Newcomb, May and June, 1927; 43 manuscript pages (retold and published in shorter form, 16 printed pages, by Mary C. Wheelwright, 1951); female and male branches.

Sam Ahkeah (OBA), Rock Point, Arizona; recorded by Aileen O'Bryan, late November, 1928; 6 printed pages (O'Bryan, 1956, pp. 131–137; probably an abstract of LH).

Hasteen Sei (HS), near Fort Defiance, Arizona; interpreter Mrs. Howard McKinley, Fort Defiance; recorded by Margot Astrov, fall and winter of 1946; 16 manuscript pages; female branch (?).

Author not given (MMC), near Fort Wingate, New Mexico (?); recorded by Washington Matthews, 1882–1884 (?); 31 printed pages (Matthews, 1887, pp. 387–417); male branch (?).

Long Mustache (CCM), Klagetoh, Arizona; interpreter Louis Watchman; recorded by Dane and Mary Roberts Coolidge, 1913 (?); 7 printed pages (Coolidge and Coolidge, 1930, pp. 202–209); Cub (female?) branch.

Sandoval (Old Man Buffalo Grass; OBS), Rock Point, Arizona (?); interpreter Sam Ahkeah (nephew); recorded by Aileen O'Bryan, late November, 1928; 5 printed pages (O'Bryan, 1956, pp. 121–126); male branch (?).

The Navajo text of YPM may be consulted in the Special Collections, University of Arizona Library, Tucson, and in the library of the Museum of Northern Arizona, Flagstaff. HM may also be seen in the same places. The manuscripts of LH and HS are in the Museum of Navaho Ceremonial Art, Santa Fe, New Mexico.

The two fragments of myth from Mrs. Louisa Wade Wetherill's notes purporting to pertain to Mountainway are of no value for comparison with the longer myths cited above. They relate very briefly a girl's ceremonial contact with bears (Wyman, 1952, pp. 51, 55–56).

The recorded myths of Mountainway present essentially only two [or three if *The Pueblo War* preliminary to the heroine's flight from Bear Man is considered separately] major mythic motifs, both of which are unique.[69] These are the *Journey of Older Sister* while she is *Pursued by Bear Man* [*Flight from Bear*] following the events of *The Pueblo War*, and the *Ute Captivity*. In Table 3 other major motifs are given, but they are in fact components of the two basic motifs mentioned above, many of them common to various chantway myths [e.g., *Visits to Supernaturals*, *Prototype Ceremonial*, *Protagonist(s) Returns Home*, etc.]. *The Pueblo War*, which introduces the myth of Beautyway as well as that of Female Mountainway and is an important part of the legend of another ceremonial, Enemyway, will be discussed at length below. Another group of major motifs, *Protagonist Feigns Death* and *Raised by Owl*, and *Dangerous Women*, which appear in only one tale (LH) and also in another brief one (OBA) which is undoubtedly derived from the first, will also be discussed below.

There is reason to believe that the *Journey of Older Sister* is fundamentally the myth of Female Mountainway, while the *Ute Captivity* is the myth of Male Mountainway. Father Berard Haile felt that this is the case, basing his opinion on the facts that the first has a female protagonist while in the second, as recorded by

---

[69] In the discussion and tables which follow here the four categories of mythic motifs distinguished according to complexity and frequency in the myths, universal, minor, major, and unique, that were defined in the analysis of the mythology of the Windways will be recognized (Wyman, 1962, pp. 36, 37). Likewise many of the same names and definitions for mythic motifs, etc., which were used in that analysis will be employed here (ibid., pp. 29–77, 55). The names of mythic motifs will be italicized, and to distinguish the minor and major motifs only the first word and proper nouns in the former will be capitalized while all important words in the latter will be capitalized.

Table 3
MAJOR MYTHIC MOTIFS OF MOUNTAINWAY

	YPM	HM	LH	HS	MMC	CCM	OBS
Locale and Personnel Established	X	X	X	X	X	X	
The Pueblo War	X	X	X	X			
Journey of Older Sister (Pursued by Bear Man; Flight from Bear)	X	X	X	X			
Ute Captivity		X	X		X	X	X
Encounters with Supernaturals (Helped by Supernaturals)	X		X	X	X	X	X
Attack by Thunder (Lightning)	X			X			
Attack by Toad (Frog)	X			X			
Visits to Supernaturals (Journey for Knowledge and Power)	X	X	X	X	X		
Prototype Trench Sweat	X			X			
Prototype Ceremonial	X	X	X	X	X	X	X
Post-ceremonial Race(s)	X			X			
Protagonist(s) Returns Home, Relates Adventures, Teaches Ceremonial	X		X	X	X	X	X
Protagonist Departs to Live with Supernaturals			X	X	X		

Matthews (MMC), the central character is a male (1946, Introduction). The story of Older Sister recorded by Father Berard (YPM) came from a singer of the female branch of the chantway and was given to him as the myth of Female Mountainway. Moreover, Lefthanded in dictating his myth (LH) said, when he had finished his account of *The Pueblo War* and the *Journey of Older Sister* [and also *Dangerous Women*], that at this point the Female Mountain Chant ends and the Male Chant begins. The ensuing portion contains the *Ute Captivity* [as well as *Protagonist Feigns Death* and *Raised by Owl*], and in these episodes the protagonists are all male, whereas the preceding portions of the story had a heroine, thus confirming Father Berard's supposition that the sex of the protagonist corresponds to that of the branch of the chant which the myth represents. Lefthanded also said that the male branch is also known as the Cub branch. The brief myth published by the Coolidges (1930, CCM), however, was said to be that of the "Cub Mountain

Chant" but two girls were captives of the Utes and no direct statement was made as to the sex of the chant although it was implied that it is female. Moreover, HM was said to be a myth of the Female Mountainway and it does begin with *The Pueblo War* and the *Journey of Older Sister*, but following these Older Sister is captured by the Utes. Perhaps the narrators of CCM and of HM, being interested in the *Ute Captivity* as a tale, intended to fit their stories to the female branch of the chant by giving them heroines instead of heroes. This could be an example of the lack of "precise standardization" in Navajo ceremonialism (McAllester, 1967, p. 237), or of flexibility like that of Navajo social organization creeping into religious affairs (see Wyman, 1970b, p. 40). In relating HS, OBA, and OBS, the informants made no statements about the sex of the corresponding chants. In spite of these apparent contradictions, it is likely that the opening statement of this paragraph is true, namely, that Older Sister is the heroine of the female branch of Mountainway while the *Ute Captivity* is fundamentally a myth of the male branch, especially when the captive is a male.

Both of the major motifs discussed above are classic examples of the standard hero-quest of Navajo mythology, the acquisition of ceremonial know-how through predicament and extrication. The longer versions (YPM, LH, HS, MMC) make much of the protagonists' encounters or visits with supernatural beings and their *Journey(s) for Knowledge and Power,* in which they are not only aided or rescued, but also are instructed, so that they may establish the chantway among earth people, that is, for the Navajo.

The distribution of the two major motifs already discussed, and of various accessory major motifs among the recorded versions of the myth of Mountainway, is given in Table 3. Father Berard's text and translation of the myth of Female Mountainway (YPM) contains, of course, the most complete account of *The Pueblo War* and the *Journey of Older Sister,* but HS, which is much shorter, also contains most of the same major mythic motifs, in fact it might almost be a digest of the former story. In HM, eight of the eighteen typewritten pages are devoted to *The Pueblo War* and seven to the *Ute Captivity,* while only three pages are given to Older Sister's *Flight from Bear* and the first *Prototype Ceremonial.* The original manuscript of Lefthanded's story (LH) [43 typewritten pages] allows about equal portions for *The Pueblo War, Journey of Older Sister,* and the *Ute Captivity* and *Prototype Ceremonial* [12, 8, and 10 pages], while the remaining thirteen or so pages are devoted to *Dangerous Women, Protagonist Feigns Death,* and *Raised by Owl.* The inclusion of these three motifs is unique (see discussion of OBA below) and will be discussed in more detail later. The brief story told to O'Bryan (1956, pp. 131–138) by Sam Ahkeah (OBA), who was interpreting Sandoval's myths (OBS) for her at the time, is so similar in every detail to Lefthanded's longer myth that he must have gotten it from a similar source, if not from Lefthanded himself. Therefore, it is of little value for comparative purposes since it may be considered essentially the same version as LH. About half of it relates to *The Pueblo War*, one page is devoted to the *Journey of Older Sister*, and two more to *Raised by Owl* and *Protagonist Feigns Death*, in that order. The *Ute Captivity*, the *Prototype Ceremonial*, and the return of the heroine or hero to her or his home, as well as several other motifs of Lefthanded's myth, are omitted entirely, and of course the motifs given are much abbreviated. For these reasons, in the Tables and in the following discussions the two myths, LH and OBA, will be treated as one, LH alone being cited.

The myth published by Matthews (1887, pp. 387–417), presumably an origin myth of Male Mountainway, is devoted entirely to the *Ute Captivity* and *Prototype Ceremonial*, and to the events surrounding them, and is the most extensive account of these motifs among the recorded versions. Their occurrence in HM and LH is mentioned above, as well as Lefthanded's remark that the portion of his tale containing them is the myth of Male Mountainway. The brief tale published by the Coolidges (CCM), as mentioned above, is somewhat deviant in that a singer gave his two daughters to the Utes, ostensibly so that the Utes would stop pestering his family but actually so that they could steal the Utes' valuables for him. Sandoval's story (OBS), although brief, is a straightforward tale not unlike that of Matthews (MMC) with a male protagonist and, therefore, perhaps a myth of the male branch.

Before discussing the major motifs of Mountainway separately and in detail, *The Pueblo War* will be analysed at some length because of the availability of new data.

The Pueblo War

THE PUEBLO WAR is one of the major mythic motifs of the Enemy-way legend (Wyman, 1962, pp. 57–58), but it also serves as an introduction to the myths of Beautyway and Female Mountainway in order to establish background for the adventures of the two sisters who are the protagonists of the two myths. An analysis of this story with a table of its minor mythic motifs was presented in the study of Beautyway by Wyman (1957, pp. 18–24, 45–62, Chart A, p. 25), but in addition to the six versions analysed in that volume, seven

Table 4
MINOR MYTHIC MOTIFS OF THE PUEBLO WAR

	MOUNTAINWAY				BEAUTYWAY					ENEMYWAY		
	YPM	HM	LH	HS	SM	WW	HG	C	OBS	SC	RJC	FG
Locale and personnel established	X	X	X	X	X	X	X	X		X	X	X
Preliminary skirmishes	X	X	X	X	X					X	X	X
Motive for war — revenge	X	X	X	X	X					X	X	
Motive for war — scalp trophies						X	X	X				X
Two sisters promised to takers of scalps												
of non-sunlight-struck girls	X	X			X		X	X		X	X	
of men			X	X		X			X			
Independent raid of Frog and Turtle Man		X	X		X		X			X		X
Attempts to kill them by												
chopping with axe		1°	1		3		1			1		1
burning		2	2		1, 4		2			2		3, 4
boiling		3	3		2					3		2
throwing off cliff		4			5							5
drowning		5	4		6		3			4		
Monster Slayer organizes and leads war	X				X	X			X	X	X	X
Hard Flint People help	X	X	X	X	X	X			X	X	X	X
Encounter with Talking God	X	X		X	X					X	X	
Details of battle	X	X	X	X	X			X	X	X	X	X
Boneless Enemies		X			X						X	
Bear and Big Snake Man get scalps	X	X	X	X	X	X		X	X	X	X	
Further contests for sisters	X	X	X	X	X	X	X	X	X	X	X	
shooting at yucca or cord	1°							1		1, 2	2	
shooting through hole in rock			3	1	1				1		3	
shooting at pine target	2	4	2	2	2	2				4	4	
putting hand in hole in rock	3	2		3	3	4		3				
shooting over high cliff	4	3		4		1		4	2	3		
distance shooting			1		4, 5		1				1	
race		1				3		2				
shinny game						4						
unspecified contests						2, 3						

	MOUNTAINWAY				BEAUTYWAY					ENEMYWAY		
	YPM	HM	LH	HS	SM	WW	HG	C	OBS	SC	RJC	FG
Postwar dance held	X	X	X	X	X	X	X	X	X	X	X	
Tobacco smoke seduction	X	X	X	X	X	X	X	X	X	X	X	
Girls flee from elders' camp	X	X			X		X	X	X		X	
Girls escape by charms			X	X	X					X		
Girls travel together	X	X		X	X			X	X	X		
Girls separate immediately		X				X	X					X
Girls tracked by magic smoke	X	X			X	X	X	X	X	X	X	
Girls meet again during travels		X				X		X				
Girls reunited at end		X		X	X							

° *The numbers show the order of the motifs in the myth. Two numbers in one space show that the same motif occurs twice in the myth.*

others, four of them concerned with Mountainway, are now available for further analysis and a new table is given here (Table 4). Of these thirteen versions, five occur in myths of Mountainway (YPM, HM, LH, OBA, HS), five in myths of Beautyway (SM, WW, HG, C, OBS), and three in Enemyway legends (SC, RJC, FG).[70] Although

[70] The Navajo author, his home locality, the recorder, date of recording, and publication data of YPM, HM, LH, OBA, and HS are given above (p. 123; as mentioned above [p. 127] LH and OBA have a common origin, so OBA is omitted from Table 4 and in the discussions of motifs LH alone is cited). Following are these data for the other versions (see also Wyman, 1957, p. 19): Singer Man (SM), Deer Spring, Arizona; recorded and translated by Father Berard Haile, O.F.M., 1932; Wyman, 1957, translation pp. 45–125, Navajo text in supplement, pp. 1–83. Wilito Wilson (WW), Mariano Lake, New Mexico; interpreter Charlie Anderson, Coolidge, New Mexico; recorded by Maud Oakes, October 1942; Wyman, 1957, pp. 131–142. Hastin Gani (HG), Beautiful Valley, Arizona; recorded by Mary C. Wheelwright; Wheelwright (retold and abbreviated), 1951, pp. 17–22. Author (C), locality and date unknown; recorded by Edward S. Curtis; Curtis, 1907, vol. 1, pp. 106–111. Sandoval (Beautyway; OBS), same data as for his Mountainway myth (p. 123 above), except for publication (O'Bryan, 1956, pp. 127–130). Slim Curly (SC), Crystal, New Mexico; recorded and translated by Father Berard Haile, winter, 1930; Haile, 1938a, pp. 140–175. River Junction Curly (RJC), Chinle, Arizona; recorded and translated by Father Berard Haile, 1929–1932; Wyman, 1970a, pp. 588–599. Frank Goldtooth (FG), near Tuba City, Arizona; interpreters his three sons; recorded by Stanley A. Fishler; Fishler, 1953, pp. 77–83.

the last (FG) is not specifically assigned to Enemyway, the statement, that "this story is used in time of war, for if a person knows
this story, he has the power to be successful in war," certainly
connects it with the war ceremonials (see Wyman and Kluckhohn,
1938, p. 7). Practices, presumably typical of tribal warfare in the
past, survive today only in the rite for exorcising alien ghosts. The
activities of Monster Slayer in *Monsterway* (Wyman, 1970a, pp.
50–59, 550–588, Table 2, p. 57) and *The Pueblo War* (ibid., pp.
59–62, 588–599) caused his illness which was cured by the prototype
of the Enemyway rite (ibid., pp. 599–605).

MINOR MYTHIC MOTIFS OF THE PUEBLO WAR

LOCALE AND PERSONNEL ESTABLISHED and *Preliminary skirmishes.*
The Mountainway myths with one exception (HM) are remarkably
uniform with regard to the Navajo group which instigates the war
with the Pueblo Indians. In four myths it is a group of ten or twelve
young men and their two beautiful sisters. All but two of the brothers
are killed by the Pueblos and the two survivors seeking revenge
promise their sisters to whoever should obtain the scalps of two
non-sunlight-struck ones among the Pueblos. To be sure in most
instances the Navajos had been having trouble with the Pueblos
before and in LH they had killed two Pueblo Eagle Dancers, so
the slaughter of the brothers was itself a matter of revenge. In HM,
however, the motive for war is revenge for the killing of two young
Turtle-dove People.

The locale of these events shows much uniformity as well, being
in the northeastern part of the Navajo country, now northwestern
New Mexico and southwestern Colorado. The Navajo group is
living in the vicinity of the La Plata Range in Colorado (YPM),
around Big Sheep, the sacred mountain of the north, perhaps
Hesperus Peak (see Wyman, 1957, p. 37; 1962, p. 78; HS), or at
Horse Lake in the Jicarilla Apache reservation in New Mexico (LH).
The besieged Pueblo is Wide House, identified as the Aztec ruins in
northwestern New Mexico (YPM, OBS), or "near Kayenta," Arizona
(LH), or Blue House [unidentified],[71] or is not specified (HS).

---

[71] One of the ruins in the Chaco Canyon, New Mexico (Wijiji, six miles east of Pueblo Bonito) is called Blue (Turquoise) House by the Navajos. Since the name Wide
House is a common descriptive term for a large open ruin it could refer to another of
the larger ruins in the Chaco Canyon such as Chettro Kettle, or perhaps to Pueblo
Pintado near the Pueblo Alto trading store. Since some myths indicate that Wide
House and Blue House were near each other, they may well have been two of the
villages in the Chaco Canyon region. On the other hand, they may have been two
settlements on the San Juan River.

As pointed out before (Wyman, 1957, p. 20), the Beautyway myths present no such uniformity with respect to the makeup of the Navajo group [SM – Gray-streak-of-earth clan people; WW – a woman and her two daughters; HG – Bear, Snake, Frog, and Turtle; C – a renowned warrior and his two beautiful sisters; OBS – the elder brother of twins]. The locale, however, is also generally in the eastern or northeastern area of the old Navajo country, although not so well circumscribed as in the Mountainway stories. The home of the Navajo group is at Huerfano Mountain, New Mexico (SM); near Hosta Butte, New Mexico (WW); near Mancos, Colorado (HG); not given (C); beyond Big Sheep (see above; OBS). The Pueblo victims are at Taos (SM); the west side of Pueblo Bonito (Chaco Canyon, New Mexico; WW); "near . . . the great ocean" (HG); not given (C); Wide House (Aztec; OBS). The Beautyway myths agree, with one exception, however, (SM), that the attack on the Pueblos is unprovoked by *Preliminary skirmishes* but is instigated frankly as a trophy hunt, a contest for warriors vying to win the two beautiful Navajo maidens as prizes for taking the scalps of the non-sunlight-struck Pueblo beings, rather than being reprisal for losses suffered in previous battles. In two of these myths (SM, HG), however, the beginning of all the trouble is the *Independent raid of Frog and Turtle Man* who capture the coveted scalps in what may be called *Preliminary skirmishes*. In one story (SM) this leads to futher killing which provokes a revenge motive on the part of the Navajo.

The three Enemyway myths likewise vary in personnel: Corn People (SC), Turtle-doves (RJC), the Slayer Twins (FG). The home localities of the Navajo group, however, on top of rock-ledge-extension [one of the mesa points on the south side of Mesa Verde] (SC), and Hard Flint Place [not identified] (FG), and the attacked Pueblo, Taos (SC), Wide House and Blue House (see footnote 71), and Blue House at River Junction (FG), are in the same general northeastern area as those in the Mountainway myths. In SC and RJC the motivation is to avenge deaths which occurred in *Preliminary skirmishes*, but in FG the attack is made for no good reason other than the joy of battle. Thus, in general the Enemyway and Mountainway myths have more in common than either does with Beautyway.

Two sisters promised to takers of scalps. The two beautiful sisters, protagonists of the myths, are members of the family or Navajo group which instigates the war in all but two myths. In HG they are summarily introduced after the raid on the Pueblos and in FG they do not appear at all since this brief myth is concerned only with the battle at Blue House without leading up to further adventures of any of the participants. The sisters are promised to the takers of the scalps of two non-sunlight-struck ones of the Pueblo. In seven myths these are girls, non-sunlight-struck being a euphemism for virgin (see Wyman, 1957, p. 21), but in the other five they are males, "twin Gods" associated with warfare (LH), the "Great Warrior" of Wide House and his chief (OBS), non-sunlight-struck boys (HS), man-eating ogres (WW). There is no constant connection between their sex and either Mountainway [females in two myths, males in three] or Beautyway [females in three, males in two]; in the two Enemyway myths, they are girls. In RJC they are called non-sunlight-struck ones without specifying their sex but, probably, they were females.

Independent raid of Frog and Turtle Man. Frog and Turtle Man go scalp hunting on their own in two Mountainway myths (HM, LH), two Beautyway stories (SM, HG), and two Enemyway tales (SC, FG). In FG this motif makes up about half of the entire story of the battle at Blue House. In RJC Turtle Man and Toad Man are merely mentioned as originators of Enemyway (Wyman, 1970a, p. 582). The raid takes place early in the campaign against the Pueblos, being the first skirmish in four myths (HM, SM, HG, SC). In SC it occurred the day previous to going to war. In fact in SM and HG Frog and Turtle Man's activities are the start of all the trouble. In both they take the scalps of the non-sunlight-struck girls, but in SM these trophies become available again in some unexplained way so that Bear Man and Big Snake Man can get them, while in HG these two old men compete for the prize maidens only in the contests held after the raid. In FG Frog Man and Turtle Man capture but do not kill the two Pueblo girls and are finally allowed to keep them as spoils of war.

The methods used and even the sequence of the unsuccessful attempts of the Pueblo people to kill Frog and Turtle Man after they had captured them are remarkably uniform in the six myths (see Table 4). Endeavors to kill them with a stone axe which rebounded off the Turtle's shell, by burning them in a fire which was quenched by Frog's urine, and boiling in a pot which was broken by Turtle's expanding shell, are the first three essays in three myths (HM, LH, SC), and they occur in the other three [boiling omitted in HG] in different order. An attempt to drown them and their escape to safety is the final event in all but FG [here the intention was to throw them off a cliff but they landed in a pool and swam away]. A second trial by fire takes place in SM and FG, and throwing them off a cliff in HM, SM, and FG.

Monster Slayer organizes and leads war party. In seven myths (see Table 4) the Slayer Twins or Monster Slayer alone direct the preparations for battle and lead the Navajos to war. In HM someone called Blackshirt plays this part and puts up his two daughters as prizes, in HS the Wind is the leader, and in C a "renowned warrior" stakes his two sisters. While searching for help the Navajos appeal to or are advised by Changing Woman, Begochidi (LH), the Holy People (HS), or Who-returns-to-look-at-the-fish, the Witch Father-in-law (RJC), and in most cases they are sent to the Slayer Twins or Monster Slayer. In two myths (WW, SC) it is Coyote who carries the news to Monster Slayer (see Wyman, 1970a, p. 22).

Hard Flint People help. In all but two myths (HG, C) Hard Flint Woman and her twelve noisy but doughty grandsons join the war party and lend immeasurable aid. Hard Flint Woman [She-whom-enemy-does-not-see] is invisible to the enemy and by raiding the Pueblos' corn fields, feeds her boys. Monster Slayer, displeased with their rowdy behavior and fearful that their noise will alert the enemy, remonstrates but is mollified and apologetic after a show of weapons and strength by them and assurances that they have come to help him.

Encounter with Talking God. Because Talking God was in the habit of receiving numerous offerings from the Pueblos, he tried to dissuade the Navajos from warring on them or flatly decreed that they should not. He agreed, however, that the Pueblos could be exterminated if the Navajos' leader could guess the significance of several [usually four] painted prayersticks or gamesticks (see Haile, 1938a, p. 30). The test was passed, and the Navajos went ahead with their plans. This motif occurs in six myths, the guessing test with sticks to determine if the Pueblos are to be attacked being in five of them [not in HS].

Boneless Enemies. Peculiar creatures, with no bones and wide eyes whose gaze or the mere sight of whom could paralyze their opponents, were brought out by the Pueblos. Monster Slayer by pretending to be crazy lured these *Boneless Enemies* to where they could be killed (SM, RJC). In FG *Boneless Enemies* are merely mentioned as the people with whom the Slayer Twins were trying to start a war.

Bear Man and Big Snake Man get scalps. Two doddering old men join the Navajos' war party, much to the latter's annoyance. The Navajos try to dissuade them from going on with them, saying that they would be useless and in the way, but they persist and turn out to be capable of becoming youthful and valiant warriors who succeed in taking the scalps of the non-sunlight-struck ones. HG is quite deviant in that the coveted scalps are taken by Frog Man and

Turtle Man. Bear Man and Big Snake Man, however, win the contests for the maidens which were held after the raid.

Further contests for the sisters. Unwilling to give their young maidens to two such undesirable old men, the Navajos propose further contests in the hope of thwarting their legitimate claims. In one myth (SM) five contests are held, in eight there are four, and in one there are three. OBS is deviant in that the people living on Mesa Verde held two contests in a competition for their maidens *before* the attack on the Pueblos. When they were won by Bear Man and Big Snake Man, the taking of scalps was set as a further contest. Shooting at a pine tree, or a target made on one, occurs in eight myths; shooting over a high cliff, ridge, or rock is in seven; running and putting a hand or finger in a hold in a rock is in six; shooting through or into a hole or crevice in a rock or at a rock thrown in the air is in five; shooting at a yucca blade or at a cord and distance shooting are in four each; a race occurs in three myths, and a shinny game and two unspecified contests in one (HG). The order of these events varies in different myths (see Table 4). The two elders are victorious in all these contests, but still the girls are not given to them so they finally resort to seduction to obtain their lawful prizes.

Postwar dance held and Tobacco smoke seduction. A war dance, held to celebrate the victory and exorcise the ghosts of slain enemies and during which the seduction episode occurs, is the one indispensable event necessary to establish the plots of Female Mountainway and Beautyway. The details are almost identical in all the myths. The two sisters choose partners, dance a while, and becoming overheated, they wander away to a stream to drink, bathe, and cool off, or else they are lured by the sweet odor of the magic tobacco smoked by the elders while still at the dance. Following the odor the girls come to the elders' camp and finding two superb youths there, they spend the night with them, the elder sister with Bear Man, the younger with Big Snake Man. The next morning the elders have reverted to their forms as Bear and Big Snake, and the horrified girls flee from these disgustingly ugly old men.

Girls flee from elders' camp and *Girls escape from people by charms.* In seven myths the sisters, sometimes warned by Wind or by overheard talk of their relatives that they would be killed if they returned home, begin their flight from the elders' camp. In the other stories they return to their people, are attacked and escape by means of charms [magic baskets, feathers, reeds] previously given to them by the elders.

Girls travel together at first and *Girls separate immediately.* The sisters travel together for a while before parting [seven myths] or separate immediately to begin their separate journeys [five myths].

Girls tracked by magic smoke. In all but three stories Bear Man and Big Snake Man track the girls by means of magic tobacco smoke which follows their victims with deadly accuracy. At this point, "The side where bear began to track her is Mountain Top Way, the side where snake began tracking her is Beauty Way" (Haile, 1938a, p. 175). The story of Younger Sister pursued by Big Snake Man and instructed in the home of the Snakes constitutes the origin myth proper of Beautyway and is the subject of Wyman, 1957. The adventures of Older Sister followed by Bear Man make up the myth of Female Mountainway which is taken up in this volume. Of course the Enemyway myths do not continue with the adventures of the sisters because these events belong to the other two chantways mentioned.

> He [Bear Man] chased the older of the two to the place called Wide Chokecherry Patch. He had done that to her, as it developed, for the purpose of [establishing] Mountainway, which at present they use in singing. On Big Snake Man's part, it developed that he had done this at Wide Rock for the purposes of Beautyway. At that place the Beautyway chant originated, they say. Over there [at their home] the search for them was quite in vain. It seems [they thought] they must simply have been chased away by the elders mentioned. That was all that happened. That done, they merely departed for their homes, they say (River Junction Curly, in Wyman, 1970a, p. 599).

> Then Bear Man left to follow, the other [Big Snake Man] also left to follow downstream. Some distance away he stopped. "Look here, the thing of which we spoke is quite unsettled! In future days it shall be called the meeting of branches sandpainting" he [Bear Man] said. "Enemyway it shall be called, we extinguished all enemies. It shall be a meeting line with Mountain-top-way," he said. "It shall be so also on your side, it shall be called Beautyway. It shall be a partner branch to Mountain-top-way, because we two did this one thing [together]" (Yucca Patch Man, see pp. 175–176).

Girls meet again during travels and *Girls reunited at end.* In three myths (LH, WW, C) the sisters meet again briefly during their journeys and in three others (HM, HS, SM) they do not meet again until they return home or just before reaching home (see Wyman, 1957, p. 23; "starting lines meet," a term applied only to Mountain-way and Beautyway). In the other tales (YPM, HG, OBS) either no mention is made of subsequent meetings or it is said that they never see each other again.

Examination of Table 4 shows quite considerable correspondence in the minor mythic motifs of the twelve [or thirteen if OBA is included; see footnote 70] versions of *The Pueblo War*. After the establishment of locale and personnel, a Navajo group decides to wage war against a certain Pueblo village. Two beautiful maidens, sisters, are promised as prizes to the takers of the scalps of two non-sunlight-struck ones of the village. Frog Man and Turtle Man make a raid on their own, are captured and subjected to a number of trials from which they escape by magical means. Monster Slayer organizes and leads the war party which is joined by the Hard Flint People. In the great battle which follows, two disgusting old men, Bear Man and Big Snake Man, capture the coveted scalps. They are refused their prizes, and further contests in the nature of sports or games are set in the hope of thwarting them. They win all of the tests and are still refused their legitimate spoils. A postwar dance is held by the Navajos during which the sisters are lured to the elders' camp by magic tobacco smoke. The next day the sisters flee in terror from their seducers, who track them by following the drift of their magic tobacco smoke (see Spencer, 1957, pp. 214–217). These events constitute the essential plot of the myth of *The Pueblo War* acceptable to most Navajos, forming a framework into which details and individual variations may be fitted.

Scrutiny of the distribution of the minor mythic motifs between the myths of the two chants and the Enemyway rite shows that in the Mountainway and Enemyway stories the motivation for the war is revenge for losses suffered in *Preliminary skirmishes* with the Pueblos, while in the Beautyway tales it is a contest for scalp trophies. In the Beautyway and Enemyway myths Monster Slayer seems to have more to do with the war than he does in the Mountain-way tales. Otherwise the mythic motifs are more or less equally distributed in the myths of the three ceremonials.

Major Mythic Motifs of Mountainway

LOCALE AND PERSONNEL ESTABLISHED. The details of this motif in setting the scene for *The Pueblo War* are given above. As in many Navajo myths Matthews' account begins with a family situation, man and wife, two sons and two daughters, moving about in the vicinity of Beautiful Mountain [in the Carrizo Mountains] and other places in northwestern New Mexico and southwestern Colorado [Shiprock, the La Plata Range, etc.], making a living with difficulty by hunting and gathering [*Impecunious wandering*].[72] In CCM a similar family group was being bothered by the Utes south of the La Plata Mountains. In OBS the captivity starts abruptly without giving the details of locale and personnel.

The Pueblo War. This has been discussed in detail. See pp. 127–136.

Journey of Older Sister [Pursued by Bear Man, Flight from Bear]. Older Sister's frantic flight from her Bear "husband," trailed by his magic smoke, parallels the adventures of her Younger Sister in her flight from Big Snake Man (see Wyman, 1957, pp. 24–27). Occasionally she stumbled unwittingly into the home of Bear Man (HM, HS). In two stories she saw a mother bear at a distance, bouncing her cubs as though teaching them to dance (YPM) or rolling them in the snow while singing (HS). In each instance the bear shook the mountain so that she nearly fell. In HM a list of twenty-three places, probably mostly mythical, which she visited in her flight is given, but the inhabitants of these places are not named. It is said, however, that in each one she was questioned, whereupon she told the story of her misadventures. This questioning, as to the protagonist's origin and intentions and his or her narration of adventures up to date, runs through all *Encounters with* or *Visits to Supernaturals* or natural beings and will not be mentioned again. Another theme which runs through all accounts of a protagonist's travels in Mountainway myths is his or her subsisting chiefly on berries of various kinds, especially those which grow in the mountains, such as chokecherries. Various berries are ingredients of Mountainway medicines (see Wyman and Harris, 1941, p. 72). Wide Chokecherry Patch is a prominent place name in Mountainway myths; it is the home of Bear Man.

Because of the emphasis upon bears in everything pertaining to Mountainway, the myths, etiological factors, medicines, and so on, we might expect the story of *Changing Bear Maiden* to appear prominently in its mythology. Such is not the case, however, for with one exception (YPM) this evil female creature is merely mentioned as being present (LH) or quite briefly as one of the many

---

[72] Prominent minor mythic motifs will be mentioned from time to time. They may be distinguished from the major motifs in that only the first word and proper nouns in their names are capitalized (see footnote 69).

supernaturals visited by the hero (MMC; Matthews, 1887, p. 407). In YPM, however, Older Sister met a cousin, the son of her mother's sister, who was one of the surviving brothers of Changing Bear Maiden. He told her the story of his wicked sister and her Coyote husband in two installments, before and after he had treated her aching body with a trench sweat. His narrative is a fairly complete version, but there is no obvious reason as to why it should have been included in YPM's myth, except perhaps the mere joy in telling an exciting tale. *Changing Bear Maiden* properly belongs to Evilway Ritual. It is one of the fundamental motifs of the myth of Upward-reachingway, the primary Evilway ceremonial. Since Mountainway, at least today, is never performed according to that ritual, there is no reason to include her story in its myths. This tale is discussed and the minor mythic motifs in seven versions of it are given in Wyman, 1973 (pp. 99–102 and Table 9; see also Wyman, 1962, pp. 33, 57).

Encounters with Supernaturals [Helped by Supernaturals]. Various supernatural beings, most of whom help but some who hinder the protagonist [or try to], are encountered during the *Flight from Bear* or the escape from the Utes. The two sisters were sheltered by the Slayer Twins (YPM). Older Sister met all the water creatures playing the hoop and pole game, Big Fly who gave her a geography lesson pointing out many places as they sat on a mountain top, and Holy Young Man and Woman who showed her their whirling log door curtain, prayersticks, paintings, and dances in their home (YPM). She also encountered Endless Snake, who blocked her way and struck her. Other beings who tried to hinder the heroine(s) were a snake who bit her and a widening creek crossed in a magic basket provided by the Bear People (HS), crushing rocks like those of *Monsterway* and a wind-made waterspout (LH), and Mountain Sheep, usually a helpful being, who dug a canyon with his horn but smoothed it out so that the pursuing Utes could cross after the heroines had crossed it in magic baskets (CCM). Crossing canyons, valleys, or rivers in magic baskets or on rainbows provided by Supernaturals are frequent minor mythic motifs in many chant myths (YPM, HM, MMC, CCM).

The *Encounters with* and *Visits to Supernaturals* occurring in the *Ute Captivity* myth will be discussed below.

Attack by Thunder [Lightning]. Attacks by Supernaturals, when the protagonist ventures into forbidden territory after being warned, are special instances of unpleasant *Encounters with Supernaturals* which provide excuses for further instruction in ceremonial lore or treatment by ritual means. *Attack [Shattered] by Thunder [Lightning]* is an important motif of many ceremonial myths (see Wyman, 1962, pp. 48, 64, 72; 1965, p. 98). Older Sister was warned by the Meal Sprinkler not to approach a certain hill but disregarding his *Injunctions [disobeyed]*, she found herself in the home of White Thunder where lightning struck near her. Suffering from painful swollen joints she returned with difficulty to her brothers' home. There they cured her with four *Trench Sweats,* one in each cardinal direction.

Attack by Toad [Frog]. Disobeying the *Injunctions* of her brothers to stay quietly at home, Older Sister went to a spring for water where she was shot by the arrows of Toad [Frog] Man (YPM, HS) and Big Snake (YPM). Her brothers found her there unconscious, brought her home in a buckskin, and tried to revive her with a *Trench Sweat* done four times. Failing, they were advised by Big Fly to try a Sweat Ceremony which they did four times but again in vain. A *Council* was held to discuss the situation and *to plan action*. A *Mysterious voice*, which turned out to be that of Bat, told them that Big Snake and Toad had shot her. Big Fly revealed the location of their home and, after the older brother had made three *Unacceptable offerings* [fawn skins], told them how to prepare a *Proper offering* [prayersticks] and was Chided by the betrayed supernaturals for his pains. The latter told the intermediary to take along the pouch which was hanging in a tree, but it proved to be an elusive item (see *Squirrel skin pouch,* Wyman, 1962, p. 70). After *Importunate appeals* to come immediately, the pair agreed to come in four nights [days] and gave directions for making the sandpainting of the *Home of Bear and Snake*. This succession—the fruitless *Council,* the *Mysterious voice* and *Big Fly monitor, Unacceptable* and *Proper offerings, Monitor chided, Importunate appeals*, agreement to begin the ceremonial in four days, the *Elusive pouch,* and directions for providing needed materials—is a standard series of events for arranging ceremonials in most Navajo myths (see Wyman, 1962, p. 70; 1970a, p. 61). These are among the minor mythic motifs common to numerous ceremonials, representative examples of which are listed and their distribution among the chants and rites given in Wyman, 1962, Table 1 (see also pp. 42–45). From this table it may be seen that most of the motifs given occur in the myths of Mountainway, and three others, *Big Fly monitor, Monitor chided,* and the *Restoration rite,* should also be checked under Mountainway. To return to YPM, Big Snake and Toad Man performed *Restoration by marking away* (see Wyman and Bailey, 1944;

Wyman, 1962, pp. 43, 225; 1973, p. 72), which revived Older Sister but left her emaciated. Later, it was decided to treat her with a complete Mountainway chant [*Prototype Ceremonial*]. Another restoration rite was performed over Bear Man who had become paralyzed, but he was incompletely restored, being left with crooked feet. In HS Frog Man alone shot Older Sister as she was getting water at his spring and after the usual series of arrangements he restored her by means of a *Shock rite*, in which she was frightened by the shouting of his children rather than by a bear (see Wyman, 1973, pp. 56–58).

Dangerous Women [*Mummifying Woman*]. Another type of *Encounter with Supernaturals* which is sometimes expanded into an independent tale is the story of the Thin Old Woman who during a *Grinding contest* with various bird maidens wins a young lover by successfully tossing a ball of cornmeal at him without breaking it and then starves him to death at her home (*Mummifying Woman*; Wyman, 1962, pp. 65–69, Table 5). Since this motif occurs only in Lefthanded's myth and the shortened version of it (OBA), it is omitted from Table 3. It occurs in the portion of the myth which he said was the story of Female Mountainway. Older Sister and her supernatural companions happened upon the corn grinding contest and witnessed the ceremonies associated with it. In this version Mummifying Woman was joined by Changing Bear maiden who also won a lover and caused him to become covered with boils and sores, thus the two dangerous women represent hunger and sickness. Why Lefthanded introduced this motif, which belongs in the Shootingway and Windway categories (see Wyman, op. cit.), into Mountainway is not clear. Perhaps he was fond of telling the story or perhaps he regarded it as an appropriate example of *Another ceremonial visited*, a minor mythic motif which is not uncommon in chant myths. Although the name of the ceremonial was not given, it could have been a Female Shootingway.

Visits to Supernaturals [*Journey for Knowledge and Power*]. This motif, as well as the *Journey of Older Sister* and her *Encounters with Supernaturals*, provides the Navajo narrators an opportunity to express the "psychological leitmotif" of their life, the concept of motion (Astrov, 1950; see Wyman, 1959, p. 22; 1962, p. 52). Worth and Adair (1970, pp. 23–25) found that motion pictures made by Navajos "portray what seems to us an inordinate amount of walking." Most of some films were composed of the central characters walking to obtain materials for such activities as silversmithing or weaving, leaving very little time for what would seem to be the principal activity; "walking was necessary to tell a story about something Navajo." The authors remark that, "In reading Navajo myths and stories we were struck by the fact that . . . the narrator spends much of his time describing the walking, the landscape, and the places he passes, and dwells only briefly on what to us are the plot lines." Along with the walking, the recital of long lists of place names makes it appear that Navajos have an inordinate interest in geography as well as in traveling (Wyman, 1957, p. 26; 1959, p. 18; 1962, p. 72; 1973, p. 98). Lefthanded mentioned no less than sixty places visited by Older Sister during her *Journey*. Place or locality is of utmost importance to the Navajo, a power which must be brought under control. The landmarks of the Navajo country are repeated in prayer and song, and their recapitulation in myth gives verisimilitude to the story and establishes a feeling of security by organizing space into manageable units (see Reichard, 1970, p. 152 ff.).[73] Many of the place names may be equated with geographical localities found on our maps but others are not recognizable in our terms and therefore may be mythical localities, although it is likely that a Navajo would be able to locate most of them in his country.

In YPM Younger Sister makes two *Journeys for Knowledge and Power*, leaving home each time in spite of the injunctions of her brothers to stay home and keep house. In HM twenty-three places which she visited are listed. At each she was questioned and told the story of her *Flight from Bear*, but the Supernaturals living in them are not named. Lefthanded (LH) gave one of the longest lists of places visited to be found in any myth, some sixty in all, naming some forty-seven Supernaturals living in them and nearly forty events witnessed or ceremonial procedures learned, such as dances, making prayersticks, grinding corn, weaving ceremonial fabrics, etc. In all of the myths relating Older Sister's *Journey* the home of the Bear People was visited; various kinds of squirrels and Holy

---

[73] Vogt (1960, p. 360), also referring to the way Navajos report movement in painstaking detail, remarked: "It also seems evident that the automobile permits an even fuller expression than before of the high value that Navahos place upon travel. They have always struck observers as a restless, traveling group of people, and there is much to suggest in their culture, mythology, and language that they conceive themselves as living, as Harry Hoijer expresses it, in a 'universe in motion' in which ' . . . both gods and culture heroes move restlessly from one holy place to the next, seeking by their motion to perfect or repair the dynamic flux which is the universe.'"

Young Man and Woman are encountered in three of the myths, and weasels, porcupine, mountain sheep, turkey, and owl in two. In LH Older Sister is accompanied by supernatural guides, in the others she travels alone. By far the greatest number of Supernaturals visited are animals or birds, in fact almost entirely so. In LH it is said that at one place there were "all the birds and all the animals." Although all sorts of ceremonial procedures are seen and learned — songs and prayers, dances, sandpaintings, the use of medicines and pollen, etc. — the most frequent ceremonial acquisition is knowledge of the manufacture and use of prayersticks, thus providing ceremonial sanction for the large number of bird and animal prayersticks employed in Mountainway (see pp. 42–56 above).

A very frequent minor mythic motif in these and most other myths is that when the protagonist is invited into some Supernatural's home, especially that of a small creature which is often underground or within a rock or cliff, the entrance is too small to pass through and has to be *Enlarged by Blowing* upon it by the inhabitant.

In two myths (LH, MMC) the protagonist is shampooed, bathed, dried with cornmeal, painted, dressed, and molded by First Earth Surface Woman (LH) or by Butterfly Woman (MMC) so as to look like the Earth Woman (LH) or like the Mountain Spirits called Reared-within-the-mountains or the Meal Sprinklers in a present day Mountain Chant (MMC).

Prototype Trench Sweat. In YPM and HS the heroine's aching body and swollen joints were treated by her brothers with a pit sudatory [trench firing, pit sudorific], four times in YPM and twice in HS. This was done after she had crawled home following her *Flight from Bear* or the *Attacks by Thunder* and *Toad [Frog]*. In this ceremony, which is like the outdoor sudorific of Nightway (Matthews, 1902, pp. 53–54, 210, 259; Wyman, 1962, p. 75), a long trench to fit the patient's body is dug outside the ceremonial hogan, ideally at the four cardinal points on four successive days, a fire is built in it and allowed to burn down, the hot ground is covered with evergreen boughs and herbs of various kinds, and the patient lies on this bed of plants covered with blankets and sweats profusely.

Prototype Ceremonial. The first Mountain chant(s) was held to finally and completely cure Older Sister of the infirmities, swollen joints, pain, and debility, incurred during her various travels or to remove the evil alien influences from the captives of the Utes. Most mythical accounts follow the main outlines of the descriptions of actual ceremonials published by Matthews (1887) and Haile (1946).

Additional details are given in the section on *Ceremonial Procedure*. The singer of the *Prototype Ceremonial* is a brother (LH, HS) or the father (CCM) of the protagonist(s), Bear Man (HM), or various unrelated singers. In YPM Older Sister herself directed the ceremonial. In LH the croaking of Frog Man and his frog companions produced the fright for the *Shock rite*, as it did in HS. Of course the Dark Circle of Branches [Corral or Fire Dance], the feature which has made the Mountain chant so well known to the world outside, was held in all the prototype chants.

An episode which is a necessary part of all Dark Circle of Branches phases is expanded almost into a major motif in four myths (YPM, HM, MMC, CCM) — the selection, dressing, and dispatching of the Meal Sprinklers [couriers] to invite distant tribes to the ceremonial and the relation of their adventures on returning. A runner known to be fleet of foot [Valley Boy in YPM] is selected to be one courier and the grandmother of a reputed lazy boy [Who-lies-under-it in YPM] proffers his services but is ridiculed. Finally he is accepted, however, and turns out to be the faster of the two because he has trained in secret. They return from their missions bringing proof of their contact with alien tribes, baked ears of corn or mescal, and tell the Navajos about their journeys. In MMC the *Reputed Lazy Boy* exchanged his bow and quiver for those of the courier from another and different ceremonial whom he had met on his journey. This was a sign to their people that they had met. The *Exchange of Quivers* in the Beadway myth is similar (Reichard, 1939, p. 33; Wyman, 1971, p. 83).

Post-ceremonial Race(s). After the *Prototype Ceremonial* in YPM, Valley Boy challenged *Reputed Lazy Boy* to a footrace around Mount Taylor. The Pueblo visitors bet on Valley Boy while the Navajos bet on Lazy Boy. Of course he won, and the Pueblos lamented the loss of their valuables. In MMC the Navajo chief learned of Lazy Boy's prowess from his grandmother and somewhat sneakily arranged the race so that the Navajos could bet on a sure thing. This time, however, the alien tribes' complaints induced the Navajos to accept another challenge so they bet half their winnings, Valley Boy won, and thus the aliens recovered half their losses.

Protagonist(s) Returns Home, Relates Adventures, Teaches Ceremonial; Protagonist Departs to Live with Supernaturals. The myths of Mountainway pay much less attention to these two mythic motifs as closing chapters than do those of most other ceremonials. Older Sister's sojourns with her brothers between her several trips

Table 5
MINOR MYTHIC MOTIFS OF UTE CAPTIVITY

	MMC	LH	OBS	HM	CCM
Hero's life saved by old man	X	X			
Old man and woman guards	X	X		X	X
Council decrees captive's death	X	X	X	X	
Captive sent for water	X	X		X	
Captive meets SN° at water	X	X		X	
Succoring SN(s) demands Utes' valuables	X	X	X	X	
Utes put to sleep by bird	X	X			X
Captive released by SN(s)	X	X	X	X	X
Escape with Utes' valuables	X	X		X	X
Pursued by Utes	X	X	X	X	X
Magic crossing of obstacle	X	X	X	X	X
Flight from Utes (protected by SNs)	X	X	X	X	X
Hidden by Wood Rat	X	X	X	X	X
Hidden under bush		X	X	X	
Destructive storm	X	X			X
Visits to SNs (Journey for Knowledge and Power)	X	X		X	
Purification from Utes	X		X		X
Utes' valuables distributed	X	X		X	X
Jicarillas arrive late	X			X	X

° *SN(s) = supernatural(s)*

are occupied with housekeeping for them — cooking, making buckskin clothing, baskets, and pots — which is described in some detail (YPM). LH and HS make mention of the birth of Bear Man's child which was left with the Supernaturals at Blanca Peak in LH and taken away by Bear Man in HS. The narrator remarked that the Cub branch of Mountainway "comes in" here. Sometimes the heroines are *Not recognized by relatives after supernatural contact* (HM). The ceremonial learned during the *Journey for Knowledge and Power* may be taught, usually to a brother (YPM, LH, HS). Only three myths acknowledge the departure to be with the Supernaturals (LH, HS, MMC).

Ute Captivity. Five of the Mountainway myths either consist entirely of this major mythic motif (MMC, OBS, CCM) or include it along with others (LH, HM). MMC is by far the most extensive and complete account. As mentioned above, this motif in LH was said to belong to the male branch of Mountainway by the narrator and MMC and OBS are presumably myths of the male branch, and all these have male protagonists. HM and CCM, with girls as chief characters, may or may not be of the female branch. The protagonists of the five myths are: the elder of two brothers who were being taught hunting magic by their father and who was captured by the Utes because of paternal *Injunctions disobeyed* (MMC); a grandson of Older Sister taken while he was guarding his family's hogans (LH); "a young man" (OBS); Older Sister herself (HM); and two sisters given to the Utes by their father with ulterior motives (CCM). In LH the *Ute Captivity* is preceded by a brief Hopi captivity from which the boy is promptly rescued by his people. Since only one of the five myths has more than one protagonist (CCM) and since the captured Navajo is male except in CCM and HM, the protagonists will be referred to as singular and masculine to avoid awkward expressions in the Table and discussion where more than one number and both sexes are involved.

Major motifs connected with the *Ute Captivity* and a few of its minor motifs which also occur in the stories of Older Sister, such as *Impecunious wandering*, protagonist made to resemble Supernaturals, *Reputed Lazy Boy courier* and *Exchange of Quivers*, and *Post-ceremonial Race(s)*, have already been discussed above. Table 5 and the following discussions take up the important minor mythic motifs of the *Ute Captivity*.

MINOR MYTHIC MOTIFS OF THE UTE CAPTIVITY

Hero's life saved by old man [chief]. An old Ute man argued the young warriors out of killing the Navajo captive and took him for a slave (MMC); the Ute chief took a fancy to the Navajo boy and adopted him (LH).

Old man and woman guards. The captive(s) was kept in a buffalo hide tepee guarded by an old man and woman, tied with a cord which was also tied to them or passed under them so that he could not move without wakening them (MMC, HM), or was sewed up in two buffalo hides (LH).

Council decrees captive's death. Angry because the boy had used some of their feathers to fletch his arrows (LH), or to obtain a scalp for a ceremony (HM), or for no stated reason (MMC, OBS), the Utes held a meeting and decided to kill the captive.

Captive sent for water. Becoming thirsty during the council, the Utes sent the captive to a spring or creek to fetch water four times (LH, HM).

Captive meets supernatural at water. Owl Man (MMC), Holy Young Man (LH), or *Talking God* (HM) appeared to the captive at the spring or creek and gave him instructions concerning his coming escape from the Utes. Holy Young Man gave the Navajo a little basket and a prayerstick which served as his monitor during his *Flight from the Utes* (LH). In OBS Talking God and Calling God appeared to the Navajo captive in his tepee prison, and in CCM Talking God in the form of a big horned owl came to the tepee to advise the Navajo girls.

Succoring supernatural(s) demands Utes' valuables. Talking God (MMC, HM), Holy Young Man (LH), or Talking God and Calling God (OBS) told the captive to steal the Utes' treasures for them before leaving. These included war bonnets, beaded buckskin clothing embroidered with feathers and porcupine quills and beaded moccasins, beaver and otter skins and collars, eagle plumes and tail feathers, and flutes and whistles.

Utes put to sleep by bird. A whippoorwill or poorwill (MMC, CCM), or a turtledove (LH) flew into the tepee through the smoke vent and over the heads of the Utes, putting them to sleep.

Captive released by supernatural(s). Talking God (MMC, HM, CCM), Turtledove (LH), or Talking God and Calling God (OBS) released the prisoner and sent him on his way. In MMC the hero followed the hoot of an owl, came to a canyon, and was helped down into it by Talking God, who then sheltered him in his home there. In OBS the Ye'i took him to the home of Otter under a creek.

Escape with Utes' valuables; Pursued by Utes. The captive fled, taking with him the stolen treasures of the Utes who began to pursue him once they had discovered his absence. In LH and HM the Utes were hampered at first by an unseasonable snowstorm.

Magic crossing of obstacle. The fleeing Navajo was sent or carried across a canyon or valley (MMC, HM), lake (LH), or river (OBS, CCM), on a rainbow (MMC, LH, CCM) or flash of lightning (MMC), on Winged Rock [Shiprock] Man's back (OBS) or in a magic basket (HM), provided by Talking God (MMC), Holy Young Man (LH), Bear (HM), or Beaver (CCM).

Flight from Utes [*protected by supernaturals*]. During the Navajo's *Flight from Utes* he was hidden, put out of reach, or otherwise protected from his pursuers by various supernaturals. From four to six of these *Encounters with Supernaturals* are described in each of the five myths. The first encounter in MMC and LH was with Talking God who hid the hero in his home or a cave in a cliff; in OBS and CCM it was with a water animal, Otter (OBS) or Beaver (CCM), who hid the Navajo in his home under the water. The second encounter in MMC and CCM and the third in HM was with Mountain Sheep, but in CCM this beast tried to hinder rather than help the fleeing captives. In HM the Navajo girl was put out of reach of the Utes on a growing rock point like the Sky-reaching-rock of other chant myths (see Wyman, 1962, p. 50), and in MMC Talking God used a hill which grew into a mountain to baffle the Utes. Other supernaturals encountered in only one myth each who hid or helped the protagonist were a "little animal" [perhaps some kind of rat] (MMC), Spider (LH), Owl and Winged Rock (OBS), Long Hair (HM), and a "black stump" man (CCM).

Hidden by Wood Rat. This is the most constant *Encounter* motif appearing in all five myths and told at more length than the others. The Navajo was invited into Rat's home; the *Entrance* was *enlarged by blowing;* Rat Woman made four offers of inedible garbage or rubbish as food which were refused by the Navajo, prompted by his Wind (MMC) or prayerstick (LH) monitor, and a final offer of food acceptable to humans; the Utes poked around in the nest with a stick but could not find their victim; and after spending the night the Navajo went on his way fortified with more ceremonial knowledge or paraphernalia.

Hidden under bush. In another motif which occurs in three myths (LH, OBS, HM), Whirl-wind (LH), White Ground Squirrel (OBS), or a young man named Long Hair (HM), uprooted a greasewood bush, blew on the hole to enlarge it, told the Navajo to enter it, and replaced the bush, thus hiding him. In MMC Whirlwind dug a hole in which the Navajo was hidden, but the bush motif was not used.

Destructive storm. In three myths (MMC, LH, CCM) the pursuing Utes were overcome and dispersed by a devastating hailstorm (see Wyman, 1970a, p. 58) brought on by the magic of Wind (MMC), Spider (LH), or Wood Rat (CCM).

Visits to Supernaturals [*Journey for Knowledge and Power*]. After the frustrated Utes had given up their pursuit and gone home, the Navajo embarked on a *Journey*, visiting various supernaturals who demonstrated ceremonial procedures or instructed him in ceremonial lore, especially, as mentioned above, the making and depositing of prayersticks. MMC has the longest series of *Visits*, some eighteen in all, LH has about eight, and HM about ten. Bears, Squirrels, and Porcupines were met in all three of these myths, Weasels in two (MMC, HM) and Holy Young Men in two (MMC, LH).

Purification from Utes. Before the returning hero was allowed to enter his family's hogan he was shampooed and bathed to remove all the alien substances and influences acquired during his captivity. Thus purified, he was received by his people.

Utes' valuables distributed. The Navajo gave the property of the Utes which he had stolen to various supernaturals met during his return home as payment for their services (MMC, LH), or gave it as a fee to the singer of the *Prototype Ceremonial* (HM, CCM).

Jicarillas arrive late. Some of the distinctive features of the *Prototype Ceremonial,* such as *Lazy Boy courier,* have been discussed above. In three myths (MMC, HM, CCM) the Jicarilla Apaches had got into a hoop and pole game and almost forgot to come to the ceremonial. Arriving late, they performed the trick of swallowing the poles used in the game, to the tops of which they had attached spruce twigs with birds in them.

Of course there are many more minor mythic motifs in the Mountainway legends, some of which are universal, shared by all or by many chant myths, and others which are peculiar to individual myths. Those discussed above are the prominent ones which form the framework of the story.

Protagonist Feigns Death and Raised by Owl

LEFTHANDED'S MOUNTAINWAY MYTH, as mentioned above, is unique among other Mountainway stories in containing the tale of *Dangerous Women* in its portion pertaining to the female branch of the chant. In the part which the informant said was the myth of the male branch, it is again unique in having the related major mythic motifs of *Protagonist Feigns Death* and *Raised by Owl.* Sam Ahkeah's short myth (OBA) which, as said before, is obviously an abbreviated version of the tale from the same source, naturally contains these motifs also although their order is reversed. The six other versions of these motifs which have been recorded, and a few fragments, are all save one (SH) either trotting Coyote stories (FBC, LSS) [an independent tale in which the protagonist was said to be an unspecified man but which is almost certainly a Coyote tale

(DS)] or independent explanatory myths [one giving the origin of the Utes (MOU) and the other said to be the myth of a ceremony for dealing with the results of witchcraft, but the protagonist of it is also Coyote and it is like the other Coyote tales in every detail (JY)]. All five, therefore, may be regarded as essentially belonging to the trotting Coyote cycle. In SH *Raised by Owl* is appended to a myth of the *Hollow Log Trip* in order to account for the eventual fate of the child born of the incestuous union of Deer-raiser (*Witch Father-in-law*) and his daughter after it had been abandoned in shame by its mother. Although it was not so stated by the informant, the story of the *Hollow Log Trip* was probably a myth of Plumeway (see Wyman, 1962, p. 50). In the introduction to his manuscript of *Raised by Owl* (FBC) Father Berard Haile remarked that the account given by the narrator of SH "was flavored with too many digressions to prove satisfactory and impressed us rather as the ramblings of one unfamiliar with the true story."

In Navajo oral "literature" there are essentially two Coyotes: one a member of the Holy People's community, companion, helper, and unofficial spy of First Man in the sacred myths, but still a being with mischievous tendencies; the other a trickster, the trotting or traveling Coyote of the more secular folktales told by older men as entertainment and instruction for children (see Wyman, 1962, p. 30). Just as there is no sharp division between natural and supernatural, secular and sacred, in Navajo thinking, a strict division between the disorderly agent of First Man of the myths and the blundering trickster of the folktales is not always maintained. Coyote's personality and outlook is that of the trickster in both roles. There is reason to suspect that certain secular tales have been incorporated into the sacred myths. It is not surprising, therefore, to find in a Navajo chant myth an episode obviously based on the folktale of Coyote Marries His Daughter and its sequel *Raised by Owl*, which is a standard favorite throughout the Indian tribes of the West and present in the mythology of all the Apachean groups (see Hill and Hill, 1945). Surprising or not, the question remains, why did Lefthanded include it in his narrative?

The protagonist of Lefthanded's *Feigns Death* story is a son of Older Sister, the heroine of the female branch part of his account, and a man from Wide House. During a time of famine starving Tracking Bears came to their home seeking food. They fled leaving the baby which the Bears seized to eat, but the female Bear, feeling sorry for him, took him home and raised him. When he was twelve years old another famine struck and the Bear decided she must kill him for food. Warned by Wind, he fled, was pursued by the Bear, and escaped from her four times. Finally she let him go, telling him where to find his people. They did not recognize him at first but after discussion they accepted him, and he grew up and married. It was he who feigned death in order to seduce his wife's sister. Their offspring, abandoned by his mother, was *Raised by Owl*, so the hero of this story was the grandson of Older Sister. It was one of his younger brothers who was stolen by the Hopi and then by the Utes, becoming the hero of the *Ute Captivity*. Occurring as they do at the beginning of the myth of the male branch of Mountainway, or in other words at the point where Lefthanded made the transition from the female to the male branch myth, it seems quite possible that he introduced these motifs to provide a male hero for the *Ute Captivity*, the essential major motif of Male Mountainway.

Four of the six recorded versions, other than LH and OBA, of *Protagonist Feigns Death* and/or *Raised by Owl* have been published (MOU, JY, LSS, SH). Three are brief English reworkings by the authors of the published papers, only two or three pages each (MOU, JY, LSS), but SH, which contains only *Raised by Owl*, consists of nineteen printed pages each of Navajo text and English translation, both recorded and made by expert linguists, in fact by the leading experts on Athabascan languages. The as yet unpublished versions are a Navajo text of twenty-three double-spaced typewritten pages and a translation of equal length recorded and translated by Father Berard Haile, also an expert linguist (FBC), and seventeen single-spaced typewritten five by seven inch cards bearing an English version in the Navajo narrator's own words (DS). The six versions are as follows:

> River Junction Curly (FBC), Chinle, Arizona; recorded and translated by Father Berard Haile, O.F.M., 1929; Raised by the Owl.
>
> Washington Matthews (MOU); The Origin of the Utes. A Navajo Myth. *American Antiquarian*, vol. 7, pp. 271–274, 1885.
>
> John Yazzi (pseudonym; JY), Tuba City, Arizona; interpreters, his three sons; recorded by Stanley A. Fishler, 1950; *Owl-Raised-Ute, An Origin Legend for Curing Sorcery*, pp. 55–59 in: *A Study of Navajo Symbolism*, Franc J. Newcomb, Papers, Peabody Museum of Harvard University, vol. 32, no. 3, 1956.

Dave Skeet (DS), Two Wells, New Mexico; told to him by his
father; recorded by A. H. Leighton, 1940; Ramah files,
Harvard University and Laboratory of Anthropology,
Santa Fe, New Mexico.

The Late Little Smith's Son (LSS), Crown Point, New Mexico;
recorded by W. W. Hill, 1933; *Coyote Marries His Daughter*, pp. 335–337 in: Navaho Coyote Tales and their Position
in the Southern Athabaskan Group, W. W. Hill and Dorothy
W. Hill, *Journal of American Folklore*, vol. 58, no. 230, 1945.

Barnie Bitsili (SH), Tohatchi, New Mexico; interpreter John
Watchman; recorded by Edward Sapir, 1929; *A Legend of
the Hollow Floating Log and of the Boy Raised by the
Owl*, pp. 36–73 in: *Navaho Texts*, Edward Sapir and Harry
Hoijer, Iowa City, 1942.

Besides these six versions, two published notes give very brief
abstracts. One, said by Kluckhohn's informant to be an account of
how the Navajo got the Jicarilla Female Shootingway (Kluckhohn
and Wyman, 1940, p. 156), is a digest of *Raised by Owl*, the other
is an abstract of *Coyote Feigns Death* told by Frank Goldtooth at
Tuba City, Arizona, in 1950 (Fishler, 1953, footnote p. 109).

Since Father Berard's text and translation constitutes the most
complete version of the two motifs that we have, the translation is
presented below, and an analysis of the minor mythic motifs of the
two tales follows here.

Minor Mythic Motifs
of Protagonist Feigns Death

Since the important minor motifs of this tale are shared in
most instances by all seven versions of it (LH, OBA, FBC, MOU,
JY, DS, LSS), there would be no point in presenting them in a table.
Instead they will be discussed briefly seriatim and exceptions
for individual versions noted.

Preliminary tale. In LH *Protagonist Feigns Death* is preceded by
Raised by Bear, and it was this bear boy who decided to seduce his
wife's sister. Sam Ahkeah (OBA) reversed the two major motifs and
told *Raised by Owl* first, making the owl boy the protagonist of
Feigns Death. Coming as it does at the end of the story, it rather
left the myth hanging without a logical sequel, and probably sensing
this, he remarked about the offspring of the owl boy and his sister-
in-law which was abandoned by its mother, "This baby was found
by the Bear." He did not, however, go on to relate *Raised by Bear*.

In FBC Coyote's illness seems to be real and was accounted for by a preliminary episode, another trotting Coyote folktale, *Coyote Swallows Horned Toad* (Hill and Hill, 1945, No. 16, pp. 331–333).

Personnel established. As explained above, the protagonists of LH and OBA were the boy who had been *Raised by Bear* and the boy *Raised by Owl* respectively. Each one had two daughters and their wives' younger sisters came to live with them. In three myths Coyote lived with his wife, son, and daughter (FBC, JY, LSS). In two others an unnamed man, who may have been Coyote since the stories are the same as the others, lived with his wife and daughter (MOU, DS).

Protagonist covets wife's sister or *his daughter.* LH and OBA are unlike all the other versions in that the protagonist plotted to "marry" [seduce] his wife's younger sister who was living with them. In all the other versions, his intended victim was his own daughter. An incest theme automatically links a story with witchcraft and one of the tales (JY) was told as the myth of a ceremony for curing illness caused by sorcery. It may be that in making this story a part of a chant myth the seducee of the trotting Coyote tales was deliberately changed from the protagonist's daughter to his sister-in-law in order to avoid the imputation of witchcraft, for sororate marriage was a socially acceptable pattern in Navajo society, whereas witchcraft, of course, was not.

Protagonist feigns illness, death. In FBC the protagonist was not in very good shape having suffered from his experience in swallowing Horned Toad, but in the other tales he pretended to be sick and fasted until he did appear to be approaching death.

Protagonist directs platform burial and cremation. Predicting his imminent death and telling his family of sure signs of death, such as worms dropping down from his body (FBC), the protagonist gave detailed instructions for a platform burial in a tree or on a rack and for firing it to burn his body. He also told them to leave the burning pyre without looking back (LH).

Protagonist advises husband like himself. The protagonist told his wife to marry her sister (LH, OBA) or daughter to a stranger who would look just like himself, wearing the same clothing and face paint (MOU) and carrying the same equipment, such as a mountain lion skin quiver (FBC), one who would hunt for them and provide them with food.

Son sees father leave platform. As they were leaving the burning burial, the protagonist's son (FBC, JY, LSS; younger daughter in LH) looked back and saw his father jump down from the platform.

He told his mother but was disbelieved and scolded for saying that, for his father was dead.

Family suffers starvation; Stranger provides food. Four years (FBC), about a year (LH, OBA), three days (DS), or almost immediately (MOU, JY, LSS) after leaving the burial, the family met a man who looked like their "late" father and who was obviously a good hunter. They were on the brink of starvation not knowing how to hunt (LH, OBA, FBC, DS) and the stranger provided them with ample supplies of deer meat. He asked them what their father had said before he died and they told him of his advice.

Mother advises marriage. Remembering her husband's "dying wishes" and because the stranger was so generous and kind to them, the mother of the family decided to give her sister or daughter to him in marriage. The girl married the stranger and became pregnant.

Girl becomes suspicious. After a time, the girl (LH, FBC, JY, DS), her mother (MOU), or the son (LSS) began to suspect that the new husband was the former father of their family. This was because of a silver ring that he used to wear when he hunted deer or a hole through his nose which the girl saw one morning when he overslept (LH, DS, LSS), or a wart on the back of his head which she discovered when she was dressing his hair (FBC, JY, LSS). She [or the son] told her mother who had been living apart from them so that she would not see the face of her son-in-law. Lefthanded (LH) remarked that this was the origin of the mother-in-law taboo, the belief that if a man looked at his mother-in-law he would go blind or become insane.

Mother recognizes husband (deceit discovered). The girl's mother went to look at the man when he was asleep and recognized him as her former husband. She scolded him and beat him (OBA, LSS) and then forgave him and they all lived together after that.

Baby abandoned. Feeling labor approaching, the girl went out into the bushes where her baby was born. Ashamed of it, she kicked it into a badger's hole (FBC, MOU, JY, LSS) or a prairie dog's hole (DS), or simply abandoned it in the bushes (LH, OBA).

Baby found by Owl. The child of the questionable marriage abandoned in shame by its mother was found by an Owl (OBA — Bear, see above) and at this point the other major mythic motif, *Raised by Owl,* begins. LSS, however, ends abruptly with this minor motif and the remark, "When the child grew up he was a monster and killed many people" (Hill and Hill, 1945, p. 337).

Minor Mythic Motifs of Raised by Owl

The seven versions of this story (LH, OBA, FBC, MOU, JY, DS, SH) ended without going on to its sequel. Again, a table will not be presented but the minor motifs will be discussed in turn.

Owl finds baby. Owl Man found the abandoned baby in the badger's hole where his mother had thrown him (FBC, MOU, SH), in the prairie dog's hole (DS), or in the bushes (LH). In JY a pair of Owls lived in the badger's hole and saved the baby from Coyote who came to eat him. In OBA the reversal of the major motifs had the baby abandoned in a time of famine, and Owl Woman found him and took him home. At first Talking God (DS) or Crow (SH) contended with Owl Man for possession of the baby.

Owl raises baby. Owl Woman (OBA, FBC, SH), the pair of Owls (JY), or Owl Man (LH, MOU, DS) raised the baby feeding him rabbit broth. When the boy became older, the Owl made a bow and arrows for him, fletching the arrows with his own feathers, and soon the boy became a skillful hunter.

Owl Man jealous, afraid. The boy began to sleep with Owl Man's wife and after a time Owl Man became jealous (FBC, JY, SH), or fearing that the boy would shoot him sometime (LH, OBA, DS), the Owl decided to send him back to his people (LH, FBC, DS) or to kill him (OBA, JY, SH). The Owl showed him the way to his old home and sent him on his way (LH, FBC, DS) or warned by the Wind of the Owl's lethal intentions, the boy ran away (OBA, JY, SH).

Guided by physical signs. At first (FBC) or later after being *Guided by Poker, etc.* (LH, OBA), whenever the boy started out in the wrong direction he was set right by various physical signs, a noise in his trachea or hiccoughs, a popping noise or tickling in his nose, ringing or buzzing in his ears, or twitching, prickling, or itching on his skin. In his introduction to FBC, Father Berard Haile expressed his opinion that:

> While the incestuous union of Coyote with his daughter is not approved, but is punished with death at the hands of their offspring, no particular emphasis is laid upon the criminal aspect of this unnatural union. The chief purpose of the story seems to be to show the origin of the several warnings mentioned therein. The moral conveyed thereby is evidently that such warnings must always be heeded. To ignore any unusual noise in one's interior, or the ringing in one's ear, twitching

of the nose, pricking of the skin or bad dreams, is to face danger at one's own risk. A journey which may have been planned, or a call upon a singer's service, a plan to engage upon a certain occupation, or the like, should be postponed for the time being until such omens cease. This practice is still faithfully observed. The educational purpose of this story in this particular is therefore evident.

Later the boy slept and dreamed that he escaped with difficulty from people who wanted to kill him (FBC). His Little Wind monitor told him not to worry about it and the boy decreed that physical warnings and bad dreams should be heeded (FBC).

Guided by poker, etc. In a succession of ruins of hogans formerly occupied and abandoned by his family, the boy was guided and sent on from one to the next by old discarded fire pokers, sticks of partly burned firewood, a torch, a cane, or old broken and discarded household utensils, such as stirring sticks, broken pots or bowls or fragments of pots, a whisk broom, dipper, metate, mano, or some ashes. These objects pointed the way, spoke to the boy, or turned into people who gave him news of his family and guided him from place to place. One or more of these inanimate guides are mentioned in all of the tales except MOU.

Camps in successively fresher hogan ruins. Each hogan or ruined windbreak of brush that the boy came across was fresher than the last until finally he reached one in which the branches were still green (FBC, JY, DS, SH). Obviously he was catching up with his family.

Pursued by Owl(s). The Owls who were pursuing the boy intending to kill him finally caught up with him. His Little Wind monitor warned him and advised him to make them an offering of white shell (FBC, SH) or jewels (JY). He did so and the Owls went away.

Boy returns to his family; Boy not recognized, ignored, disowned, by his family. The boy finally found his family who did not recognize him at first, but rejoiced once they came to realize who he was (LH, DS); or they ignored or disowned him, saying he ought to be killed (FBC, JY, SH). Throughout all this his Little Wind monitor kept him informed and advised him. In FBC and JY the boy sent his shadow among his relatives to find out what they were saying. Since only witches can project their shadows, this is another reason for linking these trotting Coyote tales with witchcraft.

Boy dangerous to his people. The boy wantonly killed an old man and woman and a young boy and girl with his arrows (LH, OBA); or he killed two children he was playing with (MOU), or a man on each of four successive days while playing the hoop and pole game with them (DS); or angry because of their treatment of him he shot his father and mother (SH) and two children (FBC), or his brothers and some other people (JY). Then he ran away pursued by angry relatives and warriors. In OBA he was helped by Porcupine Man and in SH by Owl.

Boy cuts sticks which become Utes. As he fled from his pursuers the boy cut sticks for arrows (OBA, MOU, DS, SH), or for firewood (JY), or twigs or wands to confuse his pursuers (LH, FBC). These sticks became people, either Utes or the progenitors of the Utes, and on each successive day he cut more and more sticks so the crowd of new people grew constantly larger.

Pursuers return home. Coming across the tracks or signs of an ever increasing horde of people, the Navajos who were pursuing the boy realized that they were outnumbered, so they gave up the chase and went home.

Boy joins Utes. Finally the boy joined the Utes; "He became a Ute" (LH, FBC, JY). In FBC alone, Coyote who had been killed by his illegitimate offspring was restored to life by Thunders and Winds, so that, "stories about him continue on."

The Geography
of Mountainway

MUCH OF THE ACTION of the myths of Mountainway develops in
the mountainous portions of the four corners region where Utah,
Colorado, Arizona, and New Mexico meet, with extensions along
the New Mexico-Colorado and Arizona-New Mexico borders. Big
Sheep, the sacred mountain of the north [probably Hesperus Peak
in the La Plata Range in southwestern Colorado], is an important
locality on and around which many events of all the recorded myths
of Mountainway take place. Likewise, the Chuska Range with its
subsidiaries, the Tunitcha and Lukachukai Mountains, and the
Carrizo Mountains north of it, figure importantly in the locales of
the stories. Older Sister's *Flight from Bear* in Yucca Patch Man's
narrative (YPM) is accomplished in large part in the country immediately to the north and south of the San Juan River in Colorado and
New Mexico. The *Ute Captivity* naturally begins in the Southern
Ute country of southwestern Colorado. In general, except for Lefthanded's narration (LH) which takes the heroine on a complete cir-
cuit of the entire Navajo country, old and new, the locales of the
various myths are pretty much confined to northern Apache County
in Arizona, San Juan and Rio Arriba Counties in New Mexico,
Montezuma and La Plata Counties in Colorado, with perhaps an
occasional foray into San Juan County in Utah.

[157]

Female Mountain-Top-Way

by *Yucca Patch Man*

Preamble

The fact is that this is the chant belonging to one who used to be called Forelock, then to the late Crow, then to my father who was the Late Crow's Son. Well, that Forelock was a Salt Water clansman who taught it, while Crow Man was a House-extends-up clansman, and Late Crow's Son was a Salt Water clansman. And I again am a Yucca Patch clansman, and was instructed in it by my father.

YOU SEE, THEY WANDERED ABOUT in want of everything, living on the chase, twelve of them of whom ten were men and two women, their sisters. Their food consisted of yucca syrup [from the flowers of the wide leafed yucca],[74] the seeds of goose-foot, hard seed grass [*Monolepis* or salt-bush], and drop-seed. They were occupied with this after the month of big ripening [of seeds; September], and those so engaged were of the Bitter Water Clan. It appears that the thing happened in the Big Sheep range [La Plata Mountains], across the river [San Juan]. The Pueblo Indians from a place called Wide House [Aztec Ruins, New Mexico] killed one of them, then the

---

Recorded and Translated by Father Berard Haile. Edited by Leland C. Wyman.

[74] All statements enclosed in brackets in the translation are not the words of the informant but are explanatory notes provided by the translator (Father Berard Haile) or the editor (Leland C. Wyman).

Pueblos of Blue House killed another. Those of the Small Wide House also killed one, and those of the same Wide House [Aztec Ruins] did the thing again. At a place called Wide Horizontal Belt [near the Bloomfield to Cuba, New Mexico, highway; the home of Pueblos] they killed another one, and one also on the side of Wide Chokecherry [probably a prominent slope of the La Plata range]. Then yonder where Waters-flow-across-each-other [the informant could not locate this], they killed another, and one also at the river itself [not the San Juan], the name of which I do not recall, although it was mentioned to me.

Now the older brother remarked, "Let someone avenge me!", which the younger brother seconded by saying, "I, too, am of the same opinion, my older brother! If there be anyone it is Monster Slayer and Born-for-Water who are familiar with methods of wiping out monsters [the murderous Pueblos]." "That is my feeling too, my younger brother," the elder said. That done, the elder left for the home of Monster Slayer at Waters-flow-across-each-other. When he arrived there he said to him, "My granduncle, I brought you word, because I see danger everywhere!" "Yes, my grandson, from whom do you anticipate danger?" he asked him. "Well," he answered, "to my misfortune my eight brothers were killed; take revenge for me, my granduncle, I am unequal to it. They say that there are so-called Non-sunlight-struck [virgin] Girls there; I desire only that you bring me their scalps, then I shall sleep satisfied," he told him. "Yes my grandson, what do you mean by saying this? What can we do about it, my grandson, access to it is impossible.[75] But take this news among the people, so that they may assist us. Alone I cannot do anything, my grandson. Let any number of men join us tomorrow!" he [Monster Slayer] said to him. "There will be a reward, of course!" the other said; "If you bring them out I shall give you my sisters for wives," the brother said. "From which place are you?" he [Monster Slayer] asked him. "I came from the curved rock cliff, from the place called Shooting-over-the-ridge," he said. "The two of us will go there, my grandson, and start moving from there after our arrival," he told him. The next day the two arrived, then all started out from there and camped at the place Finger-in-the-rock-hole. From here they set out for Pine Target. A space on a pine charcoaled around, with a sizable black spot in the center, this is meant by the Pine Target.

---

[75] "To its interior there is no passage," or, access to it is impossible by natural means, and I do not have the supernatural power to enter it.

From here they again moved on to Falling Dice where they again camped and Monster Slayer made this remark, "I wonder what we can do, my grandchildren? It is really not an easy matter, indications are that nothing can be accomplished," he said. And they charged on the east side, but apparently did not succeed, when they charged all around the houses. "Wonder what we can do, my grandchildren, there is certainly no passage way, we may as well return home!" he said. So they returned to their previous camp at Falling Dice, then moved on to Pine Target, on to Hand-in-rock-hole, from where they again returned to Shooting-over-the-ridge. "Strange, my grandchildren, I find it too much for me, we two will start back for home, but in three days we will return to you. We'll see about it again," he [Monster Slayer] told them. He spent three nights at his home again, then the two set out again and arrived at Over-ridge-shooting. "Just how can this be accomplished, my grandchildren?" From there again they moved and camped at Finger-in-the-rock-hole. From here they moved to Pine Target where they made camp again. Thence they moved on and camped at Falling Dice. They charged from the west again, but unsuccessfully and just returned home. "The thing is very difficult, my grandchildren, we will just return," Monster Slayer said. They then returned to Falling Dice. "I am bound to kill one at all events my grandchildren," he said.

Then again they left for Pine Target and Finger-in-the-rock-hole and made their return to the hogan. "How can it be done? I am bound to kill one yet! We two will go right back home, but return in five nights." They again spent five nights at home, but after five nights the two returned, and he had much to say. "I am bound to kill those two," he said. And again they all left for Pine Target, then again arrived at Falling Dice, where he again spoke, "We all shall kill one, and we will charge from the south side, there may be a chance there!" And they charged three times around the houses, but obtained nothing. And again they started on the return as he remarked, "We will just return now, my grandchildren!" When they returned to Falling Dice he asked, "What have you done, my grandchildren?" "Not one did we see, it was inaccessible," they said. So they set out and returned to Falling Dice. "How is this, my grandchildren, it is getting difficult," said Monster Slayer. And again they set out and reached Pine Target, then Finger-in-the-rock-hole, and finally returned home to Shooting-over-the-ridge, where the brother said to him, "How is it my granduncle, is it perhaps too much for you?" But he replied, "I am bound to get the best of them, my grandchildren, you will see!" he said. "I hope you say the truth, my granduncle," the other said. "Indications are that it will happen [as I say]," Monster Slayer said. "Now then we two will start for home, my grandchildren, but we will return in seven days," he said.

The two then returned to their home, where they again spent seven nights. "On the seventh night the two of us will leave again with every precaution, my grandchildren. This time we are moving in a holy way, indications are that we will kill some," he [Monster Slayer] said. From there all again left and camped at Finger-in-the-rock-hole, where he said a prayer, a prayer directed towards the enemy.

> Monster Slayer, by means of your dark flint shoes I shall walk,[76]
> Monster Slayer, by means of your dark flint leggings I shall walk,
> Monster Slayer, by means of your dark flint garment I shall walk,
> Monster Slayer, by means of the two dark flints which you carry I shall walk,
> Monster Slayer, by means of your dark flint hat I shall walk,
> Monster Slayer, by means of the zigzag lightnings which dart from your head top I shall walk,
> Monster Slayer, by means of the four zigzag lightnings which dart away from your head top I shall walk,
> Then the monsters shall fall down right there.

> Born-for-Water, by means of your blue flint shoes I shall walk, (etc.; with "blue flint" throughout, and "flash lightning" instead of "zigzag lightning").

> Changing Grandchild, by means of your yellow flint shoes I shall walk, (etc.; with "zigzag lightning").

> Reared Underground, by means of your serrated flint shoes I shall walk, (etc.; with "flash lightning").

They then moved on again and camped at Pine Target, where Monster Slayer again said a prayer [the same as above] towards the enemy. When they arrived at Falling Dice he repeated the prayer. "Wonder how it would be, my grandchildren. Perhaps we should attack from four sides. And yet, they may then charge among us! The plan may not do at all!" he said. So it was done, and they

---

[76] Literally futurized, "I walk here and there," having the sense of "May I continue to walk," or, to live on by means of the transformation which the invoked supernatural beings can give. These petitions are repeated over and over in the complete forms of the prayers.

charged in a wide circle, then encircled them closer, then encircled the base of the pueblo and finally next to the houses. Then they returned to their previous camp at Falling Dice. When they had all gathered there he asked, "What have you done, my grandchildren?" "We killed just three Pueblos," they said. "Well, it can be done, my grandchildren, we will finish the killing by this method. We may as well return now, as nothing else is to be done," he said. So they returned to Pine Target, thence on to Finger-in-the-rock-hole, and finally to their home at Shooting-over-the-ridge. "My grand-uncle, how is it regarding the revenge for me of which I spoke to you? Just three were slain!" "We will possibly kill some more, my grandchildren, the two of us will return again in nine days," he [Monster Slayer] said. "Let as many people as possible be gathered, then a strenuous effort will be made. That is all now, my grand-children, we two are returning, there is nothing else for us to do. In nine days we will come again," he said.

So it was done, after nine nights the two returned, and many fleet runners met there. "Now then we shall slay many," he remarked. And the great gathering moved on to Pine Target, where they camped and he said a prayer, a very forceful one [the same prayer as above]. And in their rear they saw a fire at their last camp. "Wonder who this is? Can it possibly be an enemy? Let some of you look!" But nobody went over there. And they again moved away, and here they repeated the prayer, then set out again and camped at Falling Dice. And again they saw the fire in their rear at Pine Target. Then two left to visit it. When they arrived they found two unknown elders sitting there. It developed that this was Big Bear, and the one seated behind him was Big Snake, on whose head top they noticed a red spot. As they later discovered these two were to slay the Non-sunlight-struck Girls. So it happened. At sunset several speeches were held. "We shall start the attack from four sides, then it will be accomplished, my grandchildren!" Monster Slayer said. Then [someone remarked], "How would it be if you told the two men staying over there to come here? Tell them we are in enemy country and to come, the enemy will kill them!" When two came to them they said, "We two do not fear the enemy!" Then he [Monster Slayer] spoke here again commenting upon the danger of the situation and saying that, "We are doing this in a holy way," then he sat down again. On the side opposite to them some were making noise by throwing fire at each other amid shouts of laughter. This angered Monster Slayer. "What is the idea! Evidently they have no sense who are doing this!" he said and sat down again. No sooner had he done this when they made their appearance here. "Why should this be done in a religious way when people are at war?" they said to him. It so happened that these were the boys from the Hard Flint Place. "Did I know that you were the ones doing this, when I said this?" he said. "This coming dawn we will have a real gathering, therefore I said this," Monster Slayer said. So it was done. At daylight [he said], "Let it be now, we will charge!"

But a strange woman happened along just then carrying a bundle, she carried a sizable headbag. "What is this, my grandchildren, would you suffer hunger when you charge?" she asked. "Wherever there is ripe corn in the fields I shall put it in a pit and bring it back roasted," she said. "Why do that, my grandmother? You will betray yourself to the enemy, that will not do! Yonder Pueblos are singing in their cornfields, you say the impossible!" he told her. "Persons do not see me, She-whom-enemy-does-not-see, they call me," the woman said. So she packed it over there, and her smoke floated along as soon as she kindled a fire. There she laid it in a pit and roasted the corn, and at midday packed it back. "Spread out two robes, my grandchildren!" she told Monster Slayer. She had brought two biscuits baked in ashes, they say. "This will sustain you for the night," she said. They all rushed for them and ate, but could not consume all. So she packed them away to where they were throwing fire at each other. Thus it happened. "With this same food you shall make the raid, my children!" she said. Then it seems Monster Slayer spoke, "We shall all be one group, my grandchildren, this coming dawn we shall attack." So it seems it was done. At about dawn Monster Slayer spoke. "But we have not notified Talking God about it!" their brother said.[77] "Wait until the scalps of the Non-sunlit ones have been brought. For these all of you shall be on the lookout to see who brings them," was said [by Monster Slayer]. He went to Talking God of the Striped Rock, who was in charge of all the houses. It was Wind who notified him, "as you are the fleetest one," Wind was told. He found him at home.

"What brings you here, my grandchild?" he [Talking God] asked. "Because you are not aware of it, I came to you," he [Wind] answered. "What shall be done about it, that you say this?" he asked again. "It is clear that you are in charge of the entire village, your word is final," he [Wind] told him. "If that be so, I am opposed to it. I get

---

[77] This seems to be a reminder by the older brother, interrupting Monster Slayer's speech. Monster Slayer apparently does not wish to exclude Talking God, as he allows a messenger, Wind, to be sent to him. The entire section differs from other accounts of this episode.

everything there, they have prayersticks and fine cotton cords for me," he [Talking God] said. "There is good sparkling rock [specular iron ore] for me, nice blue pollen, fine white shell, fine turquoise, fine abalone, fine jet. And I get good down feathers there, live down feathers, bluebird wing feathers, good bird feathers. There are white shell baskets for me, turquoise baskets, abalone baskets, jet baskets, all these they have for me, it cannot be as you say!" he said. "I get perfect shell discs there, reddish [abalone] shells, slim white shell beads, red [coral] beads and earbands," he said. "I'll start immediately to go there, my grandchildren," he said. The Wind then hurried away to return. Upon his return he reported the refusal. But the one who had lost his brothers said, "Although he says no, I have been badly treated, my brothers are gone." And continuing in the same strain he added, "In spite of all, you will still avenge me, even though Talking God speaks as he did!" So that happened.

By this time he [Talking God] was not far away, as the Ye'li gave his call which was faintly heard. Then they heard the call somewhat stronger, then closer this way he called unmistakably. At the fourth call he surprised them in the midst of the people. "What is it you desire of me, my grandchildren?" he asked. "Just this, that you deliver the enemies at the Wide House to us," the brothers and sisters said. "No, indeed, my grandchildren." Then he [Talking God] repeated in the same order what he had previously stated at his home. "But why do you refuse, my granduncle? Look, I live in tears because all my brothers are gone," he told him. "I see, my grandson, what can be done about it!" and Talking God wept as he said this. "I had never thought of it in this wise before," he said. He produced a prayerstick, one side of which was white, the other yellow. "Be it as you wish, but guess for me what this is?" "Tell him the white part is dawn," the Wind said, "the yellow part is evening twilight," the Wind told the brother to say. "This is dawn, and this evening twilight," he [the brother] told him. And he [Talking God] said, "It is quite true, that it is! If you had not guessed this for me, nothing would have been done, none would have been killed," he said. He produced another one, black on one side, blue on the other. "What is this?" Talking God asked him again. "Tell him it is darkness and horizontal blue," the Wind again told the brother. "True, it really is that," he replied.

He again produced the one which he had shown first, the white on one side, yellow on the other. "Tell him this white part is the dawn, in which the charge will be made. This along the west is the twilight, in which the charge will be launched." "It is true, that it is," he [Talking God] said. He again produced the black one on which the blue color joined the black. "Tell him, this is the horizontal blue, in which the charge will be launched, along the north is darkness, in which they will attack." This he [the brother] repeated to him and he [Talking God] admitted that the guess was correct. Again he produced another prayerstick, white in color with a black top. "What is this?" he asked again. "This represents their scalps which you will take, tell him that!" Wind whispered to him. He produced another which was altogether black. "What is this?" he asked him again. "Tell him it represents the enemy's death, that he is to be destroyed." "That is really true what you say, my children, it really represents that!" Talking God said. Again he felt sorry and Talking God wept. "There used to be fine prayersticks there for me. It is true what you say, go ahead then! But be sure to knock down all the houses, let none stand up, but flatten them all out!" he said. "I am now returning, you shall not do this in my presence, my grandchildren," Talking God said. He then started to leave. "How did this happen, my grandchildren? I forgot something!" he said. "When the Sun rises you shall make a sacrifice to him of a perfect, red haliotis shell disc. From then on till noon, the Sun will kill time until all are killed." It was now down. "Now then I am returning, my grandchildren, sorrow is filling me."

Monster Slayer said, "You shall attack from four sides. In the east, you Hard Flint Boys will attack." "All right, we see how it is," they said. They then left saying that they would get themselves ready. Their grandmother packed their garments there for them, flint shoes, leggings, garment, hat, and zigzag lightning arrows, in which they dressed to wipe them out in death. They held the lightning arrows in their hands. They all went eastward, where the brother again announced, "I shall give these sisters of mine to the man who returns with the scalps of the Non-sunlight-struck ones," he said. "You brothers will attack along the west side; you, Monster Slayer from the south, Born-for-Water from the north side," they were told. "Do not fail to shout along the east side, you shall do likewise in the west, and where Monster Slayer is leading you shall also shout [and likewise in the north]," they were told. So it was done. They shouted along the east, also in the west, in the south, and those with Born-for-Water in the north also shouted out.

Meanwhile the two elders, Big Bear and Big Snake, who had previously come to them entered inside of the plaza [of houses], scaling the walls by means of a rainbow. At the home of the two Non-sunlight-struck ones they waylaid them. Now the hair of the one was smoothed with turquoise reaching to the calves of her legs. The younger was likewise, her hair was smoothed with white shell and reached down to her calves. It seems they were in the habit of going for water while it was still dark. The elder would sit down on a stone on the north side, the younger sat down on the south side stone. Big Bear crawled to the bottom of the dark water, while Big Snake crawled into the blue water at the south.[78] The two Non-sunlight-struck ones left their room, opened the door, then proceeded on. When they arrived here [at the water], the younger one remained at the threshold, while the older girl stood at the west [side], both carrying their water jars. They were certainly fine girls to look at, as they stood in their garments of sewed fabric. "My older sister, the place seems to be somewhat changed, there are winds running around." But the other replied, "Who would come in here!" and she proceeded farther from where she stood, while the younger walked as far as she had been standing. The older then proceeded farther on, and the younger again stood where her sister had been standing. "The place is certainly not what it formerly was, my older sister, let us return inside, sister!" she uselessly urged.

And again she stepped forward, and her younger sister again moved to her position. Then she entered the trail to the water, her younger sister also proceeded there. They stood one behind the other, the older went to the north, the younger to the south. The ladles lay upon the water jars. Then each picked up the ladle, and when they dipped for water, they [Big Bear and Big Snake] grabbed them, and held their throats until they killed them. Then the two left the water, each produced their flints [knives], and cut their [the girls'] scalps around with their flints. The two then left and returned to their former camp. Meanwhile, shouts went up from all sides. And they [the Navajos] charged upon the houses, knocking them down and tearing out the walls. As they tore down the houses Wind ran around in the lead, he would run in the interiors shattering them. He did this looking for perfect shell discs, until he found them. These Wind picked up and brought back, because he had been told to keep those previously promised to the Sun. Thus, it happened that all houses were crushed, not one remained standing. There was a place called White Shelf House, where they were told of the killing of the enemies. Now the lower part of this was white, the upper yellow, that accounts for the name

---

[78] The water supply was in a single depression, but the water on the north side would appear darker or blacker than that of the south side.

of the place White-house-on-the-[rock]-shelf. "In days to come you shall call it the White-rock-shelf-house," it was said.

"Look this way, look eastward, my younger brother," he was told after the slaughter. When he looked there he saw a Male God, a Female God, and Talking God standing in the lead. "You have done me a great harm, my grandchildren!" he [Talking God] said. "Look here [south] again!" he [the brother] was told, and here he saw the big snakes trampling over each other. "They are the partners of those [the slain Pueblos] that formerly lived there," he [Talking God] told him. "Look to the west," he said to him. There a blue bear stood out partly, and behind it a blue young spruce stood upright. "Take another look to the north," he told him, and there a dark young spruce and a dark bear stood out again. "That is all, now go back home, go home without me."[79] There was a meeting over there, they came together again. Then it seems she [one of their sisters?] left to return and arrived over there, where many had gathered again. So the meeting was held and many were there on both sides of the brothers, both of whom had been told to come. "Let us see who brought the scalps, spread a robe here," it was said. "Who killed the Non-sunlight-struck ones, let their scalps be put on the robe." As the two [brothers] stood on either side, they passed between them. "I have undoubtedly killed them," someone said. "All right, put it down here," he told him. When he put it down, the Wind that informed both, told them, "Tell him that is not their hair!" "It is clear that this is not the one!" they said, and at once the person stepped aside. "I certainly have killed them," another announced. "That is not it," he again said. Then another repeated the same, "I undoubtedly killed it," but he again said, "It certainly is not the one," the Wind rejecting them all. And they were all engaged in merely repeating, "I killed it, and I, and I." And another threw down a scalp saying this is it, but he again rejected it. "Just put them all down which are plastered with turquoise! They are similar to them, but they are not the ones!" [the Wind said].

"There are no more, I wonder what has become of them!" the brother said. "Who has them? Clearly they are not here!" "Well, I know it, I know who took them away," Wind said. "What about the two old men sitting over there?" He meant where Big Bear and Big Snake were staying: "Suppose you tell them to come here!" And one went there and found them seated. "Someone tells you

---

[79] This statement is not clear unless we assume that the brothers addressed one of their sisters, but the girls would not fit into a meeting of warriors.

two to come!" "What for?" they asked. "You two have scalps, that is the reason!" he said. "When did our kind ever have them!" the one said. Both were seated, but one was without legs. He [the messenger] left to return over there. In a short time the two arrived. Soon they found them [the scalps] in their covers under their armpit. Then they threw the scalps down upon the spread out robe. "There it is at last," Wind said, "This finally is the one." Then, too, when Big Snake produced his the Wind repeated, "That is the one." But the people all bowed their heads in surprise.[80] So it seems it was said about Bear Man that the older woman should be given to him, and about Big Snake that the younger should be given to him. "Now then we shall move home," was announced.

Whatever it may have been, it was a small wrapped yucca, from the center of which a cord hung out, which was called *hashbį'i*.[81] "Now this will be thrown up, whoever shoots the cord part, to him the women will be given," he [the brother] said. So it seems the promise given to the elders was broken. Then he threw it high up into the air, and one missed it entirely and all that were there missed it each in turn. They did the best they could, but not one shot it. "What about you again?" the two elders were asked [in the hope that they also might miss it]. When he threw it upward, the two stood side by side as it was falling down. Before it struck the ground they shot it making it appear as one shot aside of the other. From there they moved on to Pine Target. "Whoever shoots the mark [on pine target] shall have the women," the brother said. And again they engaged in shooting at the so-called pine target. And all seemed to fail, not one struck the mark. Some just whirled them in this manner [informant showing how], and these would fall before it. Others would strike the edge of the charcoal circle and try to claim that they hit the mark, others missed the tree altogether, but all had their turn. About that time it was sunset before they noticed it. "We shall camp right here," they said, so they camped there. Then they grouped for sway-singing for the night, just as they do at present [in Enemyway].

At daylight they again set out for Finger-in-the-rock-hole and arrived there. "Now then, you shall close your eyes and walk on that way," he [the brother] said. So each one walked along extending their hand, and went up along a narrow trail. Doing this each

---

[80] Or in shame or disgust. Although the suggestion was made that the girls be given to the two old men, there appears to have been no intention of doing so.

[81] The informant could not add any of the details of this test nor the meaning of the name.

one again got his turn. "You, elders, what about you?" they were asked. With the brothers standing on either side, the two closed their eyes and set out side by side. All went up.[82] Then they moved on again to Shooting-over-the-ridge. And there was a long rock bluff the face of which appeared to be curved. "Come over here and stand in a line," they were told. "Now whoever shoots over the ridge [will get the girls]." And they went to its base and began to shoot. Some arrows began to whirl and fell off the cliff, others struck the rock, but all failed in the attempt, not one shot over the ridge. "What about you two elders?" they again asked them. And again they stood side by side, shot over the ridge and their arrows disappeared over it as black spots. "They are certainly great elders!" they said, but bowed their heads [in shame]. It was sunset then and their brother said to them, "Again you will come right here!" The sun set and darkness set in. The two elders built a fire where they sat. "This is really too bad, my sisters, I hated the sight of these strange ugly old men. But if these two elders had not come they [the Pueblo girls] would not have been killed. Still I continue to hate the sight of them."[83] Dusk then set in and it got quite dark. "Now then, you will take care of them for me all night long, so that the two [sisters] cannot go out of your midst. Stand all in a circle so that they cannot pass out through it!" he [the brother] said.

That was done and the two girls entered to be guarded by them during the night. They grouped for dancing in the same manner as they had done at Pine Target. On the other side, where the two elders had stayed, the fire had gone out. "Wonder where the two are?" someone asked. And it seems the night passed on with the group sway-singing and the two women standing in their midst. And the two elders left for Wide Chokecherry. Here, it seems, they pulled out brush, root and all, with which they built a circle in the customary sunwise fashion. And, leaning young pinyons upon it, they built the brush circle. They built a fire and piled up fuel. The doorway they made straight up with tree branches extending. After the fire was burning both entered and sat there for some time. "What is to be done, my friend, the women are withheld from us? Perhaps you have some power in this respect?" Big Snake man said. "Do it yourself, perhaps you have some power!" Big Bear said. "All

---

[82] The text is incomplete here but the informant added that the two elders, with closed eyes, put their fingers through the hole in the rock at the same time. The sentence, "All went up," meaning that each one present took his turn at trying to put his hand in the hole with his eyes closed, is out of place.

[83] The brother implied that he had tried all possible means to save his sisters from the two old men but is helpless.

right, spread a robe here!" Big Bear said.[84] He then produced his
tobacco pouch, the other also produced his. He produced his pipe,
the other did likewise. One had a turquoise pipe, the other a white
shell pipe. "Are we appearing in the shape we are?" one asked the
other.[85] And they set about to dress themselves; one dressed in
white shell, he put a slim white bead necklace around his neck. The
other, Big Snake, also adorned himself with a slim white shell
necklace, adding a white shell pendant to it. That done, Big Bear
picked up the pipe, the other also filled his pipe. The first one
lighted it with the sun, the other lighted his pipe with the moon.
And Big Bear just took a puff from it, then began a song and told
Big Snake to blow the smoke on the earth, then on the sky, then to
blow it towards the east, to the west, south and north. Then he
told him to blow around four times in a circle, the Bear singing
right along. "Blow it along where the two women are!" he said.
This he did.

It seems the tobacco [smoke] floated there to them. "What is it
that smells so sweet, my younger sister?" "Leave it alone! Can bad
things smell sweet?" the younger replied. "Blow it again over
there!" he [Bear Man] directed the Snake. And again it floated to
them. "What a sweet smell has floated to us again, my younger
sister!" she said. "Blow it there again!" he [Bear Man] told him.
When it floated to them it made her feel good. "What a fine smell,
it certainly is sweet, my younger sister!" she repeated. She perspired freely, she threw the sweat aside from her brow. Again he
said, "Blow it there again." When it floated to them she again said,
"What a sweet smell!" By that time she was bathed in sweat. "Open
up for us, let us two out, the heat is unbearable!" she said, but with
little success, it seems. "Don't say that, open up for us, we are dying
with heat!" she repeated. Then it seems they opened the circle
for them. "We shall sit right here," she said. The two spent some
time there before he blew the tobacco [smoke], which floated to
them. "Whence does the smell come," the two were saying as they
encircled the spot, then stood again where they had previously
been seated. Again he blew it to them and the two made a sunwise
circle. Again he blew it and they made the circle again. And again
he blew it so that it floated to them. "What a sweet smell this is,

---

[84] The sequence of suggestions is not complete for we would expect comments from
Big Snake Man four times as is customary in Navajo story telling.
[85] The sense is, "we ought to change our clothes," that is, "we ought to change our
appearance for this occasion."

my younger sister!" she said. As this happened no attention was
paid to them by the group dancers.

And the two girls left in the direction from which it floated to
them. "From here the smell comes, my younger sister!" And when
he blew it again they went on, again he blew it and they walked
along the path of the smell. Again he blew it and they saw the burning fire. "From here the smell came, my younger sister!" she said,
and now finally both went towards the fire and stood at the entrance.
They certainly were two fine young men unknown to them who sat
there covered with beads. "I will take that one for my husband, my
younger sister!" she said, referring to Big Bear, "You take the other,
my younger sister!" She gave her younger sister to Big Snake. "You
will be his wife," she told her. As for the Bear he was clothed in a
white robe, in a white buffalo hide, while the other wore an otterskin. So the two entered. "What do you two seek here? In this neighborhood earth surface people are not allowed!" both said. Here on
the north side, the Bear growled, and when Big Snake growled and
gave his call, they were forced to squat alongside of them in the rear
of the room. So they sat awhile, the older one sat with her husband,
while the younger also sat with her husband. "Why did you two
come? Don't you know that a careful watch was held over you?"
That done, they merely sat there until they announced, "Let us go
to sleep, we are getting drowsy!" They each lay under cover with the
men, she [Older Sister] crawled behind Big Bear and they slept,
on both sides they rolled under their covers.

They slept quite awhile. The older awoke first and lay there
with her eyes open. She heard the shouts from the place she and
her sister had left. "Why, I told you not to let them do that!" she
heard being said. When she raised herself, she noticed the first
signs of dawn. And when she got up, she found that she had been
lying under the cover of a horrible thing. He was as ugly as possible, his ears were hairless, between his toes the spaces were
peeled off, his teeth were yellow and crossed each other out of
shape. When she again looked over yonder, something strange lay
there with a wide mouth and a red spot on top of its head, but [her
sister] was still asleep. She looked this way. The one who had worn
the [hair] robe was huddled together, just too ugly and bald to look
at, even his beads were gone. The one yonder, who had worn the
otterskin, was likewise too ugly and bald for anything, even his
beads were gone. Then it seems she walked to where her younger
sister lay and tapped her foot. Her sister awoke and, after she had
awakened her, she went on. Then, after the other had followed her

out, the two continued on and stood there. "Under whose cover have we slept anyway!" "You see now why I tried to tell you not to do it! Let us return to our brothers!" she [Younger Sister] said. "No, they will kill us I think," she [Older Sister] said. "Let them kill us as they like, we will get what we deserve," the younger sister said. So it happened that they feared their brothers. "Even so, my older sister, let us return there, let them kill us. I am satisfied." "No, my younger sister, in spite of all, we shall roam around any old way," she said. "Let them kill us," the one said, while the other favored to roam anywhere. Meanwhile, the two elders were still asleep over there. "I wonder how it can be done, my younger sister!" she said.

And they left towards the east, then returned from there; again they went to the west then came back again. They also went south and returned here, then north and returned to the point where they had previously stood, then went to the east again. From there they went in a sunwise circle to the north where they stood, then started back and returned where they had stood before. Now they set out in a wider circle to the north and again stopped where they had stood the first time. Here they turned and returned to the spot where they had previously stood. Just so that happened. "But who will find us [now], my younger sister?" she said. Where they had been missed, they looked for them with firebrands. And her younger sister still insisted that their brothers should kill them. And they went towards the burning fire, but at the group dance they turned about in fear and just passed by it, and when they had gone beyond it, they stood there. About that time the two elders got up. "What has happened, which way did the women go? Where can they escape anyway? There is no place that I have not seen," Big Bear Man said.

At once he prepared another smoke, and to his tobacco itself he spoke, "What became of the women?" The other, in turn, Big Snake Man also prepared a smoke. They took a puff, then blew it out, and their tobacco [smoke] floated, one behind the other, eastward, then floated back from there. "It is quite evident that the two returned from there," he said. Then Bear tracked them with his tobacco [smoke], which floated back from there. "Both are still together," he said. And again he puffed on it and blew this westward, whence it returned floating. "Still the two are together," he said. The two went south, and after puffing again they blew it there and it returned floating. "Clearly, the two returned from there!" he said. Then he took another puff which he blew northward, where it floated on, then back again. "The two returned from there!" he said. Then both prepared the smoke and both blew it. And it floated in the surroundings of the hogan, then away east-ward and this way, a little beyond where the two girls had stood the first time. And both again took a draw on their tobacco and blowing it, it floated back. "Evidently they came back from there again," he said. And again the two proceeded farther beyond that point, drew again and both blew their smoke, which again floated around the circle which the girls had described. "Evidently the two returned from there," he said. And the two [girls] took a stand-ing position again, then left in a wider circle, and returned. Accord-ingly they [Bear and Big Snake] drew on their tobacco again, blew it out and it floated around yonder where the girls had stood and back. "Evidently they returned from there," he said.

And it seems the two girls left towards their brothers at the group dance. And the elders arose each carrying his tobacco. "They are together," he [Bear Man] said, as they followed. Near the group dance they blew the tobacco [smoke] again, which floated behind them to where the girls had gone, and they followed them. "They are still together," he said. By that time their tobacco was burnt up, so he filled the pipe again, and lit it with the sun, while Big Snake, as before, lit his with the moon. After lighting it he drew again. The other also put the tobacco in it, then blew it away. "Both are right around here," he [Bear Man] said. And the two took a drink at the Crossing Streams. When he again blew the tobacco, it stopped float-ing at the Crossing Streams. Here the two [girls] walked at the river shore. "Which way shall it be, my younger sister? Perhaps you will take downstream, I upstream?" she said. All various kinds of berries were ripe they found, red berries, chokecherry, orange gooseber-ries, sumac berries, wild rose, and hackberries. Among these the two walked eating them, getting their fill with them.

From here it seems they journeyed on to the home of Monster Slayer. There the place is called Crossing Streams which flowed below it. And where the girls had walked about, the other two [elders] also sat down and lit their tobacco. Then they drew on it again and it floated spirally four times. He [Bear Man] took another draw and it floated down the side of the San Juan River. Meanwhile the two [girls] were walking along on the other side. The bushes were as if thickly interwoven, full of fruit which they ate as they walked along. They arrived at the home of Monster Slayer and his brother, where sunset overtook them and they spent the night. While the others spent the night up above, below the Crossing Streams. On the following morning the girls set out again for what is now called Many Houses [Durango, Colorado], but is the place called Many Berries. The others also set out for Crossing Streams where the girls had spent the night. Then they set out for Many Berries where the girls had roamed about, and in the evening started right downstream. And, apparently, the elders set out for Many Berries, where they again tracked them by smoking. They again lighted their tobacco, and evidently both had their tobacco as they went along. And again [the girls] departed for the Junction of Rivers [Los Pinos and San Juan, New Mexico], and again drank some water, then walked among the hills until evening. "Right here we shall spend the night, my younger sister," she said. They journeyed on again the following morning toward the Hogback [northwestern corner of New Mexico]. Meanwhile the others again reached the camping place of the girls.

So he [Bear Man] produced his tobacco again, raked it into the pipe, which he lit with the sun, while the other did likewise. "How is it my friend, we will look at each other's tobacco pouches. Suppose you lay it down here!" he suggested to the other. Then he picked up the tobacco pouch of Big Snake and, turning it around, he looked at it. "Both are certainly alike, my friend!" he said. Both were beautifully designed. And on the one tobacco pouch the sun was figured with a turquoise pipe set on it. On the other there was the figure of the moon with a white shell pipe. "Now then, in future days, sandpaintings shall be drawn provided with tobacco pouches." Then both smoked here, where the girls had camped. That done, they again drew on it [tobacco]. "The two [girls] did not depart together it appears," [he said]. Then he blew the tobacco again, it floated spirally five times. And again he drew it, and it floated away downstream. "They are still together again," he said. Meanwhile the two [girls] spent the night at the Hogback again. And from here the two [elders] followed them and came to their camp of the previous night. Now the girls were roaming about on the side of the Hogback, camped right there, then went on again. So it happened that they [the elders] again came to the girls' camp of the previous night. So he [Bear Man] produced his tobacco, filled the pipe, lighted it with the sun, then took a puff of it. This he blew following the tracks along which the girls had journeyed. It floated around wherever they had gone. And again he took a draw, and again it floated along every track that they had made.

The two women again set out for the inflow of Slim Water Canyon [Mancos River into the San Juan]. Here both came to a stop. Then they set out for Bear Ear [unidentified mountain], along the slope of which they again traveled. In the Whirling [Carrizo] Mountains, they mixed their tracks all day long. Meanwhile the men were still at the girls' camp of the previous night. "Which way did they go? One cannot tell which side they took," he [Bear Man] said. So the girls said to each other, "How shall it be, my younger sister? Where shall we find safety?" she said. Thus they planned for each other, it seems. The older sister then said, "Yes, how shall it be? I shall return back, my younger sister! I will go this way toward the Hog-back." "I will go downstream wherever its flow terminates, my older sister," she said. Facing each other they stood after they got up. They shook hands. "Sometime or other we will meet again, my younger sister," she said as her tears flowed. The other also spoke: "It is true no doubt, my older sister, sometime we shall see each other again," she said. Then they released [embraced] each other.

The older sister then left for upstream, while the younger went downstream. After she had gone a short distance, her sister called to her, "Wait my younger sister, I forgot something. Somewhere you are to be, my younger sister. But go along now," she told her. "I suppose there are indications that we will both return to our brothers," she said. And that was the last time they saw each other.[86]

Then the older sister left upward in the direction of the Hogback. She returned to the Hogback. But the said elders set out in the opposite direction, down to the end of where the two women had been. So it happened that at Tall-grass-wide-touches-river [Ship-rock Agency] they crossed paths. Then right in their tracks they followed them where they had spent the night and at the mouth of Slim Water Canyon [Mancos River] they sat down. Again he [Bear Man] produced his tobacco, filled the pipe and lit it by the sun; both did this. He took another draw, blew it to the earth, to the sky, then eastward; both did this. Then he blew it westward, southward, northward, then sunwise around in a circle. "Which way, I wonder, did those women take, my friend?" [he said].

And he blew it around the same course the women had taken and it floated back to them [the elders]. He took another draw, blew it again, and again it floated back to them. And again he took another draw, blew it, and again the smoke floated around in every direction. And another time he took a draw, blew it, and it repeated, some floating away in all directions, crossing back and forth horizontally, then every way without order. "Which way did they go? One cannot

---

[86] This statement does not agree with the general opinion that eventually the two sisters met again and had a reunion with their brothers.

tell at all!" Just to try it again, Bear Man took another draw on his tobacco, blew it, and his tobacco smoke settled on the Hogback, the smoke which he had puffed settled opposite to him. "Mine went this way," Bear Man said. "What about you?" he asked Big Snake. He [Big Snake], it seems, lit it again by the moon, then took a draw. It began floating downward, right downstream. "Mine went this way, I see," he [Big Snake] said. "What shall we do, my friend?" Bear Man said. "Where is your home, my friend?" "On this side, to be sure, at the place called Blackrock." "So you see, in future times there will be a line of meeting [of Mountainway and Beautyway]. The medicines will be the same," he said. "That is all, what else have we to discuss?"

Then Bear Man left to follow, the other also left to follow downstream. Some distance away he stopped. "Look here, the thing of which we spoke is quite unsettled! In future days it shall be called the meeting of branches sandpainting," he [Bear Man] said. "Enemyway it shall be called, we extinguished all enemies. It shall be a meeting line with Mountain-Top-way," he said. "It shall be so also on your side, it shall be called Beautyway. It shall be a partner branch to Mountain-Top-way, because we two did this one thing [together]."

Then Bear Man set out again to follow her, while the woman again spent the night at the Hogback. Then she again left for the River Junction, arrived there, then returned here to her camp of the previous night. She was still there when she suddenly got a glimpse of him, as he came along nearby in her tracks. She started up the Hogback, then got to its summit. So again he prepared a smoke where he was, produced his pipe, lit it again and puffed on it. And the smoke hovered along the path she had taken, and from there floated back again. "Why, she came along here again!" he said. He took another puff of it, blew it along and it floated up the slope, on the side of the Hogback. "So she went up there, I see!" he said. Then he left to follow her. She went along the top, he coming along in her tracks. And she walked along the side of the rock, but he immediately followed her. That was about dusk again. And the point [of the Hogback] extended out toward Slim Water Canyon [Mancos River]; she came alongside at this point. When she reached the end of the point she descended. "Here, in the bad lands, I shall spend the night," she thought. There happened to be thickets there. Bear Man camped as far away from her, as the Out-meadows [Saint Michaels] canyon is from here [two miles]. She passed the night here. In the morning her ankles pained and she walked with difficulty. He in turn set out from there and reached her previous camp.

She set out in the lead towards Slim Water Canyon, but walked with difficulty. Her condition was such that walking was impossible, and when she reached the rim of Slim Water Canyon, she sat down, thinking that she would spend the night there. She did spend another night there.

In the morning she sat there again, and she noticed that a stream flowed there. So it happened that beavers were hoop-poling, and otters. All water inhabitants dwelt there, she found, such as various fishes, ducks, muskrats. From the other side someone spoke to her, "Bad people dwell here, the home of Changing Bear Maiden is here! Whence did you come?" the person asked her. "What about you, where is your home that you are here?" she asked him. "What are you that you say this?" he said to her. "I belong to the Bitter Water Clan, to be sure!" she said. "I, too, am Bitter Water Clan," he said. "Then we are related, I see," she said. "We used to live at the place called Red Mountain, the five of us, one woman and four men moved here from there," he told her. The woman asked, "Are our late mothers two sisters by birth?" she said. "[Yes,] we are the ones that moved out because of enemies who caused a terrible condition, they killed our mother and father. But which trouble caused you to wander around, my younger sister?" he asked her. "I am running from a strange thing after I took it for a husband," she said, "the Pueblos murdered all of us." Thus that happened. "Is there no possibility of coming to you?" "Not at all, Changing Bear Maiden killed one of us. He was our older brother, she killed our oldest one," he said. "But why should persons speak to one another from a distance?"

Then she started out using a cane. The canyon was narrow, into which she descended, then went up to where he sat. She shook hands with him. "My dear older brother," she said and he called her "my younger sister." "What trouble causes you to roam about aimlessly, my younger sister? You go where none is expected to go!" he told her. "Who knows what sort of a man I married. On that account I roam at large without aim," she said. "Who is the man?" he asked. "Bear Man, of course," she said. "I see. Where can you find safety from him? This canyon is full of them!" he said. Then the two left for the hogan and he related to her, "We also did likewise. There was no way for her [Changing Bear Maiden] to get a husband, so she herself took one." "Which [man] did she take?" she asked. "We learned that she took Coyote," he said. "We had been hunting when we returned in the rain and found no fire. So the oldest spoke out, 'What are you doing that you sit here without a fire? We are hungry,' he told his sister. She did not reply. Now a line was stretched for meat, for mountain sheep and deer venison. 'Someone make a fire, we are cold,' was said. At the time the two were seated and speaking to each other a light snow was falling. A fire was built and blazed up. So when they reached the doorway they stamped their feet."

"Meanwhile Coyote had crawled behind the bundles. So when the fire blazed they tried to speak to their sister, but she sat there angry. Soon the blazing fire filled the interior with the odor of coyote urine. 'How worthless this is, throw it out!' one said. It was thrown outside. 'The confounded Coyote ghost, he urinates everywhere!' her brother said. They threw out all of the fire. 'Break off some again higher than his reach, and build another fire!' her brother said. Two walked out there and broke limbs off beyond his reach, then built another fire. When that blazed up again there was the same odor of coyote urine. Again he scolded, 'You confounded ghost of First Scolder, Coyote ghost! Where is it that you don't run to urinate!' he said. Running outside they stood there. 'Break off the tips of the tree there again, perhaps he urinates there too!' So they again broke them off almost at the tip, brought the fuel inside and again built a fire. It blazed up again, and although there was a fine blaze, the same odor of coyote urine remained. The oldest one then scolded, 'Confound him, even at the tree tips he urinates! Way at the tip you will break off the small ones!' So it was done again, the fire blazed up again. The oldest was very angry. Anything that came to his mind he said: 'Ghost of first scolder, what a useless thing! He even urinates on wood when he pays his visits to us!' When that had happened, the Coyote's ears stuck out a little from behind the bundles. And they merely nudged each other and walked out. 'What are you saying, my brothers-in-law?'" While the two were seated there and relating this, the sun set. "Let us go to the hogan, my younger sister!" he said to her. "How far is it to the hogan?" she asked. She must have gotten stiff from sitting, since they had talked on from early morning. And, as she had difficulty, he dragged her to her feet and they set out together. The hogan, a real hogan, happened to be right there. So that happened. As the two entered, her [cousin] brothers looked at her. It developed that these were the people who had separated from them, as he had told, the ones who had departed from them at Red Mountain. So they shook hands calling her "younger sister." It was sunset and darkness set in. Then a place was prepared and robes spread out for her. But, as she was in pain, she did not sleep all night long.

It was daylight. Then, as she remained reclined, she related [what] they [she and her brothers or she and her sister?] had done.

She told where she had gone until she had come here; just as it had happened she told about herself. "I see how it is, but from where did you start out at the time?" he asked. "I left Shooting-over-the-ridge." "You certainly made good time, you came around in a circle." When daylight appeared, she failed to get up.[87] "What can be done, my younger sister?" he said to her. "I shall do something or other for you, stay over night!" he said. That was done. He dug a trench her size, large enough for her from head to foot. Boughs to fit of pinyon, juniper, and spruce [Douglas fir] reaching from her muscle down [to her fingertips]. Down in the pit he built a fire. "Something is still missing, I shall go after it," he said. Apparently he referred to rock sage, estafiata, snakeweed, and grama grass, for which he searched.[88] He uprooted wild buckwheat, he plucked four black medicine [gromwell], and red medicine [also gromwell], then pounded up all these where he found them. Then he returned to the hogan. He built a fire, then laid the pinyon across it, and the juniper, spruce [Douglas fir], rock sage, estafiata, snakeweed, and grama grass. "Now lie down on it there, my younger sister." But she tried uselessly to rise, her ankles and knees were swollen. So he accompanied her there. "Undress now," he told her. She removed her garment. "Now lie on top of it!" he told her. She lay down there, then he covered her with blankets. He then brought the medicine, put it in water, then gave it to her in his hand. She drank it all, and he added more water. "Is that enough, my younger sister?" he asked. "I want to lie here a while longer. I like it very much," she said. "Now perhaps?" he asked her. "Just wait, my older brother, I want to lie a while longer." Then he removed the blankets from her little by little. He handed the medicine bowl to her, she bathed her whole body with it. "Put the blankets on me, I want to lie here a while!" By that time it was toward late afternoon. Then she herself got up, and the two returned to the hogan. And nothing ailed her as she arrived there with him. Here she ate.

Now it was sunset, then dusk set in, and they sat around till it became quite dark, then they lay down to sleep. Daylight came. "Where do you intend to go now?" he asked her. "I do not know

[87] This implies that they kept her relating her story all night long, although she was in pain, thus causing her stiffness.

[88] The common names for plants used in this translation are those used by Thomas H. Kearney and Robert H. Peebles in their *Arizona Flora*, University of California Press, Berkeley and Los Angeles, 1951. The plants mentioned by the informant were identified by comparing the Navajo names for them in the text with those in Leland C. Wyman and Stuart K. Harris, *Navajo Indian Medical Ethnobotany*, University of New Mexico Bulletin No. 366, 1941.

definitely where I am going, my older brother," she said. "How is it, my younger sister? When we tell you to do things, you just do not do them. Here you go around aimlessly." "Am I to blame, my older brother? My older brother is to blame!" "Across here, close by, you can return to Shooting-over-the-ridge!" "All right," she said. "So it should be, my younger sister," he said to her. "We also are doing that, we are going to return. Our late older brother was killed, she bit off his neck. I will tell you this only to a certain point, you will remember it." So that happened. "We have enemies where we live, my younger sister, although we did not do this thing," he said, "although we did not kill her husband. His sister hated him for his words at the time they made the first fire," [he said]. "Then the men all stepped outside, made a brush circle [saying], 'let them lie by themselves, we do not care to lie opposite to where the two persons lie.' So that happened. Then they again went on the chase, they put wraps on their feet. Just when they were ready to set out, Coyote came along. 'Where are you going?' he asked. 'Where would we be going? We are just going around here, we are going on the chase, that is clear,' he told him. 'My brothers-in-law, I want to go with you, I am very fleet,' he said. 'Not at all, you stay at home!' 'No, no, I am very fleet, my brothers-in-law. Even very speedy deer do not run away from me,' he said. 'Even so, do not talk, stay at home, you are always in the way of anything, run back there,' he told him."

"Then they set out and went along the rim of Slim Water Canyon [Mancos River]. But here he [Coyote] overtook them and he [the brother] said to him, 'You go this way, while we are going right down the rim.' Before they had gone very far they killed a mountain sheep. While they were skinning it he came along. 'My brothers-in-law, I want the breast meat,' he said. It so happened that its horns were quite large. Their horns used to be nothing but fat, they say. Upon this he insisted. 'I want the horn marrow, my brothers-in-law,' he said. He set his knife around the base of the horn. 'Turn into bone!' he [Coyote] said. Just as he cut along, it turned into bone. 'You are always in the way, what can be done with you [useless thing],' he [the brother] told him. He was very angry. They finished skinning it, then fixed up a bundle for him, slapped it together and made it into a small size for him. 'Now run home!' he [the brother] told him, we are proceeding to the mouth of Slim Water Canyon. He [Coyote] then started to pack it home. As he set out with the pack, he [the brother] called his attention, and he came back. 'Do not pack it along the cliff rim, bad people dwell down in the canyon. Be sure to keep it off the ground during the whole time

you are returning,' he told him. And he [Coyote] set out with the
pack, but set it down on the ground anyway. He tried but could not
lift it, so he squatted down with it. He left half of it there. Then
he packed it away again, but sat down again. He crawled around on
hands and feet with it but failed to get up, and left the spine there.
Then he sat out with the pack and sat down again. He left both
front quarters there, then packed the rest on again. Then he carried
it out to the rim of Slim Water Canyon, where he sat down again."

"Down at the base of the canyon a hoop-pole game was on. 'I
wonder who are hoop-poling there!' he [Coyote] said, 'Coyotes
must be hoop-poling, I suppose, one just as ugly as the other!' he
said. 'Where all of you tried but failed to marry, I succeeded in
marriage' [he said]. Then he kept up this abuse as he sat there. So
the hoop-polers got angry with him and moved up towards him.
Even when they about reached him, he remained sitting there. 'Are
any of you equal to these?' he said as he worked his legs. When they
reached the rim, he ran some distance away and, running back to
them, he taunted them in the same way. So they returned down into
the canyon to their hoop-pole game, while he ran back to the canyon
rim, where he stood again abusing them. 'Where you failed in marriage I succeeded!' he said again. But they now sent word to Spider
Woman, who wove four webs around him. Then they again moved
towards him, but when they had about reached the top he began
his abuse again. There was the otter, the beaver, muskrat, the swallows, cliff swallows and black swallows. These appeared over the
rim. At a short distance away, he turned about, stood there and
abused them. Then, finally, they moved upon him and began to run
him down. Just when they were about to grab him, he ran through
the web. And again they set out after him. They scratched around
on him, as he managed to pierce the [second] web. And again they
set out after him, but he managed to crawl through it again. And
again they set out after him and this time exerted all their energies.
But he ran on, bumped against the web and fell back in the midst of
these people. They caught him, sliced up his hide into strips with
flint points, then cut up his hide into narrow strips. One was cut
for beaver, who put it around his neck. Another was cut for otter, who
put it on his chest. Another was cut for the swallow who spread it
over his chest. Another was cut for the cliff swallow, who slung it
along his arm."

"Then they moved back and down the canyon. Meanwhile the
hunters set out for home from the rim of Slim Water Canyon, where
they killed a big buck and returned packing it home. He has no

sense at all, the people of Slim Water Canyon have killed him, the oldest mentioned. When they returned here, the place was in complete disorder, the earth was torn up in spots. And they set out for home and returned there. A fire was built, they busied themselves with frying the venison which they had brought. The woman [Changing Bear Maiden] stepped out of the other place, walked over here to them and stood at the hogan entrance. 'Where is the one with whom you left?' she asked. 'Who would be with us, we left alone,' he answered. 'There is no doubt but that you went with him,' she said again, then returned and entered her hogan. At dusk she stood there again. 'Where did you leave him?' she asked again. 'Why ask, when it is known that he started back with the bundle today before noon!' he replied. Then, without saying another word, she returned to her hogan. Then they slept and slept all night. About daylight she returned. 'What became of him?' she said. That was all she said, then started back again. They then set out on the chase again, spent the whole day in hunting, and returned at sunset. Again she came to them. 'Which way did he go?' she asked. The people of Slim Water Canyon killed him, he told her. Then she continued to come to bother them, but at the time nothing else occurred."

And the woman [Older Sister], for whom medicine had been made two days before, now left. Here, where she had been told to start for home, she met her husband, the Bear Man. The woman ran back past that hogan and started out towards Bear Ear. She continued along in that direction till sunset and till dusk, then camped there for the night. Then she ate various wrinkled berries and walked around there till it warmed up. She then went up to the top of the mountain. When she almost reached the summit, the sun set. Here she munched whatever pinyon nuts lay on the ground and again spent the night there, and here, too, sunrise found her. She then left and reached the mountain summit. When she started this way the Bear Man again met her, and on his account she started back along the same path on which she had come. On the following morning, she left again towards the east, where she went up to the rim of Bear Ear, then sat down in the late afternoon and remained there till sunset. "Where shall I spend the night," she sat thinking. She spent the night and stayed there till daylight and sunrise. And she sat there looking out over the distant mountains, then intoned a song.

She started down and went down to the bottom. From there she left and somewhere, while she walked along the middle of a meadow, it got to be late afternoon, so she walked around there till sundown again. Dusk overtook her here and she lay down there till daylight. There she walked around until midday, then left again. There was a canyon and a small hill. "I may reach the top of that hill," she thought, and started out toward it right along the rim of the canyon. But before she reached the hill, it was sunset. About this time [5:00 P.M.] she was still walking toward it, and soon dusk set in. "I shall spend the night right here," she thought. And as she sat there dusk set in, so that she spent the night there. Daylight appeared, the sun set [she thought], but in reality the sun stood high up in the skies. She then went straight towards the canyon and sat down at its rim. From here she looked across to the other side, when suddenly the mountain shook her, so that she almost fell over. On the opposite side there were black spots, which she discovered to be bears. It so happened that the she-bear was leading her cubs. And she picked up her cubs and danced them up and down, while she sang. But she [Older Sister] sat right there looking across. By this time it was almost midday. "What shall I swallow, what shall I eat," she thought. So she left in the direction of the mountain, mentioned before, and continued on until she reached it. To her surprise she found berry bushes aplenty, but only here and there a berry hung and their leaves had dropped. Finding them thus, she went among them and ate whichever were dried, thus getting some satisfaction out of this meal. Now she went up to the summit, where she traveled on until late afternoon, then walked on to the very summit, which she reached at sunset with little to spare. Here she noticed a wide valley. As she walked along carefully looking around, the mountain contours were visible in all directions. And when she stood there looking at the ground, she noticed pinyonnuts scattered everywhere. "Here I shall spend the night," she thought. And she sat there gathering pinyonnuts.

By that time dusk set in and she got somewhat chilled. "Well, I shall make a fire," she thought and set her drill right there. Her drill was quite small, they say. After she had made a fire, she opened the dried leaves and lay down there, then slept. At midnight she awoke and sat at the fire. "Where am I going that I do this," she thought. Then she sat there till the first signs of dawn, without going to sleep again. At full daylight [she decided] to use these for the home journey: chokecherry, orange gooseberry, service-berry, and wild currants. But [she] found that nothing was to be done, the berries had all fallen off. Then she got up and walked around, then sat down. She began gathering pinyonnuts. When she had gathered a fair quantity in her dress, she returned to the fire, sat facing it, and opened up the ashes. In there, she shook the pinyonnuts. After a time, she went to them again and stirred them. Some would pop out and she raked them out of the fire. She sat down again and picked them all up and now began to eat them. She found that they were nicely cooked. She then arose, "Wonder how conditions are," she thought. She went up towards the east, but found precipices everywhere. Then nearby someone spoke to her, "What are you doing here? This is a forbidden place." "I am pursued, therefore I am here." "What have you done to be pursued?" he said to her. "I am in flight from Bear Man," she said. "Well he met you two days ago, then returned back yonder, he returned to Wide Choke-cherry." Big Fly happened to be speaking. "I want to stay around this vicinity, my granduncle," she said. "All right, my grandchild. I live closeby," he told her.

She then went southward, then passed that point to the west. From there she returned south and went up the slope again. From here she again went north and up the slope, and looked out over the landscape and the contour of the mountains. Then she returned to her stopping place of the previous night. A large tree stood there, below which she rested again, gathering pinyonnuts as she sat there. She then went back to the fire which she had built before. With her hand she opened it again and dumped the pinyonnuts into it, then let time go on as she watched them. Occasionally she stirred them with a stick. When they finally cooled off she gathered them into her dress. Somewhere or other I will use these for food she thought. "Now I recall that in the east I have not seen places well, I wonder how it looks there," she thought. She went there, sat down and looked around. As she sat there looking, she noticed a white mountain peak. Looking to the side she saw Horizontal Black Belt [Blanca Peak, Sangre de Cristo Range]. "Wish I could go there to see things there," she thought. Suddenly nearby Big Fly spoke again. "This rock canyon is called Sacred Canyon," he told her. "This mouth of the canyon is called White-Streak-in-the-rock-shelf [White House in the Canyon de Chelly, Arizona], while that, to the side, used to be called Wide House, but people destroyed the houses, therefore the enemies are all wiped out. It is quite a big place, a wide place, one cannot get there from any point. The peak yonder is called White Mountain, the other peak this way is called Horizontal Black Belt," he told her. "I see how it is, my granduncle," she said.

She then returned to the west, where she went up to the top. From there she looked out and Big Fly, as before, again came to her. Pointing with his finger this way he said, "That mountain point is called the Black-down-streak Mountain. The one beyond that is called Fuzzy Mountain. Opposite to it, in there, your sister entered," he told her. Here she wept in sorrow. "Wonder where my younger sister has gone," she thought. "Do not say that, my grandchild, probably she will return to you! She went into that canyon, along the Roundrock into Chinle [rivershed], then went up along Wide Rock. She is there now in the Blackrock rincon," he told her. She then went back again to the south, went up the summit and stood there. "Yonder is the point from which you left, Over-ridge-shooter, your brothers are there. Yonder hill, this side of Tongue Mountain [Mount Taylor, San Mateo Range, New Mexico], is called Red Mountain," [he told her]. At once she left again for the north and looked at the sun. It was just about to disappear. She went up to the rim at the north, which she reached and stood looking out. She saw many canyons which appeared to be turned upside down. "That point extending is called Bear Ear. It is the Utes' mountain. Have care not to go there!" he said. It was sunset then, and as she sat there the sun went down.

She then returned to her former fireplace and was picking up pinyonnuts, as she had done the day before. Again she opened the ashes and emptied the nuts into it, then covered them up. After a while she went over to them and stirred them, then raked them out. Returning aside she sat down again and remained sitting for sometime. They had cooled off nicely, she found, and were roasted yellow, so now she gathered them all. She then arose and went to the east, stood there, then finally started downward. There she stood again. "I will go yonder to the meadow," she thought, then set out and continued walking without interruption. What she had thought of going to over there proved to be a valley below Big Sheep [Hesperus Peak, La Plata Range, Colorado], which she was approaching. A long distance still remained to be covered. And again she set out and when she finally arrived much grass stood there, tall in size. "How can it be done," she thought as she stood there. "I will go to the east," she decided, set out and was walking along. Where points of the foothills extended she stood again. "Despite all, I will go to the east," she thought as she stood there.

And again she set out and stood still, when something moved some distance ahead. She then proceeded there, but a large thing lay there; it was black spotted white. When she looked this and that way, she found no end to the line. When she looked the other way the same endless line met her view. The grass was open as if mowed; the thing just lay there with its head to the south, while its tail was to the north. This kind of squares were on it, yellow spotted, blue and red spotted she found it. Going away from it, she stood about as far away as that hollow. I will still go to the east she thought as she stood there. Just as she had first thought, so she thought now of going to the east. Then she set out and walked to the thing lying there. And when she thought of running across it, one foot behind the other, it raised and curved its back. She returned back there and stood beyond where she had been standing before. She prepared herself there and set out for it again. Just when she wanted to make a step again, it curved up. And again she returned yonder and stood there. She ran toward it again, but again it repeated. It struck her as far as her stomach. "Once more I shall try it," she thought, and returned beyond where she had been standing. From here she set out again toward it, it struck her in the neck, she fell down backwards. The man who had come to her on the mountain at times, now came to her again. "Why are you doing this, my grandchild? You will cause it to wind around you, it is dangerous!" he told her. "The Endless Snake it is called, it is the slave of Big Bear, who strung it out to stop you!" he said, then told her to go back. So she started back and went up the slope. About that time it was late afternoon. And she continued along until she saw a small hill in the distance, which she thought to reach.

She went up the hill there, and sat down eating pinyon nuts for some time. "I will go to the top of it," she thought as she sat there. She arose and stood there. She would look up and along where she had come down and decided that it was too much for her. "I had better go this way," she thought, "right along the side of it." There was a narrow gulch there thick with brush. "I will return to my brothers, I will return home this way," she thought. She went down this gulch and found it deep, but it was a kind of nice place. The chokecherry bushes were full of green leaves, and service-berries, currants, wild rose, sumac, all of these happened to be there. "Perhaps there are all kinds," she thought, so she walked around eating them. They appeared recently ripened as she walked among them. Then she started down, but found none there and returned to where she had been eating. Then she went up again and found that it was only a short distance to the curved rock and that there was a seepage of water. So she prepared to collect the water, and when quite an amount was caught she drank. That was about sunset. There were bear tracks everywhere, some of cubs, some showed that they led the cubs, which scared her. "Where shall I sleep tonight," she thought. So she went up to the summit, where she found another elevation about the size of this [hill; informant pointed to one near

Saint Michaels]. Here a sizable cedar, walled in on both sides, had grown together with another and had formed something like a hogan on both sides. "This looks suitable," she thought.

But on account of the many tracks just mentioned she was afraid and decided to build a fire. Therefore she got busy breaking off limbs. Then she rubbed the bark together, drilled a fire with her flint, and laid the fuel upon it to start the fire. She stood at the fire, then sat down and remained seated facing the fire, where the trees nicely grew together. After it got quite dark, she lay down and went to sleep. But suddenly she awakened after she had been sleeping. She heard them going where she had been eating berries, and she lay there with her eyes open. "What if one came here to me!" she thought. And she finally arose when dawn appeared. She lit the fire and it blazed up, and she heard them leaving. She sat there till full daylight, then produced her lunch bag of pinyonnuts. It was then near sunrise. The sun rose, but she stayed there till the sun was well up, then went down there again and stood along the rim. Here she picked up stones which she threw down into the canyon, but there was no sound. Then she went down into the canyon, but found that they had eaten almost everything from them quite a distance up the bushes. She then picked the berries by pulling the branches down and after getting a handful she decided to return home supplied with them. She returned to the water, drank some, then walked around there, and went up to her camp of the previous night. When she returned there she sat down, revolving in her mind which way she should go.

Finally she arose and set out. "I will go directly up there," she thought. She looked about as she walked along. As she looked along the sunny side she noticed two pretty hills side by side. "Something may be down there," she thought as she stood there. In that direction she went and arriving there, found a beautiful basin. From there she left and went along the east side. Standing there she beheld a great sight, a thicket of cat-tail flag, willows, chokecherries, service-berries, orange gooseberries, currants, and sumac, which presented an inviting spot. At the base of there was a circle of thicket, inside of which there was a fine round meadow. Suddenly there was a movement [in there] and it moved sunwise in a circle. "Come down, my grandchild," she heard somebody say. She descended from there, and while this thing was circling around she stood facing it. After some time it increased its whirling speed. Now something or other evidently lay there, one across the other, and she discovered that they were two logs. At their ends in the east, two children sat, in the west, south and north also [i.e. at each cardinal point]. Somebody approached her here. "Whence do you come, my grandchild?" he said to her. So that happened. But she motioned with her hand [as she explained] to him, "I came this way along the river, along the Hogback, the Bear Ear, and the Sacred Canyon. From there I arrived in the valley. Then I returned to the foothills where something or other lay, which induced me to return to the foothills again," [she said]. "Perhaps that was your fire we saw?" he said to her. "It was mine, to be sure!" she said. "What are you seeking that you are here?" "It is just that I am chasing around on account of some strange man."

"As for me, I am called Holy Young Man. Inside here there is Holy Young Woman, you see in here I have my home." He, it developed, was the head [of the family]. "Perhaps you will enter, my grandchild? Choose for yourself," he told her. "This whirling part is called the place of the whirling babies." "But how will I enter?" she said. "That is an entrance curtain!" he told her. Suddenly the whirling logs came to a stop, and when she looked closely, she found that they were of wood. "Get down!" he told the children. Stepping down, the children of Holy Young Man walked away, she saw that their faces were altogether white, arms and legs were black, and they were speckled all over their bodies. Then Holy Young Man went along the east, stood there and blew. He went to the west again and blew. He went back to the south and blew again, and also blew at the north. When he stood at the east again it turned this way on edge, which revealed nice, over lapping [stairs] leading down. "Now enter inside, my grandchild!" he told her. She then entered, he followed, and she heard it fall down again, that was all. In the rear of the room she sat down again, and by that time it was sunset. There were house [rooms]. So she entered after he had opened for her, and sat in the rear of the room. It was too dark when she entered, so that she was unable to recognize things. But a woman sat there, the Holy Young Woman. "At dawn today they left us in different directions," the woman said. They merely sat there with her as the night passed. Suddenly the children ran in again saying, "it is getting dark," and they sat around talking to each other.

"What have we to eat for the person?" Holy Young Man said. Then Holy Young Woman went into the rear room, from which she brought a dish. She brought a white shell basket out, which happened to contain chokecherries, service-berries, orange gooseberries, wild rose berries, pinyonnuts, tree pollen, cat-tail flag pollen, which she set before her. She sat before it a while, then began to eat. "This is our only food," [Holy Young Woman said as] she placed it before her. "Thanks for the food," she said. "Is this the same as your food on your journeys?" he asked her. "Yes," she said. It was quite late then, when the door was heard and two entered. It so happened that their faces were all white, and they entered, just carrying their clothes on their arms. "The sun set on us a long distance away," they said, "it set at White Spruce [Chuska Peak]." Two others also entered, who just sat down there carrying their clothes. "Far away, on the side of [Tohatchi] point the sun set on us," they also said. Food was placed for them, and they ate. By that time midnight had passed. After eating they merely sat around. Then the man [Holy Young Man] stepped outside.

"Where have you been?" he asked. "We were in the vicinity of Sumac Patch," said the two who had first entered. "Then we went this way, right along the mountain range, toward the north. Quite a number of earth surface people live there, a chant was on when we arrived. Four prayersticks were given to us here," he said. Reaching inside their garments they laid them down, each laying down two. Picking them up, Holy Young Man held them up, saying, "This is really my prayerstick!" The two that had entered last also produced prayersticks, which happened to be the woman's prayersticks, Holy Young Woman's, to whom they were given. "In truth, they are my own," she said. "The condition that prevails is just terrible! An earth surface man is sick, his feet are swollen, and his knees and wrists likewise," [they reported]. "What will happen to him, he will recover I guess," she said. "You see, they have really made the prayersticks as prescribed for me!" she said. When that had happened, four others entered. They were colored as the others, their faces were white again. "We two went to Tongue Mountain [Mount Taylor]," two of them said, while the others said again, "We went around on Bear Ear to the homes of earth surface people. Their language was very abusive; earth surface people have no regard for holy things, that is evident!" they said. The two who had visited in the other place, around Bear Ear, said, "They have much respect there, they prayed to us when we visited among them." These had no prayersticks, they had brought none. The two who had gone to White Mountain had not yet returned. So that happened. "We are getting sleepy, let us go to sleep," Holy Young Man said. So they slept the rest of the night.

When it was daylight, she noticed sandpaintings on the east side, on which the figures stood with their heads upward. "That white

one is Holy Young Man, the yellow one Holy Young Woman, the
blue one is Exhibit Killer,[89] the one standing toward the north is
He-who-acquires-holy-things," she explained to the woman who
had entered. So that happened. At dawn the others left to return,
while she invited the woman to accompany her outside. "We will
go on top of the mountain," she told her. The woman went outside with her and there they went up the slope and were sitting
on the mountain side. Then she [Holy Young Woman] explained to
her, "That is called Dark Mountain, those that left this past morning visit there. Another two went to Black Mountain, two others to
Striped Rock," she said. Then they descended from above, and
found a place with all sorts of berries, where they walked about
picking them. From there they returned up and sat in the same
place. Then they proceeded to the sunny side where again berries
were found, which they picked as they went along, then returned
up above, continuing to pick them. By that time it was well towards
evening. "Let us return inside now," she [Holy Young Woman]
said to the woman. They entered and sat about inside. Thus another
sunset had come on. During this time nothing had worried her
[Older Sister], she got accustomed to the people. She spent this
night there again, and at daylight ate a meal. "We will go out again,"
she [Holy Young Woman] told her. And they went outside. They
went to places where she had traveled and spent the night. Down
where berries were reported to be, they went again, when suddenly
she saw the woman's tracks. "Whose tracks are these? They are
tracks of an earth surface person!" [Holy Young Woman said]. "They
are mine of course!" the woman replied. Although all berries had
been eaten from them before, many again were on the bushes. So
they went among the bushes picking berries. They lived exclusively on berries which they picked.

Then they ascended the slope. "This particular place is called
Ripe Berries," she [Holy Young Woman] said. They reached the
summit and from there she came to her camping place with them.
They sat there for some time. "Down here they resent visitors
much," she said. "These two places will be the same all winter,
this place and that one. Yonder, from where you set out, your older
brothers still are," she told her. When they returned to the hogan
the sun had set again. At dusk those who had gone out had not

---

[89] "Exhibit killer" is a literal translation. The exhibit of power as in the acts in the
Dark Circle of Branches (Corral Dance) is meant.

yet returned. When it was about time to retire, she told her children to dance and they lined up in a row, porcupines stood at either end. She [Holy Young Woman] then began to sing for them and pounded the basket which lay bottom up. The six of them did a fine dance, moving back and forth.[90] The dancers ceased. "Just the two of you," she again told the porcupines. And with the basket set down for them, the two danced surprisingly well facing each other, doing as exhibit dancers [in the Dark Circle of Branches] at present do. So that happened and they ceased. She again spent the night with them. Daylight set in again and they ate. "We shall go outside somewhere again," [Holy Young Woman said] and at once they left, and down at the head of the canyon, they again found all sorts of berries. There they again walked and set out from there taking a small amount with them. And when they came out of it to the top, they sat down.

She [Holy Young Woman] then began to question the woman [Older Sister], as at daylight the full number would be reached.[91] "Just on whose account do you wander about aimlessly?" "That is because I took Bear Man for husband I run around everywhere," she replied, "On that account my brothers threatened me with death." Although they were informed of all, yet they questioned her. The sun set. "What a surprise, we are still here, although it happens to be sunset. Despite all, you had better set out in the morning for your brother's home. He doesn't mean to threaten you, everywhere he has been searching for you. As for him [Bear Man], his home is at Wide Chokecherry patch. Have no fear, return there to him [your brother]." So she spent the night there, which, at daylight, would be the fourth night she had spent here. After dark they again retired and slept till daylight, then ate. "We shall go with you up to that hill," [Holy Young Woman said]. They went up there with her, then sat down. "We got accustomed to one another, but now you leave us for your home, my younger sister!" [she said]. "That is true, my older sister!" Then she pointed out the hill for her saying, "You will return on the lower side of it," she told her, "yonder below the farther hill there, you will return. Although quite a distance, you will be at home in two days," she [Holy Young Woman] told her. Then she [Older Sister] set out and walked along. Continuing on and on, she was quite close to it by afternoon. Then she set out again and reached it just when the sun was over the horizon.

---

[90] This indicates that there were four children with a porcupine at either end.

[91] That is she would have spent four nights with them.

At sunset she was very tired and spent the night there. She opened the leaves on the ground and lay down in there, and covered herself with the leaves. She slept soundly.

When the sun rose she got up, but with difficulty. Her ankles and feet were swollen. She sat there munching berries she had with her. But the woman's clothes on her were all threadbare. Here she ate part of her lunch she had with her, then set out towards the farther hill. She walked along with the utmost difficulty due to her swollen ankles, and the sun set before she reached it. Still she continued on. At dusk finally she reached the hill, then busied herself building a fire with dried wood she broke off and rubbing bark. For this she drilled fire with her firedrill and put fuel to it. She sat with her soles to the fire, produced her lunch again and ate. After eating, she continued to sit there till midnight, then finally lay down. At daylight she piled up the remnants of the fire and after it blazed up she sat facing it. But now little remained of her lunch, of which she ate a small portion. Then she set out again with the utmost difficulty. Where she and her sister had parted, she found the place of their camp, but set out again. She was in the neighborhood of where the two had gone at the time. "I am at the spot to which we came then," she thought. And she walked along following the same course they had at that time taken. And she started out again, then rested at a small hill there. It was not far now from the point to which she was returning, and the thought came to her as she sat there, that her brothers might club her to death. And she arose with difficulty and walked to the hogan. It was perhaps about this time of the day [4:00 P.M.] that she was returning to the hogan. But when she arrived nobody was at home, her brothers were gone. She entered and lay down. It was sunset. Having made a fire, she lay down and noticed a large supply of venison there.

At dusk the two returned. The bundles of venison which they had, they threw to the side. Approaching, her brother embraced her.[92] "My dear younger sister, where have you been all this time?" he said as they wept. After saying this to one another, they released their embrace. Then the two busied themselves with the food, cutting the meat for pot-boiling. That finished, they just sat there while it boiled. They had brought a very fat one which they were now boiling. They had biscuits made of grass seeds. It was taken out of the pot, they began to eat, and some time passed while they ate. They did not bother her, they did not speak to her, they just ate.

---

[92] The embrace seems to have been the traditional form of greeting after a long absence.

After the meal was finished, he finally said, "Where have you been going around, my younger sister? Tell us about it," he said. "What is there to tell? We two [the sisters] passed by here to River Junction, she said with a mere gesture, "then went on to the Hogback and Slim Water Canyon [Mancos River], then to Bear Ear mountain. That we ascended and went to the other side across to Sacred Canyon, where we spent two nights. Coming down the mountain something obstructed my path." She referred to Endless Snake. As she was in pain, she said, "Wait, some other time I will tell you the details." Then she also told of coming to the said hill, and of another hill to which the two had come. "Now I returned and entered to you here. A person cannot tell it carefully, I am aching, my older brother," she said. They did nothing else but retired and went to sleep. Without sleeping at all, she passed the night, and when she arose, her feet and legs were much swollen, the venison which she had eaten had made her sick. "Did you ever get in this shape, when you made these journeys?" he asked her. "I got that way, at Slim Water Canyon. I was in the same shape," she said. Now the people who had moved away from Red Mountain [still] dwelt there.[93] "And what did they do to you then?" "They dug a pit for me this way [of my size], built a fire down there, and when the fire had burnt out they laid a number of pinyon branches down, and juniper, spruce [Douglas fir], rock sage, estafiata, snakeweed, and grama grass. This they did for me." "Tomorrow morning then, let it be so done," he said.

At daylight then they dug a pit in that shape, fired it, then broke branches from pinyon, juniper, spruce [Douglas fir], and rock sage, estafiata, snakeweed, and grama grass. "Nevertheless let chokecherry and willow branches be broken off, let these two be added to them." Many small plants also were added, and black medicine [gromwell], and red medicine [also gromwell] also, that was all of these medicines, and then he [the older brother] placed the boughs for her. But when he bid her come, she just crawled out, and crawling along, she crept to the spot. She removed her garments, then lay there and remained there for some time. The said medicines he pounded up for her, then she asked for the medicine bowl. After she drank some, he covered her. "Is that sufficient?" he asked her. "I will stay lying a while," she said, and he sat waiting for her. "Is it sufficient now?" he asked her again, then dragged her out of it.

---

[93] This phrase, which interrupts the narrative, seems to have been inserted as a reminder of her first treatment by her clansmen from Red Mountain. She may have said that she had met them.

She perspired freely all over her body, and with the medicine, she bathed herself. That done, she put her clothes on again, then they left with her and returned inside. It was then about midday. "At daylight you shall do the same to me, my older brother," she said, to which he consented. They were roasting venison, then ate again. "I presume you feel better now, tell us your story!" "What is the hurry!" she said. When this all had been done, she had spent another sunset there. "Wait a while, I shall tell it to you when I feel better." "All right," he consented. So it happened and daylight appeared. At daylight they ate again, then dug a pit for her in the west. He built a fire again, broke off pinyon branches, juniper and spruce, and rock sage, estafiata, snakeweed, grama grass, and choke-cherry, willow and service-berry branches, all of which they placed there for her. After the twigs had been placed for her, he bid her to come, and she went out. Arriving there he told her, "Remove your jacket," which she did. "Lie down here," he said to her. When she lay there he covered her.

As she lay there, he sat attending her for quite a while. "Is that sufficient?" he asked her. "Wait, I will stay here a while longer, my older brother." He handed the medicine bowl to her, and after some time she drank again. Much sweat ran from her. "Lie down again!" he told her. She lay down again while he sat watching her. Some time passed again. "Perhaps that will do," he said to her. "Wait, let me lie here a while, I like it very much, as it has warmed me up," she said. So he just sat beside her. "That will do, I suppose," he said to her when it was midday. Now finally she arose and washed her whole body and her hair with the medicine. Then she vested herself again, and now set out in the lead and they all entered. "My younger sister, boil some meat this time!" So she got up and she herself prepared the pot. "Put some grass seed [meal] in ashes, my younger sister!" he directed her. After kneading it, she set it in the ground. They waited while it baked. When baked they found that she had placed four [biscuits] in the ashes. These she took out, washed them off and placed them in a dish where her brothers sat. She also went to the dish of boiling venison, dipped from it, added salt to it, and set it where they were seated. She sat there and they began to eat. They finished the meal. "What about it? We will go out, my younger brother, somewhere there may be a forked horn," [he said]. So they set out. "Wait for us quietly here, my younger sister, food should be prepared again!" So she was alone here, but [he remarked], "The contents of that bag one may put in the pot [to boil]. That is a sweet dish, meat cut with tallow in small pieces." So she ground slim-grass [drop-seed] seeds, which she dropped into the water, and sat there, making a thin gruel. She took this gruel out of the pot about sunset.

At dusk she heard her two brothers returning. "Take this bundle from me," she heard said there. "Remove it from me also," she heard the other say. Then both brought their bundles inside and laid them in the rear of the room. They cleaned the heart, blood, and entrails nicely. "Thanks, my older brother, I shall eat meat," she said. Then she placed the dish before them, the gruel with the prepared meat, she set before them. They began to eat and finished the meal. "Now then, my younger sister, let us have your story!" Nothing ailed her then, she was well again. "All right, very disagreeable things happened to me. True, at the time of the group dance here, the two of us walked out when we were really heated. We sat there for a time, then started out from there." She said nothing of the tobacco smell. "Then we went to some fire in a mountain pocket, where we found two strange men seated within a brush circle. They certainly were two fine young men. One had an earband of turquoise in his ears, the finest slender white beads hung around his neck. He was clothed in a white robe [a white buffalo hide]. The other was similarly adorned and clothed in an otterskin. His white shell earband was this wide, he also had beads, slender white beads with red beads were his necklace. So the two of us stood at the entrance, without we being seen by them. As we stood there the Bear gave his call on the north side, the Big Snake on the other side. Then to the rear of the enclosure, we rushed together. I squatted there next to him [Bear Man], while my younger sister squatted next to this one [Big Snake Man] and we sat with them for some time. There the two of us slept."

"About the time of dawn I awakened. When I raised up, it was full dawn I found. 'Where are the two [girls], look for them,' I heard said, 'as soon as found they shall be killed,' I heard said. 'Yucca torn into four strips and wrapped, with that the oldest shall be whipped to death,' I heard said, 'while the younger shall be beaten to death with willows wrapped with yucca,' was heard said of us. Then the older woman [herself] raised up. When she looked at the prostrate figure, his teeth were yellow and protruding over the lower ones, his ears were completely bare. Then I left this way and awakened my younger sister. She awoke to find herself lying under cover of something whose mouth was its front, whose head-top had a red spot. At once we left there and came right here next to the dancing group. 'Let us return there,' my younger sister strove to tell me, but I refused her," she said. "The grass stood high there, therefore a person could not easily be tracked." So it happened. "That is true, it really was so planned at the time, my younger sister." "On that account we two started out anywhere, and again set out and arrived at River Junction, where we got a drink. Around there we were walking around eating berries, then left again for Crossing Streams. It so happened that Monster Slayer had his home there up in midrock, and on this side, Born-for-Water lived in midrock. At a place called Many Berries, we again walked around eating berries, then left downstream for Between Rivers [Farmington, New Mexico]. While we were in that vicinity we again ate berries. From there we went towards Hogback, and then towards the Slim Water Canyon confluence [Mancos River]. There we were walking around in the direction of Whirling Mountain [Carrizo Mountains]. Then without any plan we were walking around," the woman said.

"And my younger sister went downstream towards Fuzzy Mountain, while I turned back this way. 'Who knows where the river terminal may be, there I am going. Some time or other we shall meet again, my older sister,' she said to me. I left there and returned to the Hogback. There I sat for a while," she said. "Suddenly behind me a bear came along, it happened to be Bear Man," she said. "And I ran away and ran up to the top of the Hogback and came to the top of the rock. And the range ended towards Slim Water Canyon, and I sat down up there," she said. "Then I went down and walked out to the valley, but it was sunset then," she said. "I thought I would spend the night there, but my feet and legs ached, my knees were swollen. As I sat there dusk set in, then I lay down," she said. "At daylight I looked, and at full daylight I set out from there with difficulty, but I went up to the rim of Slim Water Canyon and sat down. It happened that below me, down in the canyon, several were moving, so I sat right there," she said. "It developed that a hoop-pole game was on, beavers, and otters, and muskrats were hoop-poling for their clothes," she said. "But there was a small rock canyon running out into the main one. Suddenly someone called to me from there, 'From where do you come that you are here,' he said to me, 'people are not allowed here. What are you doing here?' he said to me. 'Come across over here, it is too far for persons to talk to each other, that is evident.'"

"So I started down and found it quite a distance to the bottom. Then I went up the other side towards him and found him sitting there. 'What are you? I am Bitter Water Clan,' [I] said. 'I too am Bitter Water Clan,' he said, 'long ago we moved away from a place called Red Mountain, we moved on account of the Pueblos at the time. Those women, two sisters, were evidently our mothers, the youngest was my mother,' the man said, 'while the oldest is your mother,' he told the woman [me]. 'You are my younger sister, I see,' he said shaking hands with me. 'Yes, my older brother,' I said. About that time, it was well along afternoon. 'We just live over there nearby, there at the hogan,' he said. Then I arose with difficulty and followed him. He entered ahead of me, I required time to get there. When I entered, I found people sitting there. The man then informed them. 'This is one of those people from whom we moved long ago. Leaving here, I set out for the top [of the canyon], when someone happened along and I discovered it was she,' he said. 'But she sat down over there. Where do you come from to be here? People are not allowed here, I told her. Cross over here, we will speak together here, I told her. Then she crossed over to me. On whose account do you go around anywhere? I asked her. What are you? I asked her [the man speaking]. To be sure I am Bitter Water Clan. Even so, on whose account are you going about, I said to her. It is just that on Bear Man's account I am pursued, she said. Then I invited her to come with me to the hogan, here we are.'"

"Now those who had moved away from them at Red Mountain, I found these were. 'It is clear, this is our sister,' and again they pressed hands calling me 'younger sister.' It so happened that men alone were there. 'Our sister got mad, she was the only sister we had, but she got mad at us,' they said, 'when she took Coyote for a husband.' Then darkness set in. As they had returned from the chase, meat was abundant. 'Why do we not eat,' the oldest of the men said. 'Boil some venison,' he said. That was done and the meat boiled. 'Are there still any slap cakes?' he said. The meat was brought for her [me]. Some they set before the men, some before the women. The slap cakes mentioned were slim-grass [drop-seed] seed slap cakes. 'Go ahead eat, my younger sister,' they said. They all ate. Then I went outside, but arose with difficulty. When I returned inside the oldest said to me, 'What ails you, my younger sister?' he said. My feet and knee regions are swollen and ache me. 'What then can be done? we cannot let her remain in this condition,' he said. At daylight food was prepared again, venison was again boiled. 'Why do you do this? You go in any old place, my younger sister,' he said. 'From which point did you set out at the time?' 'From Shooting-over-the-ridge it was,' I said. 'Well, then start back to your brothers! To the other side it is quite close,' he said. So I set out to return and started toward the mountain. Suddenly there was a movement among the trees and I stopped. Standing there I looked and discovered a bear. 'That must be the one from whom I am fleeing,' I thought and returned towards the hogan. But I passed the hogan, then started out toward Bear Ear mountain."

"Then I left this way towards my older brother, but he came towards me. Then I turned back, and returned where I had walked previously. I thought of going along the summit but, as I walked along looking at the ground, I realized that I was where I had first gone. I was returning along my own tracks. So I was afraid as it was late in the afternoon. As I continued on towards Bear Ear mountain the sun set. 'I wonder where I shall spend the night,' I thought as I walked along," she said telling her brother about it. "'I shall spend the night on the side of the mountain,' I thought as I walked along," she said. "I went there, but walking along I thought of how it could be done. 'Clearly, if I have a fire nobody will approach me,' I thought as I went along," she said, "Dusk set in before I could reach the summit. Then I engaged in breaking fuel and tearing off bark, drilled for fire and got it started," she said. "I sat at the fire for some time, some time passed. Then I finally lay down and went to sleep," she said. "At daylight I sat up looking and investigating. At sunrise I left again and following my former tracks I went to the summit and stood there," she said. "Then I crossed the mountain, and went down to Sacred Canyon, then rested there again. Suddenly, on my opposite side I noticed some moving, and discovered bears walking there, she said. It so happened that the bear was leading her small cubs out along there. Picking one up, she made it dance up and down, while she sang for it. That shook the mountain, and I almost fell over."

"Then I returned towards a hill," she said, "but I found myself in a spot where berries were plentiful again," she said. "Here I began eating berries until dusk set in," she said. "There I spent the night and when daylight appeared I went up the slope," she said, "and reached the top. Up there was a valley to which I went and found pinyon nuts which I ate," she said. "I filled up fairly well with them, then went towards the east, ascended the summit and sat there," she said. "And there was White Mountain peak, and Horizontal Black Belt [Blanca Peak] in the distance. Just then some strange man came to me, who happened to be Big Fly," she said. "'Why do you sit here, my grandchild,' he said to me. 'Yonder peak is called White Mountain, the other which sets to this side is called

Horizontal Black Belt,' he said to me. I then went to the west again, ascended the mountain and sat down again. The same man came to me again. 'Yonder is Black-down-streak Mountain [Sleeping Ute Mountain, Colorado], and the one farther on is called Fuzzy Mountain,' he explained to me," she said. "'Yonder canyon running up across there is the canyon into which your younger sister went,' he told me," she said. "'From there she went along the Round Rock, then into Chinle and along Wide Rock,' he told me," she said. "'From there she went to Blackrock, then down off it, there your younger sister is now,' he told me, and my tears flowed. 'What can happen to her, my grandchild,' he said to me; 'no doubt she will return to you, my grandchild,' he said to me. 'Songs will originate as she goes along and indications are that she will learn them, then return to you,' he told me," she said. "'Do not grieve for her,' he said to me," she said.

"Then I went to the south again, went up there and was sitting there when he came to me again," she said. "'That yonder is called Open Mouthed Bear [rock in the Tsaile, Arizona, area], the mountain this side is called Red Mountain,' he told me, 'the range forming a circle there is the point from which you two set out at the time,' he said to me. 'Here is the home of your brothers, undoubtedly you will return there to them,' he told me," she said. "Then I went north again, ascended the mountain and sat down again. There he came to me again. 'Beyond that mountain range running out is the mountain called Bear Ear, it is the Utes' mountain,' he told me. 'Do not go there,' he told me. Then I turned back, again," she said, "and went to the place where I had previously gathered pinyon nuts. So that happened. From there I went to the east and down the mountain. In the distance there was a beautiful valley into which I went and as I stood there I decided that I wanted to go to the east. But when I set out something moved ahead of me. And when I came upon it there, some black thing lay along there speckled with white, blue, yellow and red spots. And I thought I should step over it and walk back. But when I set out toward it, it suddenly curved its back and I moved away from it again. Then I moved toward it again, but it acted the same way, it curved itself somewhat higher. Then I returned beyond my starting point. When I again approached it, it struck my thighs. Then I returned still farther back, and when I approached it again it struck my neck throwing me down. Then I returned away from it," she said. "But Big Fly came to me again. 'What are you doing, my grandchild?' he said to me. 'That is to be feared, it will twist itself around you,' he told me," she said. "Then I returned, went up the slope and thought I would return on top," she said.

"So I continued up the slope, but found the grade too much for me and sat down there. Here I ate the lunch I had with me. And I thought I would return here," she said. "But there happened to be a slim canyon there with many berry bushes. I went down there picking them and satisfied my hunger. I came down there, when the sun was still high in the skies. As I proceeded farther down, I found that its outlet was close by, and I went up again. Up there, nearby, there was a curved cliff from which water oozed out. I prepared a place nicely and in a short time much water had collected from which I drank," she said. "Right there I spent the night and slept. When the night had passed half way, I woke up and lay with my eyes open. Then some beings or other were moving down into many berry bushes. After a while, the sound of their footsteps retreating could be heard. When I raised up, it was about time for sunrise, so I got up, built a fire and sat eating what berries I had picked the day before," she said. "Meanwhile the sun stood high up. 'Perhaps I ought to return down there,' I thought, and when I set out, I was surprised to see many coming on this side again. There I walked up to the rim. 'Perhaps some are down there,' I thought, then gathered some stones and threw one down, then another and another and another one, four all told. 'There are none evidently,' I thought. So I went down," she said, "but found everything eaten from them. Higher up only there were some on them. By bending the branches down I could pick them off, and I picked this much [showing two hands full]."

"Then I went up the hill again and when I reached the top it was afternoon. 'I will go up above,' I thought then and went back, but noticed two nice hills, which stood side by side and I turned around. When I came close there I stood up a while, then went on. The place was very beautiful I found. I made a circle, came to the east and stood there looking. I saw a nice round place at the base of them, while around the edges it was thick with all bushes, chokecherry, service-berry, orange gooseberries, currants and red bush [sumac], so I found it," she said. "'My grandchild, come down,' I heard someone say to me. So I set out and went there," she said. "When I arrived someone stood along there among the bushes. 'From where are you coming my grandchild?' he asked me. 'What do you seek, my grandchild?' he asked me. 'Just because I am pursued, I am here,' I told him. 'Inside here is the hogan, perhaps

you care to enter?' he said to me. 'You have your own choice, if
you say no, it is all right too.' 'I will enter I suppose,' I told him.
'Me they call Holy Young Man, one called Holy Young Woman is
my wife,' he told me. 'Inside is our home,' he said. In this [sunwise]
manner logs whirled in a circle. 'This place is called Baby-floating-
around,' he told me. Suddenly the said logs slowed down. At the
east point sat two children, two also at the west, and also at the
south and north points. 'These are my children,' he said to me,"
she said. "'Get down,' he told them. They came down and went
aside. Their arms and legs happened to be black, their faces white,
they were spotted," she said.

"He now went to the east and blew at it, then went to the west
and again blew at it, and also blew at it from the south and north.
Then it turned on its side, revealing their home inside of it. It was
terraced down and led to another door which he opened for me.
When I entered it was too dark to recognize anything. 'Sit down,' he
told me, and when I sat down, I discovered a woman there. We just
sat there. 'This morning they left us' [she said]. While sitting there
the children ran in saying that it was dusk. 'What shall be done, why
not give the person something to eat' [he said]. Then it was quite a
while before the woman left to go into the rear room which she had
opened. When she brought the dish out, it happened to be a white
shell basket with chokecherries, service-berries, orange gooseberries, tree and cat-tail flag pollens which, as I learned, was their
ordinary food. 'This exclusively is our food,' she said. Then I began
to eat, but could not eat it all. Then they ate. That done, we sat in
the rear room, when suddenly the door was heard outside and two
entered. They carried their clothes [on their arms] and I saw that
their faces were white, their arms and legs black. Surprised, I
looked at them," she told. "They hung up their clothes, bear garments they were, very pretty garments. The next morning I made a
careful survey. And we were just sitting around, when the door
sounded again and two others entered. Their faces, too, were white,
their arms and legs black, and they also hung up their clothes.
Holy Young Man walked out, following him, she [Holy Young
Woman] brought the dishes out and they ate. So it happened."

"The dishes were removed and brought inside. 'At White Spruce
[Chuska Peak] the sun set on us, while it overtook us [who entered
last] along the point,' the first two that had entered [said]. 'We left
here [and came] to the homes of people. Then we went on this way
and came to another range, where some kind of chant was on. Here
prayersticks were given to us, to the one, two, to the other, also

two.' 'We two also left here, walked around on the mountain, and came to the homes of some earth surface people. These prayersticks were given to us there, to the one, two, and two to the other. From there we returned. Quite well the earth surface people show their respect,' they said. 'They prayed to us when we were there.' He gave the sticks to Holy Young Man, who looked at them. 'They are mine, I see,' he said. 'We found the man in quite serious condition, he was sick, his feet, legs and knees were swollen,' they reported. 'Evidently my stick has nicely been made for me. Nothing will happen to him, he will certainly recover,' he [Holy Young Man] said. The other two, who had entered last, also produced some and gave them to him. 'These are not mine evidently,' and he gave them to the woman [Holy Young Woman]. She looked at them and said, 'It is true they are mine.' So that happened. They then lay down and slept until daylight. And the sun rose, then they ate again. After that, two left again for Dark Mountain and Black Range, while the other two went along White Mountain. That done, the woman said, 'Let us walk around here.' It was not far up the slope where we went, but berry bushes were abundant, which we picked until we had sufficient. We went up on top, where we sat down. Then we returned home and went inside, and it was then near sunset. Soon the sun disappeared, and when darkness set in, we sat around. When quite dark, she invited her children to dance. The men, who had gone out, had not yet returned."

"So she turned the basket down for her children; a porcupine stood at either end of their line up. She then sang for them, they danced nicely in a row from one side to the other. After they quit, they merely sat around. Then, after some time, the two porcupines faced each other. While she again beat the basket they danced and also quit. Then they lay down and slept again. At daylight they ate again. 'We will go along the ripe berry patch,' the woman suggested. We went there, but when we arrived, we found that they had come back again, many of their tracks showed. We went down there. As we went along she saw footprints. 'I wonder whose footprints these are?' 'They are mine,' I told her. We then busied ourselves with picking berries, and when we finished we had picked a considerable number. Then we returned home and after entering, just sat around. After it was quite dark, they had not yet returned. And they ate again, lay down and went to sleep. At daylight, after we had eaten she again suggested to go down into a certain hollow. There we found chokecherries again, and serviceberries, and orange gooseberries. These we picked again, until we had a good supply, then set out to return. We went on top, sat down and remained seated. 'That yonder is called Dark Mountain,' she said to me. 'The range ahead of it is called Black Mountain,' she said to me. We then set out to return home. It was another sunset then, and we sat around until dusk set in, then we ate again, lay down and slept all night. Daylight appeared and at sunrise we ate again."

"Now she pointed with her finger to the east, where a painting of standing figures hung. 'The white one is called Holy Young Man, that yellow one is Holy Young Woman. This is their home, these are we ourselves. That blue one is called Exhibit Killer,' she told me, 'the dark one, standing on the north side, is called He-who-acquires-holy-things,' she told me. 'Wherever in future times a chant with Dark Circle of Branches is held, this sandpainting shall be used,' she said to me. Then the woman said to me, 'Let us go up on top,' so I went with them. And we sat there. 'Now then you will return to your older brother, my younger sister,' she said to me," she said. "'We were getting accustomed to one another, but now you are leaving us. Go there, on the lower side of that distant hill,' she told me pointing with her finger at it. 'You will return on the lower side of the hill beyond this one. Now go on, return my younger sister,' she said to me. Then, going down from above, I set out, but as I walked on and on I found that the distance was quite considerable. It was quite late in the afternoon when I arrived there. I thought I would spend the night there, because I found a thick layer of leaves. These I nicely raked apart, then slept right there, as I was tired." In this manner she was relating the story. "And I again ate my lunch, then arose with some pain in my ankles. Then I set out again on my return, and started out for the mountain which had been pointed out to me," she said. "Going along I walked with utmost difficulty toward that mountain and arrived there at sunset. There I sat down, as I had become unable to walk on," she said. "'I ought to build a fire,' I thought, then went about breaking off twigs. Then I sat with my feet to the fire and sat there till dark. Then finally I lay down," she said. "I slept till dawn appeared and awaited full daylight," she said.

"The fire had gone out, so I piled up the remnants of the fire and lit it. I had a very small quantity of pinyonnuts then and I ate again. When I managed to arise with some difficulty, I set out, but found walking difficult. And I stood looking at the ground and recognized that I was where the two of us [she and her sister] had come along previously. So I set out to follow the course the two of us had taken at the time. On some small hill I lay down. 'My brothers will perhaps kill me,' I thought as I sat there. So it happened that I entered here," she said to him. "That is my whole story," she said. "I entered here and did not sleep all night. But that you know already [and] placing me in the fire pit."

"There certainly is not a thing that you did not do, I see," [he said]. Meanwhile the sun set again. After food had been prepared again, they lay down and slept. "Well, so it happened I see, my younger sister," he said. Then he threw buckskins toward her. "You left a long time ago, all clothes on you are shredded, they are dirty. Make some clothes for yourself of these buckskins!" he said. So it happened that she was nicely cutting them out till sunset, when she had them all cut out. "You know, of course, how to sew," [he said], and she began to sew. On both sides she added nice fringes and made the sleeves. So that happened again. She was busy with this till sunset, but did not finish the sewing at sunset. After dark she laid the fabric aside. After dark they prepared food and while it was boiling they sat there, then ate when it was ready. A while passed again in which they sat around, then finally lay down and slept all night. Daylight appeared. In the morning he said to her, "Prepare some food, my younger sister, we are going hunting somewhere." So she busied herself with the food, cutting meat for the pot. She then put water on the fire, put the cut up pieces into it and stirred it and repeated this occasionally. Then she dipped some mush into a bowl and took the meat out of the pot again.

They then began to eat, and after finishing the meal, the dishes were set aside. "Now then we two are going hunting again, my younger sister, stay at home quietly," he said to her. "Do not think of going to places, but make your clothes carefully. Tomorrow you will make me a pair of pants," he said to her. The other brother then added, "On the following day you may make me a pair," he said to her. The two then left and spent the day walking around along the side of Wide Chokecherry, but it appears that they had not bagged any game. At sunset they returned and arrived at home about dusk. "We failed," they said to her, "there were tracks, of course, but we did not get sight of one." She was wearing the clothes she had made. This time they made the food, set it before her, then they all ate, then went to sleep. They slept the whole night and arose at daylight. She then busied herself with the food, she again prepared the food, then they ate. "Will it be as I said about the pants?" he said to her. "All right, cut them out," she said. "You too cut yours out," she told the younger brother. They did this till noon, when the two had finished. She just laid them aside saying,

"After a while I shall sew them." "We two are going around in the immediate neighborhood, perhaps we will have no success again," he said. After the two had left, she began to sew and sat sewing until, close to sunset, she had finished one of them. Then she picked up the other, which required till sunset to finish one side. Then she set about to prepare food.

She put some cactus fruit in the pot, kneaded it and separated the seeds from it. Into this she put slim-grass [drop-seed] seed flour, mixed it with water, and by that time darkness had set in. Suddenly she heard the two returning at the entrance. "Hey there, remove this fabric from me! You, too, take it from me," [she heard]. Then they brought them inside. "I made a gruel without gravy," [she said]. "Well, here are ribs, fry them," [he said]. So she fried them, turned them over, then took them from the fire. She sprinkled salt over them, then they sat down facing each other. It so happened that they had brought a very fat one. The older brother cut off a rib, put his finger into the mush and ate it. "She certainly made a very tasty mush," he remarked, as he again dipped his finger into it. "It is the truth, it is very tasty." "Of what did she make the gruel?" [he asked]. "Oh there was some dried cactus around here, I mixed that with it," [she said]. "It certainly has a fine flavor," [he remarked]. So this happened, and they finished the meal. About that time darkness had well set in, and they retired and went to sleep. They slept all night. At daylight she again busied herself with the food. She set water on the fire, kneaded the said grass seed flour and baked biscuits in ashes. She then picked up another side of ribs, cut them small so that they required only a short time to boil. When boiled, she removed the pot from the fire. The biscuits she removed from the ground, washed them by scraping the ashes from them. Then she set about to prepare the meat, took it from the pot and placed it into a bowl and set the biscuit dish aside. Again they sat down facing each other and ate, then put the dishes away again. Then the two left saying that they would hunt somewhere. But at sunset they returned empty-handed. "We had no success," he said. Meanwhile she had sewed the fabrics any old way, but that was all that happened about it [that is the brothers said nothing]. She had cooked venison only, the dish of which she set before them. Apparently she was displeased and moved around restlessly where she sat. In time they lay down and slept through the night.

The following morning they arose and early she went outside. The two themselves had to roast the vension, but she sat nearby in view on a ridge. "Go out there and ask her to come!" he said. Presumably he told her to come and she entered. "Why do you

grieve, my younger sister?" "I do not grieve for anything," she
said. "Right in the neighborhood we plan to go hunting all day.
Stay quietly here, my younger sister. Do not think of other places,
my younger sister!" he said to her. The two then left and walked
around hunting in the hills. They came to the spot where the woman
had spent the last night. Quite late in the afternoon, they set out
for home without having bagged one. Immediately after they had
gone, the women had left, the fire was out. "She certainly is a
great one!" he said. But she had gone along over the ridge to the
other end of the mountain range. There was a hill there, to the very
summit of which she had gone. "I wonder which way she went
again, my younger brother!" he said. "Suppose you go this way, I
will take the other and we will meet in the west, her tracks may be
somewhere!" [he said]. They found her tracks leading toward the
east, there were four of her footprints, then they lost them because
of the abundant grass. But she had left there and set out for this
side of Big Sheep [Hesperus Peak in the La Plata Range] towards
Slim Water Canyon [Mancos River]. As she was walking along, she
suddenly stopped when something or other called. She looked
around but saw nobody. When she went on again she heard the
call again [but found nothing]. Again she proceeded and again
heard the call. She stood and wondered who might be calling,
when she noticed him sitting on a tree. "What are you here for, my
grandchild?" he said. "Nothing at all, I am just going around here,
my granduncle," she said. "They said that you were at Slim Water
Canyon several days ago, and what are you seeking as you go everywhere!" he said to her. "You are going this way, you are going for
prayersticks, to be told about them, for that you are here," he
said to her.

And she went on again. At some distance she stopped again and
when she proceeded again there was a call. "What did you come for,
my grandchild?" "For nothing in particular," she said. "Around
here, going used not to be allowed, my grandchild," he said to
her. "Where are you bound for that you are here?" he asked again.
"I am on my way there, beyond that jagged mountain," she said.
"This main canyon is Slim Water Canyon, the canyon to which you
came before, this is," he told her. Thus she had come upon two
persons. "I am Chipmunk, so they call me," he said. Then he
repeated the same, "Your purpose in going is to have prayersticks
told to you. As for us, we shall tell you later about them," he said.
"Now go on, continue on," he told her. When she was walking
along again, someone called to her again. She stopped again,
wondering who it might be that called. And she discovered that

White Pine Squirrel had called. "What are you doing here, my grandchild?" he also asked her. "Where are you bound for that you are here?" he asked her. Then it seems she journeyed on again. At some distance she stopped again. "What causes you to be here, my grandchild?" he said. "I am just visiting here, my granduncle," she said to him. She learned that Black Pine Squirrel was speaking. "You are going on account of prayersticks, I see. That they be told to you is your purpose in going, that is evident," he said. "Just continue walking on, my grandchild," he told her, and she walked on again. After this had occurred, she set out again, and when she had gone some distance, she saw a rock peak, from the top of which she heard a call. Suddenly someone poked his head out at the top of the rock. "What are you seeking that you are here, my grandchild?" he also said. "They call me Ground Squirrel. What are you doing here? Earth surface people are not allowed around here," he said. "Wherever is the place you are bound for?" he said again. "Right around here I am going about, my granduncle," she said to him. "Go this way toward the east. Prayersticks will be told to you, that is your purpose in going. As for us, we will inform you later, we will not inform you for the present," he told her. "From where you started till here, there are five of us who have our prayersticks," Ground Squirrel told her. "Now go on, my grandchild," he said to her.

And she set out again, but as she walked along, she suddenly stopped. Her thought went back to the home of the Chipmunk where she had passed. I will catch it, she thought, it will be nice to have it for my pet. So she returned there but had no success in finding it, it was gone. Then she walked sunwise in a circle, but suddenly, back where she had started, she heard a call. When she returned there she found him at home. Inside of a hole through the rock he had his home. She reached inside, but her arm was too short. Then, after she broke off a stick, she poked in there after it. It ran up a tree, so when she set out to follow it, she found it sitting at the tip of the tree. She encircled it but to no avail, so she simply started away from there. There was a small mountain in the distance. When she came to it a strange white something ran along, its breast was black. She learned that this was a weasel. Another yellow one ran along right behind the other. Then a blue one ran along again, then a black one again, and a spotted one again ran along. When that had happened he said, "They call us all Weasel, we all have a prayerstick, no doubt. Which place are you bound for, my grandchild?" he said. One of them was speaking. "Prayersticks will be told to you, for that purpose you evidently started out," he said to her. It so happened that one was walking behind the other, Porcupine walked in the lead, Badger followed. So it happened. "For which purpose did you come, my grandchild?" he asked her. "Nothing in particular," she said again. "There is evidence that we have our prayersticks for all days to come," he said. "Just now you came below that mountain," he said. "In yonder big depression some people have their homes," he said. Then she left in that direction. When she arrived there it happened to be a bear's home with a small opening. "Enter, my grandchild," he told her. After she entered she remained for quite a length of time. "Whence did you come to be here now, my grandchild?" he said to her. It happened to be dusk then.

Just one night she had spent there again but in reality she had spent it there without realizing the fact. He owned fire she found out and they were stones, a dark one, blue one, yellow and white one. So that happened. "There is evidence of the existence of my prayerstick. Later on I shall give you this information," he said. "Since you came inside here four nights have passed in reality. The interior here is called Burrow-lying [place]," he said. The entrance had been screwed [shut off from the outside] for her, it developed that this was a door. "Prayersticks will be told to you, for that purpose you are really going," he said. "Walk upward, on the summit everything is to be had," he said. But she did not make very good time going up, she found the up grade long. After she reached the summit, large red cedar-tree berries lay scattered around, with which she busied herself for some time, eating some and tieing others to her skirt as she gathered them. Then she heard somebody's call and discovered that the Turkey had been calling. Many of them were there, and she noticed a Turkey gobbler encircling them. After they nicely got together in a bunch they stopped, and when she sat down just looking at them, he came toward her. "Why did you come, my grandchild?" he said to her. "I am just going around here, my granduncle" she replied. "Information on prayersticks will be given to you, for that purpose you are going," he said. "As for us, our prayersticks are existing, my grandchild," he said. "Later on, you will get information about ours too," he told her. From there she set out again in the direction where Mountain Sheep were roaming, one of which came to her. "What are you doing here, my grandchild?" he said to her. "We also are in possession of our prayersticks," he said.

Then she went up to the summit and sat down along the point of the mountain. She sat there looking out over the landscape. 'I will go to the east,' she thought, but then again decided not to go. Suddenly someone came to her. "What did you come here for, my grandchild?" he said to her. Presumably he had guessed that she sat there thinking of going to the east. She learned that this was the Sun. "It is a very long distance, you gain nothing by going," he told her, "it is an awful distance away. I too have a prayerstick in my possession, we, the Moon and I, have our prayersticks," he told her. "Continue around here, but do not think of going over there!" he said to her. Then she bethought herself of her brothers' home, 'there I shall return,' she thought. Then, it seems, she set out. The badlands were very much cut up, there were many small canyons. When she was walking along without having made a single stop, she was suddenly checked by the river, large waves were rolling along. So she sat down there. Here somebody came to her. "The distance is very great, all kinds of rock canyons are there," one called Rain Weasel [some describe this as a bird] said to her.[94] "Over here there is a hogan, that particular hill there is a hogan, go there!" he told her. So she left for that point. Arriving there she encircled the said hill, but found no opening to it. She learned later that this belonged to Meal Sprinkler. It so happened that along its tip there was a hole, therefore she encircled it with no result. "Walk up here!" he called to her, and she found him lying prone. "Whence did you come?" he asked her. "I came around sunwise from yonder and was checked by the river. From there, on this side of Slim Water Canyon, I went up the center of the mountain this way, but when I came here I was checked by the river [unable to pass]," she said.

"There it happened that someone came to me, who told me that a hogan is over here. I am encircling this hogan, but find no opening," she said. "So it happens that this is a hogan, is it yours perhaps?" she said. "Over night perhaps the water will be down, then I will return," she said to him. "In any event, you cannot cross," he told her. "I presume there is no hogan here as they said," he said. He was speaking as he lay prone on the ground. "Where else can I spend the night? I set out thinking that here I would spend the night," she said. "I see!" he replied. Then he got up, and she saw that there was a hole of [his] size. A ladder extended out of it. And when he had stepped away from it she went down. There she found a beautiful place, similar to sand smoothed out. And after the two

---

[94] "It is assumed that the bird of this name is *drawn on by rain* but is not indigenous to the Navaho country. The late . . . stick dice gambler described it as having red eyes, medium sized tail like a road-runner, glittering plumage like a peacock. . . . The *pheasant* may be meant" (Haile, 1950, p. 152).

had entered, they sat talking of various things. "The one whom you met first, after you started out this way, is called Striped Rock Squirrel," he told her. "The one who came to you farther on is called Chipmunk," he told her. "The one who again met you when you proceeded farther is called White Pine Squirrel," he told her. "The one who met you still farther on again is called Black Pine Squirrel," he said to her. "The one whom you met again still farther on is called the Ground Squirrel," he told her. "Their prayersticks are five all told. The stick of Striped Rock Squirrel is colored white, the stick of Chipmunk is yellow, the stick of White Pine Squirrel blue, next, the stick of Black Pine Squirrel is black, Ground Squirrel's stick is gray," he explained to her. "So they are without a doubt! This is a terrible condition, when coughing is a disease at large," he explained. "Therefore, if a person desire that they [prayersticks] be cut in the course of a ceremonial [chant], these are the first ones [to be cut]. From there on [any] cutting may be done. That is the situation, remember that!" he said to her.

"And the one whom you met, when you proceeded still farther on, is called Weasel," he told her. "The one who ran out the very first is called White Weasel," he explained. "Next a yellow one, that is called Yellow Weasel," he explained. "Next a blue one, which is called Blue Weasel, then a dark one, as a last one, that is called Dark Weasel and he is their leader," he explained. "The stick of White Weasel is white, the yellow one has a yellow prayerstick," he explained. "Next, the blue one has a blue stick, the dark one a dark stick," he told her. "Following, there is a spotted one. That is the stick of Spotted Weasel," he said. "This disease is very dangerous and affects a person in this manner," he explained. "Whenever it dries up a person in disease, remember that these [weasels] are doing it. Whenever earth surface people suffer [in this manner], let these [prayersticks] be cut for them," he explained. "And concerning the one to whom you came again in the Burrow-lying-place home, he is called He-lies-in-a-burrow," he told her. "His prayerstick is dark, while his female's stick is blue," he said. "On the summit of this mountain some also live," he said. [She went up above and, after she reached the top, she walked on some distance. As she walked along, she heard voices and stopped. And when she started out again, she heard the voices also, setting up a great noise. She walked on quite slowly, then sat down, and learned that Turkeys were giving their calls.][95] "Those Turkeys upon which you came

---

[95] These bracketed sentences seem out of place because the informant apparently forgot that Meal Sprinkler was still explaining matters to the woman.

there also have prayersticks," he told her. "The stick of the [gobbler]
is dark, that of the female blue, so it is," he said. Then she also met
the Mountain Sheep. "They are called Mountain Sheep, one of
them also has a dark stick, that of the female is blue," he said. From
there she went to the summit. "The one, of whom you mentioned
that he came to you, is evidently the Sun," he told her. "His stick
is blue, while that of the Moon is white," he said.

So, it seems, that happened. "Be sure that earth surface people
will use them in days to come, therefore I am informing you," he
said. "How is it, don't you ever eat here at home? I am just dying of
hunger," she said. "There is no food, why should there be when I
am at home alone?" he said. But then, it seems, he went into the
rear room and brought some out in a dish, chokecherries, sumac
berries, and fruits of all bushes, which appeared to have ripened
quite recently. She then ate. It became quite dark as they sat con-
versing with one another. "It is time we should sleep," he said.
And the two lay down separately, they slept on grass-woven mats.
Then it seems she slept, but some time during the night he crawled
under her cover, he crawled under the woman's cover. So it happened and daylight appeared. 'Now then I shall set out to return,'
she thought. And he accompanied her outside, and some distance
away, the two sat down. "When will you be around here again?" he
asked her. "I do not know definitely," she said. "You and I will
cross over there again," she said to him. "That stream is not to be
trifled with," he said to her. "The stream flows with Holy Young
Man," he said, "it flows with Holy Woman, it flows with magpie
tail feathers," he told her.[96] Then she left with him, and the two
came to the edge of the stream. He then produced a basket and tail
feathered arrow. "I will give you just a little information about it,"
he told her. "And over there you are going toward it.[97] After you
set out again the sandpainting will also be told to you." She stood
on the small basket, in which a pair of talking prayersticks lay. And
then he blew her across. There, on the other side, it landed with
her. "Release it to me here on this side," which she did, she blew
it towards him. Then he pointed to the hill and said to her, "Bad
people dwell there, do not go there by any means!"

Now finally she started out. As she walked along, the thought
struck her, "Why, I wonder, did he say that, I will go there," she

---

[96] The informant explained that Holy Young Man and Holy Woman would move
with feathers of the magpie and red-tailed hawk in the stream. Here they would grab
people and drown them, but Father Berard doubted this interpretation.

[97] It is not clear what she is approaching over there.

thought. So she started that way. When she reached it, there was a great noise within the said mountain. Then a cloud formed above her, and the said cloud hovered over the ground, and lightning struck near her. And it chased her thus [sunwise], and repeatedly struck near her, wherever she walked. Here she stopped and stood a while. It happened to be the home of White Thunder. The Rain Weasel again came to her. "That is the home of White Thunder, to which approach is forbidden," he told her. Then she started out again, and a pain struck her ankle, and haltingly she moved on. She was then returning towards her brother's home, but walked along haltingly, she walked along with difficulty and on fours along the top of the hills. It was well at sunset when she returned with difficulty at her brother's home. When she returned there, they again prepared food and ate. "You certainly are the limit to be our sister who goes around aimlessly!" he said to her. "Tell us your story," he said, but she refused, saying that she was in pain. After that had occurred, they paid no attention to her all night, and were angry with her on that account. "Did we not tell you to stay quietly at home when we two left?" But it seems she spent the night in that condition, she lay there with swollen ankles and wrists. But in the same manner, too, the night passed without them paying any attention to her. Again, daylight appeared each of four days without paying any attention to her. The two occupied themselves only with tanning and soaking hides in water. After another sunset they again spent the night there, so that five nights had passed.

The oldest of the men left as soon as they had eaten. He was now thoroughly angry with her. But the one, who had remained there, went to her. "What shall be done about our younger sister, my older brother, shall we leave her in this condition?" he said to him. "But what can we two do for her, we know nothing of this, perhaps she knows," he replied. So the one who had walked out second returned, then finally spoke [to her], "What shall be done, my younger sister? The manner in which this is to be done by a person is not known to us," he said to her. "I suppose you ought to treat me again in the same manner as you two did the first time," she said. Then he returned to his older brother. "All right then, you dig the trench in the east, while I break off tree branches," he said. After that had occurred, he dug a trench and laid the branches in it for her. Then again they plucked [branches] of pinyon, juniper, spruce [Douglas fir], rock sage, estafiata, snakeweed, grama grass, chokecherry, service-berry, orange gooseberry, wild currant, willow, buck-brush. All of these should be pounded up. They did this and pounded them fine. They then started the fire burning, then placed all the branches there. When they told her to come, she failed in her effort, she was unable to rise. So then the two went inside, where they placed a real buckskin on the ground and put her upon it. In this fabric they then carried her over there. Then they laid her upon the branches and covered her. She lay there for some time. And, "It is a long time till evening," he said to her.[98] Then they bathed her, having pounded the said herbs with a stone. But she failed in her effort to rise. Then again they spread the buckskin and placed her upon it, then carried her inside with it. There they prepared food again and ate. He put some in her mouth, but she failed [to swallow it]. While she remained in this shape, they went to sleep again.

On the following morning they repeated the same, they dug a trench for her in the west. "This time you gather the herbs, while I shall break off only three [kinds of] branches. But gather all [the rest], they are not far away," he said. "So get them all." He gathered them all and brought the various bundles of herbs. Then they placed them in position and the two went over there to get her. They entered inside and brought her out in a blanket again. Here they placed her on the branches, then covered her. They left her lying there until the sun was low down on the horizon. Then they brought the dish with herbs to her and she bathed herself with it. She now arose with difficulty, then set out for the hogan, entered there, and the two brothers followed her. It was then about sunset. When dusk set in they retired. At daylight they took a bite to eat again and after they had eaten the meal, they again dug a trench in the south. They built a fire again just as they had done in the first instance. After the fire was burnt up they laid the branches, all of which they had brought as before. And when they bid her come, she walked over there [unassisted]. She arrived there, they covered her up, then the two sat there for quite a time. After that they again gave her the herb dish, with which she bathed herself. "Now for home," she said. After she entered, the two followed her inside. At daylight you shall repeat the same treatment for me," she said.

At daylight they prepared food again, then he opened up a trench for her at the north. "I shall break off the branches," the older said. When that was done the fire was kindled. Then they again brought

---

[98] It seems the older brother is speaking, but his remark, "It is a long time till evening," seems out of place, unless he intends to keep her in the pit sudatory until dusk.

bundles of pinyon, juniper, spruce, rock sage, estafiata, snakeweed, grama grass, chokecherry, service-berry, orange gooseberry, buckbrush, willow, and cat-tail flag, this number had again been secured and laid in position for her. And when they called her, she again came over. When she arrived there, she removed her garments and he told her to lie down. She lay down there, they covered her, and she remained lying there for some time. Then again they put herbs in water for her. "Now remove the cover from me," she said. So they put the blankets aside. Now then she bathed herself all over with the medicine and then left for the hogan. She returned to the hogan, and it developed that her swellings had all been reduced. Then, apparently she sat there [unoccupied] and when he told her to do some tanning, she began to tan hides. Then it seems they again went out hunting on the mountain side. Possibly three nights after that, she ran away again. "Which homes did you visit again?" he asked her [after her return]. She had run over the ridge, then on farther again. "There were four of your footprints, but from there where did you go?" "From Slim Water Canyon [Mancos River] to the center of the mountain, where something or other was running around." She had reference to the Striped Rock Squirrel and Chipmunk. "I received information on five prayersticks," she said. So that happened. Then she merely mentioned the sticks to them, the Squirrel sticks. "Further on, of the Weasel sticks there are five again," she said. "Farther on is the Burrow-place, where two were mentioned to me. Then on the summit again the Turkeys were found," she said.

"It so happened that they also had two sticks, a dark and a blue one. Farther on the Mountain Sheep were roaming at the rim, and they had two sticks, one dark the other blue. And I left there again and went to the rim towards the east, where I sat down. But here someone came to me again, who happened to be the Sun. And one of his sticks is blue, the other white belonging to Moon. 'Your particular thought of going to the east, must not be,' he told me. 'It is a long distance, so go along the sunny south and stay along this neighborhood,' he told me," she said. "Then I set out to return, as I wanted to return to my brothers' home. From there I left to return here," she said. "And there were many small canyons among which I walked, and when I was returning in this direction, I was confronted by water [a river]," she said. "Here someone came out to me and said, 'This stream here is called It-lies-across [natural stone bridge]. On that side there is a hogan, that hill yonder is a hogan, you will find,' he said. Then I went over there.'" "Who was it that came to tell you this?" her brother asked her. "I learned that this was the Rain Weasel speaking," she said. "So I went to that hogan, but merely encircled it, as there was no opening to it," she said. "Suddenly someone spoke above me. 'Come up here,' he told me, and when I went up there I found him lying face down. I spent the night inside. It was a beautiful home, a home much like sand raked together [smoothly]," she said. "Here he enumerated the prayersticks to me which I had obtained at the various points I had visited. In future days earth surface people will make use of the sticks which he enumerated to me. Inside there I spent the night," she said.

"At daylight of the next day he accompanied me to the river shore. Here he produced a small basket from his garment, also a tail feathered arrow and a talking prayerstick. Then he blew it with me across to other shore. 'This is called the bridge, a sandpainting exists of it,' he told me.[99] Then it landed me on the other side. 'Send it back to me,' he told me. This I did, I blew [the basket] towards him and it floated back to him. Then I started out again, but he called to me over there. When I looked back that former stream had disappeared. 'Where has that water flown,' I wondered as I stood there. I then went back to the rim, where I discovered that far down below a very slim stream flowed, which looked much like a thin line drawn by somebody. From his side of the stream he again said to me, 'Do not go to that hill over there, evil people live there,' he said. I thought then of going down the valley, but I turned back. I thought to myself, 'I wonder who they are of whom he said this.' So I went there," she said. "There was a rumbling noise within the mountain, and above me a cloud had formed. A thick massive cloud hovered along the ground, and lightning struck next to me. A second time lightning struck nearby, then I ran away as fast as I could, but again and a fourth time lightning struck nearby me. Then I ran back along the route I had just come and stood for a while breathing heavily. I discovered then that this was the home of White Thunder. From there I started for home and now I returned here. So it happened just as I have related it," she said.

After they had suggested to her to tan hides, she busied herself with tanning, and probably was solely occupied with this for three days. "We two are going around over yonder to hunt, we may kill another fawn," [he said]. About the same time she had again left, and when they returned at sunset they found her gone again. "She

---

[99] The informant refused to tell the details of the sandpainting of "the Bridge."

certainly is a great one, who knows when she will return this time!"
he remarked. So that happened, but they had not bagged one. And
when she had left, they were unconcerned about her. "Let her
alone, she goes as she pleases anyway," the younger brother remarked. The Wide Chokecherry Patch is a big bulk of a mountain
and here, as they learned afterwards, she had gone along its sunny
side, then passed over it to the shady side of the mountain and
farther on. "Around here is the home of him [Bear Man] from whom
you are fleeing," Big Fly again told her. "For goodness sake," she
thought as she continued on and on. She surely was making good
time before the sun set. Meanwhile he [Bear Man] was following
her tracks. Looking back after she reached the summit, she saw him
following her. Walking along the slope of Big Sheep [Hesperus
Peak], she almost had reached the summit when some unknown
woman confronted her. "From where did you come running along,
my grandchild?" she asked her. "Inside of this is my home," she
said. "What is chasing you to bring you here?" she asked. "It is
Bear Man that is chasing me along," she replied. She entered inside,
into the home of the other, but stood still thinking that he might
come in to them. "He really fears me, my grandchild," she [the
unknown woman] said, and with that produced something or other
of woven spruce [Douglas fir; fir garment]. "This is what he really
fears," she said. "Lie down here," she told her, then nicely rolled
her sunwise up in it. She [Older Sister] was looking through the
woven spruce and saw him enter yonder. At the same instant he
fell backwards and continued rolling on and on, and finally ran
away. Now she unwound it from her and said, "He is gone, get up,
my grandchild!"

She spent that night in her home. "What I have here made earth
surface people [the Navajo] shall make," she [the unknown woman]
said. "Of this alone he is much in dread. You shall do it as I have
directed," she said. When daylight appeared, she [Older Sister]
asked her, "What is your food, my grandmother?" And when she
reached aside, she brought out a dish of chokecherry slap cakes.
These she found very tasty and sat there munching them. After she
had finished eating, the other put down four medicines of which
one happened to be jet black, another blue, another yellow, another
white. "This one is called sparkling medicine, this one is called
cold medicine," she said. So there were six all told. "This jet black
medicine shall belong to the earth surface people [the Navajo],
also this blue one, and the yellow one, and the white one, and the
sparkling one, and also the cold medicine. These ground together

shall be your medicine" she said. "Also all berries, the chokecherry, orange gooseberry, service-berry, wild currant, also the hackberry and juniper.[100] These also, ground up, shall be your medicine," she said. In this manner she informed her of the medicines. "But what about this thing in which you put me, what is it?" she [Older Sister] asked her. "It is called fir garment, my grandchild," she told her. "But what are you that you say these things, my grandmother?" she asked her. "The White-circle-of-teeth-woman they call me. With these things earth surface people shall perform ceremonially in future days, that is their purpose," she said. Then she tied the medicines given to her on herself and left to set out again. When she reached the summit, she noticed a long row, which she discovered were small black ants. Coming to them, she just stood there looking at them as they ran back and forth. Some time elapsed before the line was opened and she could then pass through it. Next she also met a column of red-headed black ants which also were running back and forth, but finally set out again, only to be stopped by very large jet black ants. And when their line opened up, she again passed on through them. Nothing else happened, but all of these have their sticks, which are completely jet black.

Then she continued on again, but two strangers came from the side to meet her. One of these was black with a white striped spine and sides, Big Skunk, the other was spotted and the female, called Spotted Skunk. And these passed alongside of her because, as is well known, their urine is malodorous if they urinate on something. "Their prayerstick too, is jet black spotted with white dots," he said.[101] And when she set out again to journey on, something or other ran up to her. It happened to be gray, with forearms and lower legs black, a black stripe on its breast, its front arm blackish, and it is called Marmot. "It also has a prayerstick which is jet black," he said, the other [the female] is white [the prayerstick]. It is known that they live down there, go around this way," he told her. Then she set out to go right along the side, that is, the sunny side of [the mountain]. And again she was walking along, and found the mountain side very thick with underbrush. Evidently they [bears] had been there quite recently and had been

---

[100] The Navajo word translated here as "juniper" means "which starts to pop" and refers to a juniper-like bush or tree found in southern Arizona. Apparently it does not grow in the Navajo country. Its Navajo name refers to the fact that in the heat its bark pops off and covers the ground roundabout (Haile, 1950, p. 89).

[101] The informant did not say who "he" is, but possibly Big Fly was still instructing her.

leading their cubs. "This place is called Shrubbery," he told her. Trails from all sides led into it. "Walk into it, my grandchild," he told her. When she entered, darkness settled, it got so that she could not see, the thicket was filled with quaking aspen, spruce [Douglas fir], ponderosa pine, and Rocky Mountain juniper. They went into the rear of the room with her, where she discovered it to be the home of Holy Woman and Holy Young Man.[102] Right here she spent the night. They say it was a fine home, the openings were closed with rock mica similar to the windows here. "What did you come for, my grandchild?" she [Holy Woman] asked. "I just came around here for no particular purpose," she replied. "Who is the cause for your going about in this manner? Earth surface people are not allowed here," she said to her. "I have no particular purpose in coming, my grandmother, I just wanted to know how conditions are, therefore I came," she said. So she again spent a night in their home.[103] "As for us, our prayersticks are this size of the outstretched fingers, thumb and index finger stretched out. One is jet black, the other blue. At sometime or other earth surface people shall make use of it," she told her.

So it happened that she spent the night there and in the morning again journeyed out. And as she again walked along she came to a hill which, small though it was, was called Where-bear-squats. She sat down on the top of this hill, from where she looked out over the valley. And she sat there looking out over Jet Black Mountain, over Black Mountain and yonder out over Red Mountain, wondering how conditions might be there. Then she started out again from there, and continued to walk on until she reached the place again, which is called Striped Rock. By that time it was sunset and she learned that this was a home where many people, Bear People, were gathered. She remained standing some distance away. "Come in, my grandchild," an unknown said, and she went in. They walked about in human form. The woman led her to the rear room and she followed her. There she sat down with her. "From where did you come to be here?" she asked her. "I am running [away] from somebody," she replied. "Who is it that is chasing you?" she asked.

---

[102] The informant was not explicit here, but the context implies that the she-bear and her cubs led Older Sister into this home. Some of the songs of Female Mountainway mention a Holy Woman who is different from Holy Young Woman. At times the Holy Young Man, Holy Woman, and Holy Young Woman seem to be identified with the bear.

[103] "She again spent a night" does not mean that this was her second night in the bear home. The informant was merely repeating himself.

"Bear Man himself," she replied. "Oh, that is the man from here, the man from Wide Chokecherry Patch who travels back and forth. Evidently then, you are our daughter-in-law, I see," she told her. So it was sunset then. "For what did you come here? Those that are quite to be feared travel in this vicinity," she said. She lay down to sleep with the women and children only, while the others remained outside. She discovered that this woman was their chief, therefore they feared her. When darkness set in, she [Bear Woman] scratched around there a while, then set a dish of food before her [Older Sister]. To her surprise she discovered that she owned berries, and that she had placed before her tree pollen and cat-tail flag pollen. "Do you, by any chance, eat this?" she asked. "Certainly I eat it," she replied. She ate. "The fact is, that the purpose [to secure prayersticks?] for which you came will be of use to earth surface people," [Bear Woman said].

When daylight appeared, the voices of many speakers were heard outside, they spoke to each other like humans. "Now then you may set out to return, your home is over there," she [Bear Woman] told her. Then it seems she [Older Sister] left to return, and this time she returned in good health, she returned without feeling any pains. It happened to be afternoon when she returned, and her two brothers returned later in the evening. "Where have you been again, my younger sister?" "I was just around in places," she told him. Then she prepared the food, the woman herself who had just returned prepared it. They ate and it was evident that they had bagged game. "Tell us your story," he [her brother] said to her. Then she told her story from the time that she had left. "I went this way in a sunwise circle," she said, then told them of the various places she had visited. "So now I have returned," she said. On the following day they spent the day walking around the hill till sunset. Another night passed. Four times she spiralled sunwise around on the side of Big Sheep. And they stayed another day right at home.[104] "Let us go to the top of Wide Chokecherry," he said after this had occurred. Then they began to pack their bundles over there, then went up the mountain. As they were occupied with this and that, the woman busied herself with the berries left here and there. Then the men went back for their baggage and packed this in at sunset. And at sunset they again prepared food. The two men were always busy

---

[104] The point which the informant wished to make here is that the brothers and their sister spent two days at home, during which time the woman had gone up the side of Big Sheep (Hesperus Peak in the La Plata Range, Colorado), describing a sunwise spiral circle as she did so. Just why, he did not say.

with the chase, and they all spent four nights in this place. Small streams flowed close to each other, [and] some of these were springs. That being so he said to his brother, "Let us go hunting again," and to his sister, "Stay quietly at home, do not go around anywhere," he told her. But after the two had gone, she would go to various points extending out and sit up there. [On the top of Blackrock there was a flat tableland, and there they lived.]

So it seems she would visit these points, then return to the hogan again. They spent ten nights in that vicinity and had moved into a circular recess with a single entrance. From here the two had again left hoping to find one or other mountain sheep. The two ran upon one, which would pass back and forth nearby. Telling his brother to stay behind, he again ran off to [follow and] head it off. Thus, trying to head it off the two brothers met again, while it ran off yonder toward the Blackrock. There, without checking its speed, it jumped from the cliff. The two went up there, thinking that most probably it had died. But when they reached the rim it was walking away from the rim. "How is this possible," he thought, "that anyone should fall from such a distance unhurt!" The two then did nothing more at the time but leave and return yonder to their home. It was then late in the afternoon. She had been occupied with various things till sunset, and had made a basket, she had made a basket of *Parryella*. The sewing of another had also been begun and lay there. "That is as it should be, my younger sister, you should be busy with various things!" he said. So she had made two of them. "We two are leaving again along the trail of that mountain sheep, it may be lying somewhere!" he said. So the two left and proceeded to the spot. When they reached it, they found a large hole in the ground, where it had left the imprint of its horns. Thus they stood there looking up and trying to figure it out. Although the rock bluff ran along there, the hole in the ground was far out of line with the bluff. But where can it go they thought as they set out to follow it. And when they followed it, they found that it had gone in a straight line. In time it had started to run towards the Black-down-streak-mountain [Sleeping Ute Mountain, Colorado]. So they gave up the chase and started to return home. They did return from there and late in the evening they went to the top and got home. "It got away from us," they remarked upon their return. When they ate it was sunset and then they slept all night.

On the following morning they arose again. "We two are going down and make a circle this way [sunwise]. Somewhere there may be one. You stay here nicely, my younger sister," he again said to her. "You may get lost, this is thick underbrush to all appearances, although the place is small," he said to her. She made a small earthen bowl of mud and also a small ladle with a handle extending from it. Meanwhile the two left and went down the cliff. When they had gone sunwise around it they just got a glimpse of one running along, and again they took after it. It again ran in the direction of Slim Water Canyon, and again they gave up and turned back. Just yonder, when they got half way up the mountain, darkness overtook them, but they continued on from there and returned to the hogan. They came up to the entrance trail, but inside the hogan it was pitch dark and she was gone. They made a fire, but still nobody was there and their search was useless. "She certainly is a great one!" he remarked. Some distance away there was a spring, where she was accustomed to go back and forth for water. So the two went out wondering which way she had gone. But they went this way, sunwise as usual, and walked in a circle right along the rim. Tracking, however, was impossible due to the high grass. And the next morning the two set out again. They again went around, but made the circle shorter than where they had gone the evening before. At sunset they returned home. "I wonder which way she went! Maybe she is not here," they remarked as they sat there. She would sleep on that side, the south side, while opposite her, in the north side the two men were accustomed to lie down. "We should have various articles here, search around my younger brother," he said to him. But when he felt around he found them in their places. "I wonder what this means, my younger brother!" he said. "Evidently the waterjug also is gone, with which she used to fetch water. The ladle, too, is gone! She may be right around here!" he said. "Suppose you take a look at the spring!" he said.

When he arrived there she lay prone some distance away, the waterjug was completely shattered, he saw, and she lay there motionless, just able to wink. "What has happened to you, my younger sister," he said to her, but she did not answer. Four times he tried to speak to her, but she failed to answer. Then he returned to the hogan to report that she lay at the spring. "I see, wonder what she has done again!" he said. "Although she lies there continually winking, she did not speak to me," he said. Then the two proceeded over there and after he failed to get her to speak, he stood facing her. He spread out a buckskin on which they laid her, then carried her back in this fabric. And wherever they got tired they let her down on the ground. Then they would pick her up in the buckskin and carry her along again for a stretch, then let her down on the ground again; she was terribly heavy. After they took another rest they would carry her along and let her down again, then stand and get their breath. Then they carried her on again and let her down at the entrance. From here they carried her inside, but it proved useless to ask her what had happened to her, she made no reply. It was late evening then and they prepared food for themselves. "Do you want to eat something perhaps?" he asked, and she then shook her head in consent. So he poured broth into her mouth. Still she could not move. "What can be done!" the brothers wondered as they sat there. "We will treat you again as we treated you the other time?" he said to her, and she then shook her head in consent. So they did this for her, her younger brother dug the trench, while he offered to break the limbs for her.

He dug the trench on the east side, he brought the fuel again, and the pinyon [and other] branches. Following the same order as they had previously done to her, they now proceeded with her. They applied the full numbers of herbs to her; rock sage, estafiata, snakeweed, grama grass, chokecherry, service-berry, orange gooseberry, wild currant, buck-brush, willow, cat-tail flag, all these were again secured in bundles. Then they laid these down for her again, laid her on them, then covered her up. She lay thus for a considerable time. "Is that sufficient?" he asked her. Then she shook her head in consent, but could not speak to them. After some time they removed the covers from her and carried her inside again in the buckskin. Then they just sat around, the two sitting, she lying there. On the following morning they repeated the same on the west side, then on the south and north sides, with a night intervening each time, as it was not done in a single day but on each of three days. But now she had given up food, she would not eat. "What can be done now? This is as much as we can do, we have done everything known to us, but it has no effect whatsoever," they said as they sat there. So they sat with her doing nothing else. At midday they were again seated facing each other, when they heard a voice at the smokehole. "You ought to have a fire ceremony for her," Big Fly told them. This again they did on the following morning. They went around breaking very slim twigs. This time fire was drilled, and this they used for the fire ceremony. They set fire to the stack, and in a very short time the fuel which they had brought in was gone. They raised the door curtain and carried her out in the blanket, she was covered with sweat. On the following morning they repeated, and on the next two days, making it four times again. This too failed, not once did it take effect on her. So it happened, and the number was completed again.

"I wonder who is causing this, my younger brother?" he said to him. "Ordinarily one can learn a thing [by speaking to a person], but if a person does not speak to another [how can one know?]," he said. "Do notify the people near Red Mountain, so that they may discuss the matter for us. Whoever can be secured, let them come to us," he said. At sunset some came with him, there were quite a number with whom he returned. After that had happened, they discussed the matter. "Nothing is known about that, absolutely nothing," they were saying. "About her journeys, when she first left at the time and went along the river and from there returned to the Hogback and then came to Slim Water Canyon and traveled around there, nobody has definite knowledge. It appears, however, that she must have traveled about in the tracks of some wicked thing," some were saying, and they discussed nothing else all night long. And although it was still night, they set out to return, saying, "tomorrow at sunset we will come again." It happened that the sun set and daylight appeared. On the following day, when they returned at sunset, quite a number had come. So here again they discussed the matter. Thus it happened that they met again. "The fact is, that absolutely nothing definite is known about it," they said. "About the time when she sat up at Slim Water Canyon nothing is definitely known," they said. "Possibly something or other may have been told to you two." So they [the brothers] repeated to them the incident from the beginning when the accident had befallen her, and told what action they had taken, but that they had failed in their efforts. "This is pretty difficult, since she has been roaming among various people," they [the people] said. That done they set out to return home in the night. But while these people were passing along somewhere one was heard to say, "The two things that were lying at the spring, they are the ones that did this to her," they heard said. "Who said that?" they were inquiring of one another, but with no result, so that they came back again. "Who of you spoke there?" they asked. "We are now going home, but this coming sunset we shall return to see who said that," [they decided]. At daylight [of that day] they again returned [at sunset]. And as soon as they had all arrived they said to them, "I suppose you are all here now?" "Yes, we are all here," they said. Then again they discussed that same point. "What can be done? Absolutely nothing is known about it! Evidently there is no manner of getting this knowledge," they said.

It appears that those that were discussing this reached no conclusion, and by that time it was midnight. "We may as well go home now as there is no means of getting at the facts. So let us leave now

to return home, at daylight we shall come back again," [they said].
At sunset of that [next] day they came back again. "But who was
speaking the night before last?" [they said]. So that happened.
They [the brothers] again related to them who had come here about
all the places which she had visited. "This is certainly a difficult
situation, she has visited places that were forbidden to be visited."
So again they failed to reach a decision. "Well, nobody knows, we
will go home now," they said. So the crowd left and started for
home. "Suppose the two of you step outside!" her brothers were
told. "Stand right here!" they were told. Stepping outside, one
at either side of the entrance, they held a blanket between them as
the people were passing out. All had presumably passed out, when
suddenly the elder brother felt something moving in his armpit.
And when the two returned inside he said. "It appears that he has
been found, come in again," he told them. So again they came
inside. And he sat there as he had come inside, with his arms
pressed together [against his body]. When they had all re-entered
he reached under his arm, and there under his armpit he was sitting.
This happened to be the Bat. "From the farther side of the spring
she is being injured," he said. "Who is doing this injury to her?"
they asked. "Beyond that spring is the home of Big Snake and Toad.
They are the cause of her injury, my grandchildren. And although
she visited various places, these visits have nothing to do with
her present condition," he said. "Big Snake shot her in her sole,
while Toad shot her in her kneecap. Big Snake shot her in the hip,
while Toad dispatched his arrow into the back of her head. This
they did to her," he said. "This is all I have to tell," he said. "Why
did you not tell us this long ago, instead of allowing us to lose sleep
over it! But what should be done in this case?" [they asked]. "That
is as far as my knowledge goes, beyond that I do not know, my
grandchildren," he said.

   Then it seems they dispersed [even] in the night. And as they
began to return home, he [the brother] said to them, "Regardless of
the things told, you must continue to look us up [secure help by
means of a ceremonial], her condition is terrible." Now, she was
dried out, she was nothing but bones, her former flesh was gone,
she was dried out. "I wonder what she can swallow? There is nothing that she can eat," he remarked. After that had occurred they
dispersed, and the three merely sat around till sunset. And in this
condition she remained two nights, and when they would offer to
put broth into her mouth, she would turn her head away. "What
can be done," they wondered. A dish with slim-grass [drop-seed]

seed broth stood there, so they offered her this. Just then it was
noon, and a voice spoke at the smokehole. "What are you two doing,
my grandchildren?" it said. "It is just this, that we are busy with our
sister who is very sick," he replied. "I see!" it said. "Those two
elders at the spring put shots into her," Big Fly said. "I am just on
my way home. This is all I am going to tell you. They scold me
much, I fear them," he said. "I wonder where their home is, of
whom he spoke. You will search around there, my younger brother!"
he [older brother] said to him. At once he set out in that direction.
After a long while he returned saying, "There is nothing, you cannot
tell, I tried, but found nothing. So another night passed with conditions unchanged. "Go ahead, search again over there!" he [older
brother] told him the next morning. It was a very long time before
he again returned. "You certainly cannot recognize anything, who
knows what kind of home they have," he said. Another night
passed. "Suppose you go there again. Search closely by opening
the grass there!" he told him. So again he set out and after a long
time in the afternoon, he returned. "There is nothing at all, I tried
hard," he said. And again the sun set and another night passed. At
noon on the following day they were again seated facing each other
and feeding her corn gravy [or] slim-grass seed broth, when that
voice was heard again at the smokehole. "Why do you search for their
home beyond it?" it said to them. "Don't you know that grass covered hill beyond the spring? That is their home," it [Big Fly] said.

Then it seems the older one set out for it and went straight to it.
He encircled it, but failed four times to find anything. Returning
along the east side of it he was looking at it, when suddenly the
grass raised up and a young toad ran out of it. Without flopping it
sat there, but as soon as he made a move, it dashed inside. "Some
strange earth surface man is standing out there, my father," it said.
When that had happened he walked toward it and stood at the open
hole. "Come in here, my grandchild, the opening is large," he
[Toad Man] said. So he started to go down. It opened sufficiently
and he entered inside and sat down along the side. There he noticed
that the two lay opposite each other, the Big Snake lay on the north
side, Toad Man lay on the south side. "For what did you come, my
grandchild? Don't you know that earth surface man is not allowed
here?" Toad Man said to him. "That is so, but I am on my way
looking for help, my granduncle. My sister is pretty sick," he said.
"We two certainly do not know anything, what should we two know
sitting here!" he replied. So he left to return and entered over
there again. "Their home is near, but I found that you went beyond

it!" he told [his brother]. Then added, "I wonder what they desire, my younger brother? Go over there to them with fawn skins, two for the one, and two for the other." So he went there to them and entered their home. He placed two of them on the tip of Big Snake's foot, then did the same to Toad. They did not take a look at them. "What would the two of us know, we live here without much knowledge of anything," he [Toad Man] told him. So it seems he just brought them back. "They have no desire for them," he said when he returned. That sunset the two sat at home discussing the matter. "Wonder what they want," they were saying as they sat there.

On the following morning he went to them again and did as he had done before, he placed the fabrics on the tips of their feet. They just kicked them aside and would not even look at them. "We two told you that we know nothing!" he said. So he merely set out to return home. "They do not want them at all, what kind of old things are they anyway!" he said. Another night passed, so that four nights had passed. "What kind of confounded old things are those two lying in there! Let them lie where they are!" the elder remarked. "Once more we will try again, my older brother!" the younger said. "All right, you go there again, I shall not go!" he said. This time he packed four bundles to them, for each of them four. These he placed on the top of their feet, but they would not look at them. "What do you mean running here to us? We do not know a thing! Did we two not tell you this?" he said. Then he left for home and brought all bundles back. By that time the sun was high up when he returned home. "Those two are certainly mean things!" the elder brother said. It was then midday. "Are you really in a critical condition, my younger sister?" he said to her. But she just moved her head up and down. Just then they heard the voice again at the smokehole. Later they learned that the two usually slept at noon. "Why bother with goods? They are not worth them, the two are not worth anything [like that]!" he [Big Fly] said. "Cut prayersticks for them, for Big Snake cut a big reed, while for the Toad an ordinary reed" he [Big Fly] said. "These are both rubbed with chokecherry. One cut is made on [back of] the big reed, while the ordinary reed is white," he said. "You should make them sparkling with specular iron ore. You should make four fawn feet [on big reed], while the ordinary reed is speckled with jet black, blue, yellow and red spots. Make both of them pointed. Around the rim, at both ends, a blue and a red line is drawn. You must put down white shell, turquoise, jet jewels with it, and do likewise for the Toad stick."

"Upon what are these [placed]?" he asked him [Big Fly]. "Upon cornhusks," he said. "You must also bring specular iron ore, blue pollen, and tree pollen, and cat-tail flag pollen, and ordinary pollen, turkey down also and white [eagle] down, and bluebird wing feathers, and cotton cords, and turkey beard, that is all. You then roll two down feathers in a ball [for a stopper for the ends of the reed], and roll this in chokecherry juice," he said. "You must insert mountain tobacco into them," he said. So that happened. Then they prepared it nicely, with pollen shaken from a bluebird it was touched up. Meanwhile Big Fly had left to return, he returned without telling them details. "Have care not to tell on me, under no consideration must this be done, my grandchildren!" he said. Then it seems Big Fly returned and the other followed him bringing the prayersticks. He found the one lying on this side with legs crossed, his left leg resting on top. This leg he threw down on the ground, then placed the stick container on this foot. On that [Toad's] side he did likewise, but placed the [cornhusk] container on his right foot. Their looks were fastened on these places, and some time elapsed before they sat upright. Then he [Big Snake] looked at it, turned it around and removed the [down feather] stopper [to extract the tobacco] from the prayerstick. Then spreading out a fabric he placed the [tobacco] upon it, took the downy feather ball out of it, while he smelled the stick. "It is true, it is really my own," he said. "It is my prayerstick, I see. But you, Big Fly, are the one who directed this! Where are the places you do not visit for a purpose! You alone know my prayerstick, that I know," he said to him. "No, my granduncle, we ourselves did this, on our own initiative," [the messenger said]. "Well, over there the pouch is hanging outside, to be sure!" he [Big Snake] said. "Go around this [sunwise] way, as you pass by there take it along," he said. Over there he [the messenger] tried to find it along the trees that stood there, then returned inside. "It is not there, my granduncle!" he told him. "Why, of course it is hung there!" [Big Snake said]. But again he entered [without it]. "Why, of course it is hung there," he again said. Again he went outside, made the rounds, but again failed and re-entered. "It is not there, my granduncle!" he said. "Of course it hangs there, why do you run in here saying that?" he told him. Again he went along there, then returned inside. "It is absolutely not there, my granduncle!" "What are you saying, have you no sense at all running in here time and again?" he said. "I know it is up there! Take it with you, and be gone!" he said.

So that happened. Something black stood in one of the tree forks.

"Is that what you mean perhaps?" he [the messenger] said to him [Big Snake]. "Of course that is it! Pick it up and be gone with it!" he told him. "Let it be immediately, my granduncle, it [Older Sister's illness] is a pretty serious condition," he said. "In four days, to be sure!" he replied. "No, my granduncle, don't say that, let it be immediately," he said to him. "What can happen to her? She will very likely recover," he said. So he could not do anything with him, he continued to say in four nights [days]. "In four nights you must have a sandpainting waiting for me," he said. "At the center you must put a circle, strew a line across the center, the south side [half] white, the north half jet black. Four border lines are strewn around the circle, first blue, then red, then yellow, then white, thus four borders are strewn. Four reflected sunray [bars] are placed on it, in the south half two, in the north half also two. At the east two Big Snakes lie on the outlook [that is they look out towards the cardinal points]; they are zigzagged with four angles [as are all snakes in the painting]; their tails alone come together," [he said]. "On the west side too, there are two yellow snakes, while those in the east are white, the ones on the south side blue, those on the north side jet black," [he told him]. "On the south side a white one lies with its head sunwise, then a blue one again lies there, then a yellow one, and towards the north side a jet black one again lies [the four forming an encircling guardian around the painting]. And towards the north bear lies facing away from it [the center; walking towards the northeast]. And the pursued one lies [in the northwest quadrant] with her head toward the east, and towards her the Bear Man is walking [see Fig. 3]. Thus the sandpainting must be made as a rule," he instructed him. So it happened, I suppose, and he merely gave him these instructions. Here [in the brothers' home] a dish was brought [to contain the sands for the painting]. "Well, my younger brother, they will be a long time in coming, you had better spread the news among the people, so that they may make the sandpainting," he said.

So at daylight he left in the direction toward Red Mountain. "In two nights you may come over to help with the sandpainting," he told them. At sunset he returned, saying that they had promised to come after two nights. They themselves spent these two nights right at home taking care of her. After the two nights had passed, just three came. These also stayed with them here that night. At daylight they ground the stone [into powder], they ground white and red, black, blue and yellow, all told five kinds, as this was the day which had been set for them. Then it seems they busied themselves with the sandpainting and were occupied with it from noon on till sunset, when they had finished the sandpainting. After that they sat around until after dusk, but he [Big Snake] was not there, he had not yet come. Then, after some time they came, to wit, Big Snake, Toad, and Toad's children. Then Big Snake went over to the place where his pouch was and sat there. He put medicine in the water and foot liniment [chant lotion; see footnote 29], then he got up and looked at the sandpainting. "That is as it should be," he said. Many had filled the place. The Toad and his children sat at the doorway, although they had been invited to the rear of the room. Then it seems they carried her in a blanket upon the sandpainting. "Let it be a sign to all of you to shout out when I strike the basket," he [Big Snake] said. Then he began to sing and was singing with all his might. By that time it had twisted her around, her back was turned to her front. He finished quite a number of songs, but they did not yet know what had caused [this twisting]. Then he again beat the basket, the young toads and people were shouting with all their might [shock rite]. That done, he finished singing, and just put the medicine and foot liniment aside. Her hands and her feet were drawn together. "Put her back in shape, my grand-uncle!" he [the brother] said to him. "All right," he said. "Blanket this drawing out," he directed. They blanketed all of it outside.

All dishes which had previously been set aside [informant did not complete this statement]. Now finally he [Big Snake] said, "Lay her down here! Have you an unwounded buckskin perhaps?" [he asked]. "Is there perhaps a white cotton fabric?" he asked. "There is one here," they told him. "Spread it over her!" he said. Then he again intoned a song and made a four-angled mark on her east side. He then extracted his arrow out of her sole, then stepped aside and stood there. "What about you there?" he said to Toad. He, in turn, stood over her along the west side where he made a straight line, [then crossed it] at its tip. Out of her knee he extracted his [own] arrow. Again Big Snake stood along the south side, where he made a zigzag line, then extracted his arrow out of her hip. "You do it again," he told Toad. He [Toad] again made a straight line with a straight mark drawn across its tip. Then he extracted an arrow from the back of her head. "This zigzag one represents a zigzag lightning arrow," [Big Snake said]. "This straight line represents a flash lightning arrow," he explained. He then pressed her arms and legs and her trunk with a mountain sheep horn, and used the same for marking the lines away from her [that is both Big Snake and Toad used it]. Now finally she arose. "This [her sickness] is certainly a great condition!" the woman said, over whom the cere-mony had been performed. "What a relief!" she said. She then threw the white cotton fabric upon Toad Man and blew it [fast] upon him. For that reason, I suppose, the rough toad has a white garment. Meanwhile she was a pitiful sight, because she was [like] a standing stick, without even one particle of flesh on her. "Yes, it still requires time, it will be some time yet before you all are informed of the prayersticks." Time passed on till midnight as the two men alone performed. Then finally they gave her the medicine. "This now is the first night ceremony.[105] As for us, we are now leaving for home, what else can we do here?" Big Snake said. "You see she who is sitting here knows the songs," he said. They had just left, when someone crawled from the rear [room] and sat down along the fireplace. "I myself shall sing," he said, and this happened to be Bear Man, by whom she had been pursued. But here Wind said to him, "Refuse him!"

So her brother told him, "No, a person should not sing over his own wife," he [Wind] told him to say this. "Nonetheless I myself shall sing," he said. When they told him this, he ran outside and sat there. "Why are you doing this, man? Come inside again!" she said to him. But he did not as much as raise his head. So she returned inside. "He does not speak to me. I wonder what will happen if he acts in this manner!" she said. Then she again went out after him, but he was sitting farther on again, where he had made a dugout, around which he had walled himself in with stones. Inside of this he sat. "Why are you doing this, old man, come inside again!" she told him. Again her words failed with him, so she merely returned inside. "I failed to induce him, he does not speak to me," she said. "Wonder what his reason for doing this is!" She remained inside a while again, in fact, quite a long time elapsed. When she returned there his ears alone showed out of the hole. "What do you mean by doing this, old man? Return inside," she told him. Then she left him again and returned in the hogan. This made it the third time. A very long time passed again before she returned there, and found that he had crawled under a rock. He had uprooted two young spruce, and had planted them crosswise before his entrance. She remained standing where she was, she did not return to him this time, but went inside again. "What has the old man in mind doing this?" she said. And they just sat there. "What can be

---

[105] This statement is ambiguous. The sense seems to be that Big Snake told them to perform a one-night ceremonial immediately. Later in the text the brother refers to this command when he suggests the chant with the Dark Circle of Branches. It may be understood that Big Snake told Older Sister herself to sing, since she "knows the songs."

done? Let one of you take word to Talking God of Striped Rock, whatever he says is directive in this matter," she said.

"Who of you will go?" was asked. "Who shall it be? You, of course, you alone are fleet," he told the Wind. So he left and arrived over there, but found him asleep. "For what did you come my grandchild?" he asked. "It is merely that they are begging Bear Man, but cannot succeed. They are wondering what he means by doing this," he answered. "You may return now, I will be over there immediately" he told him. Just then there were faint signs of approaching dawn. "Does it require much time? I will be there," he said. The Wind returned saying that he had promised to come at once. Only a short time after that the call of Ye'i was heard. The same call was heard again, and another time. Quite close the call was heard again, he had arrived at the entrance, and now entered. "What is your purpose in calling me, my grandchildren?" he said. "We have had no success in begging the old man lying under the rock," she said. "Wonder why he acts that way?" he said. "Have you a basket?" he asked. "There is one, to be sure," she told him. "Let him lie there, I do not care to go back," Talking God said.[106] Then it seems he intoned a song to him and, at mention of a certain word, he would strike the basket. He finished that song. "Go and see him again," he said. When somebody went there, he found him making efforts to crawl along, because his feet were out of shape. "Something is wrong with him, he lies there with his feet turned around and out of shape," he reported. "Well, he is paralyzed," Talking God said. "As for me, I am setting out for home, my grandchild," Talking God, who had paralyzed him said. When he was about to leave they asked him, "What is to be done, my granduncle?" "Draw lines away from him after you have dragged him inside!" he told them. So two of them walked over there, but they tried and failed to do anything. And they took hold of his legs and dragged him along until they got him inside, where they left him. There they drew the lines away from him; I suppose the elder brother treated him.

That done they drew the lines away from him, then he got up, but his feet remained in that shape. Meanwhile the sun was well up. "My!" he said. "It is true, I see, that earth surface people have power! I used to consider everything my slave, I used to think of thunder, I used to think of all kinds of winds as slaves to me, and

---

[106] Bear probably said, "I do not care to go back," and Talking God repeated his words.

of the sky, and of the earth, and of darkness and of dawn, but I see that you on your side are powerful," he said. As soon as this had occurred they told him, "Now go and return wherever your home may be!" He started out dragging his arms and legs along, and outside he raised himself, then began to lope away awkwardly and with his legs flopping in every direction, he disappeared over the ridge. He left at the time never to return, his feet remained crooked, they were never straightened out for him, so that he still travels that way. Then she would just stay at home, while they would prepare food for her. And they stayed at home without doing anything in particular. Probably ten nights had passed, in which she had not been doing anything else than walk around in places, getting more emaciated right along. About that time the elder brother remarked again, "We were told about a one-night chant," meaning that Big Snake had told them this previously. "He referred to the Dark Bough Circle," he said. "But in that event who will do the singing? There is no singer," he said. "Do that yourself, you must direct it," Wind told her. "All right!" she said. "You see, those songs that were sung for you when you reached the top of the Hogback are used here. There is a sandpainting for the place previously called Whirling Babes.[107] Their sandpainting is first, these figures are laid down in the painting," [he said]. "Then wherever you set out again and heard other songs [these are used]. At the place called the Bridge, where the Meal Sprinkler mentioned a sandpainting there are fifteen songs to be sung on this painting. Do you happen to know them?" he asked her. "I know them quite [well]," she said.

"There is also a sandpainting at the place called Striped Rock," [Wind told her].[108] "Those of Red Mountain, although you did not go there, also have a painting," [he said]. "There is also a painting of the place called Young Spruce Round Hill" [he said]. "Now that is all [to be used]," he said. After this had occurred she walked around in that neighborhood only. "The songs of the incidents at Slim Water Canyon shall be employed in the fire ceremony. The songs, descriptive of how Changing Bear Maiden swallowed her

[107] The informant could not give any details concerning this painting. He said, "It is just told in legend." He asked to be allowed to reserve the following sandpainting of the Bridge for himself.

[108] Since there is no sandpainting from Striped Rock this probably refers to a prayer-stick for Talking God of that place.

brothers consecutively, shall be the fire ceremony songs. The songs
which she used to kill her brothers shall be used in the fire ceremony." That was all the information he gave her, Wind speaking.
"Now that is all," [he said]. "How would it be, my younger brother,
if you went back to Red Mountain, to have them come to us again.
A nine-night chant shall be held including the Dark Circle of
Branches. Therefore, tell them to return here this sunset. Your
sister got well again and walks about," she said. And he set out for
that place. Meanwhile she was telling her brother the songs which
she had heard while visiting the Hogback, also those songs at the
Bridge. Without any loss of time, she fixed the songs of both places.
That done, she told him, "Yonder in the valley is a place called the
Hill, which has the sandpainting of the Arrows. Upon this thirty-
four songs are sung. Then somewhere, in a real mountain recess,
there is a place called Young Spruce Round Hill. It has the Young
Spruce painting," she told him. It was then sunset, and he returned,
bringing very many back with him. When dusk set in, the older
brother was relating various things to them. "Our sister was almost
taken away from us," [he was telling them]. "You were present,
you know. You were gathered around here." "That we know happened as you say," some said. "In fact, she never seemed to be
able to be the same woman again, when she lay there at the time."
"I want you to discuss this for me," he said; "we cannot allow
things to go [unnoticed] as they happened to us," he said. "All
right, what else is there to be done!" they said.

"But of which place do you think that you say this?" he asked.
"Well, let it be done right here," the younger brother said. "I think
this is not a good place," [someone objected]. "That is quite true,"
they said. "Since the time that they shot into her they will do various
things [again]. Therefore I think that, although some people dwell
there, it ought to be done below Red Mountain," [someone sug-
gested]. Those of you who suggest this locality here suggest a difficult thing, [because] you are camped in a rock bluff with a single
entrance," they told them [the brothers].[109] "That is my purpose
in saying this to you, my friends, finish this for me," he [older

---

[109] Their camp in the bluff enclosure with one entrance or exit was not suitable because a sick person would have to pass over the same path after his recovery, and
thus chance an encounter with the cause of his illness. Some in the party from Red
Mountain told this to the brothers, suggesting that they choose a better place for the
chant.

brother] said. "You will now leave here, and presumably will reach
the home in Red Mountain at sunset. At once you may begin to
build for us, make us a hogan in a suitable place," he said. Then
it seemed they grouped together again. But while they were going
along over there, she ran out after them. "When you have finished
the building let some come here to us again," [she said]. The
menfolk, her brothers, then spent their time in food gathering, and
in hunting rabbits for her. In this manner another night passed. "We
two will go along the rim again, by some chance or other game may
have run in here again," he said. So the two brothers were over
there all day long again, because there was no meat. So it happened
that at sunset they packed a doe home, which they had killed. This
was boiled, and they ate till they had their fill. This happened to be
a bluff enclosure where deer could not escape. "Let us go over
there again, there may be another one roaming there," he said.
Sure enough, they killed another, this time a buck, and the two
returned while the sun was still well up in the skies. Along the
rear of the room, she put pinyon twigs down, upon which they
carried the venison in. "Why do you do this, my younger sister,
you have not yet recovered your strength," he told her. "What
do you mean? Why, I run along those points over there," the
woman said.

Then it was sunset and again they prepared food. That done,
they lay down to sleep and slept all night long. And it was one more
day to the time set for those people to come. "We are going over
there again, beyond where we were before, my younger sister."
And the two set out again, and happened to kill another one, a
small fawn. Late at sunset they returned, bringing the vension
inside. And again they ate meat. "Tomorrow is the day the people
set for us," he said. Again they went to sleep until daylight appeared.
Early in the morning they said, "Let us eat, here the men are
coming to us." They ate. "We set out from yonder way before dawn,"
[the party from Red Mountain said]. So they arrived here, just when
the sun peeped over the horizon. "We came without having eaten,"
they said. So food was boiled for them, and when ready, they ate.
Then they busied themselves with bundles, which they tied up.
And putting these on their backs, they set out. The woman offered
to carry some, but they refused to permit her. They kept moving
along packing their bundles a long way. "What is needed for it
[out of the mountains]?" he asked her. And when they were going
along the valley, he asked her, "What is used in the ceremony?"

"Well, of course, chokecherry for the emetic, service-berry, orange gooseberry, wild currant, and cat-tail flag, willow, dinas too, and big dinas, and slender dinas [box-leaf or manzanita], all of these," she said, "pounded up in this amount." After securing these they went on again. Spruce [Douglas fir] was found at the place itself. They arrived at the hogan. It was nicely built with braced points [conical hogan] into which they packed their bundles. Sunset, then daylight appeared, but they laid off all day without doing anything. "This night the ceremonial will begin," she said. The sun set. Wavyleaf oak should extend in the crevices, one extends along the east, in the west also, and one extends in the south and north," [she said]. "Out of which will the emetic be drunk?" "Out of a basket, to be sure."

So it was done and when dusk set in he who was to begin the ceremonial asked, "What are we to do now?" "Nothing more than to give some medicine, then go to sleep," [she said]. So it was done. At daylight she directed them to break off twigs for fuel, which they did. "What has happened here, we forgot something I see, there are no pokers," she said. "You must break off four lightning struck limbs, one along the east, and along the west, south and north sides," [she said]. Then the emetic was set on the fire, and when boiled, it was set before her. They put some cold water in it for her, then she drank, and drank as much as possible of it. Then she vomited while songs were sung at the side. When she finished the emesis, she stepped back and forth across the pokers. "Now then you may raise the curtain." She stepped outside then returned inside again. "You must do the water sprinkling now," [she said]. There were then eight more nights left. "The prayer-sticks of Rock Squirrel of that place will be cut, five in number," she said. These were cut for her. The woman over whom the chant was performed went about with nothing ailing her. The sun set again here. "Bring some spruce [Douglas fir]," the woman said. They brought in a quantity and she told them to wall up the fir and that it would be cut up. This was finished after darkness set in. When it was quite dark she said, "Let it be done now." They tore yucca leaves into strips, and the four fir walls were tied together, one along the east, one along the west, one along the south, one along the north. "My voice shall be used, my songs also shall be used," Monster Slayer and Born-for-Water said. After they had twisted the yucca this was laid in the fir. "You two shall be used, you shall do the cutting, there is fear of you, my granduncle," she told him. "All right," he consented. "What is used for the cutting, my granduncle?" she asked him. "Songs, of course, and the flint points."

Then it seems he [Monster Slayer] himself intoned the song. Along the east he made this motion and moved the flint club down her front, accompanying his motion with his haha-call. Born-for-Water gave his haha-call with an upward motion. Then they went along the west and repeated the same. Then repeated along the south and north sides. From there they turned back and stood in the east again. Now he [they] moved the flint point again and holding the flint club in his hand, repeated his call, and just made a cut in it. Then the two went to west and made the cuts, then south and north also. Thus Monster Slayer finished his part of the ceremony [garment ceremony]. Then medicine was administered. "Carry the spruce out," Monster Slayer said. After it had been carried outside, the medicine was administered, which finished two nights of ceremonies. At the following daylight the fire ceremony was repeated, the emetic was boiled again, poured out for her and cooled. Then she drank it again, and stepped over the four pokers around the fire. The curtain was then raised again, she stepped outside, then re-entered, and water was sprinkled over her again. That done, she directed the five Weasel sticks to be cut. These were cut again and the prayer said for her, then the sacrifice was offered to them. She herself gave directions as the ceremonies proceeded over her. "Bring some fir and yucca again," [she said]. The fir garment was to be made with that according to the woman's directions. That done, they again made it after darkness set in. Then many had gathered there. The two men to do the cutting had come again. So again they covered her with it [the fir garment], the two stood along the east giving their calls. Again they went along the west and repeated their calls, repeating this also in the south and north. Then they made cuts upwards across it, and did likewise in the west, and south and north. Then he told them to carry the fir out. Then medicine was given to her and they lay down to sleep again. On the following morning the fire ceremony was repeated, the emetic was boiled again, set before her and she drank it again, then vomited it. After that she stepped over the four pokers in the circle, the curtain was raised again and water was sprinkled on her. The prayersticks of the One-lying-in-the-burrow [bear], the Turkey prayersticks, the Mountain Sheep prayersticks, making six all told, were cut.

In the evening twelve unravelings were made and unraveled

over her. Pinyon, fir, juniper, rock sage, estafiata, snakeweed, grama grass [were employed]. The cotton cord being just looped together, one draws at the tip and pulls the cord out. So at dusk they were made again and unraveled over her, and the bundles of weeds were carried out. Then medicine was administered with the arrow songs. At daylight the fire ceremony was repeated in the same manner, as there is only one way of doing this part. The prayer-sticks alone vary. The sticks of Holy Young Man, of Holy Young Woman, the stick of Magic which Kills [striped rock squirrel] and the stick of He-acquires-holy-things [chipmunk] were cut. Thus four times it was done, the number of times for the fire was complete. "Extinguish the fire completely, pour water on it and carry it out," she said, "the poker you can take away later." That done, she said, "The fire you may upset along the ridge. Beginning with the morrow, the sandpaintings will string out and meal will be strewn." So that happened. "After dusk you shall gather again," she said, and after dusk they gathered again. On the following day the meal was strewn. The Valley Boy, they say, strewed the meal. He was very fleet, the antelopes having raised and suckled him. Now this very one had been secured. "But who will be the other one to make it two?" they were saying. But it so happened that there was one called Who-lies-under-it [a mountain]. He, too, was very fast, according to report, and had practiced in secret. "Let him also be one," they said.

After this had thus happened the two entered as soon as daylight appeared, that is the woman, his mother, entered with The-one-who-lies-under-it. "My son will do the meal strewing," she said. "What is he going to do!" they whispered into each other's ears. "Why, he is always sleeping till noon." So it happened that he washed his whole body and his hair. Then burnt herb mixture was burned, and white clay was set aside in a bowl of water. "Let my son sit first," the woman said. "No," they said, "Let Valley Boy be first." But the woman said, "No, in that case my son will not strew meal," and the two walked out. That started a discussion among them. "Let it be that way, who else is there to join the other? Let him sit ahead, there is nothing out of order if he does," they argued. One of them then followed them out to bring them inside again. There he sat in the lead as they blackened parts of their bodies, then spotted them with white clay. Their faces they painted white. Then they put on their moccasins, which completed their preparations.

The sun was then a trifle above the horizon. They had bags of speckled fawns [skins], into which they put meal for both. They stood one behind the other a short distance away. "You will go in this direction northward among the Holy People," he [older brother] said to The-one-who-lies-under-it, "while you," he said to Valley Boy, "will go around in the direction of the river towards Sky-reaching Rock where a Shootingway singer lives. You will then go up the river among the Pueblos, let many of them gather here with us. Then you will go to Young Spruce Round Hill," [he said]. After these instructions, the two set out together and left, then met yonder behind Black Mountain. From here one ran south, the other left in the direction north. Just before sunset the two returned.

Meanwhile the sandpainting of the Meal Sprinklers had been made. This was blanketed out, then food was brought in to the two Meal Sprinklers who now ate. "You two may tell us now where you have been," they said, and some remarked that both were about equal in speed. "You who are seated ahead may relate first," they said. "What is there to tell? Was that any distance to go? Well, from here I left and reached Wide Chokecherry, where these two sticks were given to me," he said as he laid them down there. "Of these you will make uprights they said," he explained.[110] "I left there again and came to the place called Up-the-coyote-trail, where one wild cherry [wild-olive] stick was given to me," he said, as he again laid it down. "That too you shall use as an upright you are told. Then I left there again and came to the place called Striped Rock, where a desert-thorn stick was given to me." He threw this down there. "This you will use as an upright, you are told," he said. "I left there again and reached Rock Center where another stick of an orange gooseberry bush was given to me. Then I set out again and reached the place called Young Spruce Round Hill. 'Our group will move in at dawn with spruce therefore we shall be there,' [they said]. Then I set out again and reached Sumac Corner. 'Our group will come in as those who turn white again [Re-whitening dancers], for that we will come. We will be the First Dancers just after sunset,' they said. I then left for a place called Whirling Babes and arrived at the home of Holy Young Man. 'We shall have our own exhibit, they will dance,' he said."

"From there I then left in the direction of White Mountain, they will also dance [they said]. From there I started out again for Jet Black Mountain. They also will [come] for the purpose of dancing,

---

[110] Uprights for the setting-out ceremony and the sandpainting set-up (see Kluckhohn and Wyman, 1940, pp. 81, 94).

[they said]. Then I set out again for the Black Mountain where I found the home of Mountain Sheep. 'Our purpose in coming will be to have our group move in,' [they said]. Several other people had their homes there, the Yavapai [Cracked Voice] lived there, I found. 'Our group too will come in,' they said. Somewhat to the side three people had their homes. They happened to be the Porcupine, the Badger and the Jumping Rat." "Our group too will enter, to be sure. In days to come earth surface people shall make use of it," they told him.[111] All of them said this. The Yavapai said, "My songs shall be used"; the Mountain Sheep also said this.

He then began to return home as he was told to do so. But as he was coming along the edge of the valley he heard somebody calling. He stood in his track, thinking that somebody coming along there may have called. And when he wanted to set out again, there was another call. This happened to be Turkey Man that had called. When he came up to him, he found him rolled up in a ball, his wing and tail feathers spread out. He was biting out many of his feathers, of which he made quite a heap. "Of these you will fix uprights. I shall sing just two songs when I arrive there," he said. From these places they [the people invited] set the time to follow him, some setting the next day, others two days, others the day of the close of the ceremonial. Then he set out to return home, but nearby found a hogan at a farm which belonged to real Navajo. When he gave his call with the whistle, someone ran out. It was then exactly midday. When he entered there, he found the other Meal Sprinkler, who had taken the south side, already seated there. He strewed meal before them in a circle saying, "I am come to you to ask the help of your travel food and your ordinary food." So that happened. "I shall return this way [over the same route he had taken], you too will return on that route," he said. "I shall return first," Valley Boy thought as he ran with all his might. Then it seems the two kept on running until just about sunset, when they returned and both met at the hogan. He-who-lies-under-it entered first, Valley Boy entered next, and there both bathed themselves.

Then the one who entered second told his story. "I came to Mountain-which-fell-out [from the range; Dropped-put Mountain]," he said. "I found Holy Young Man at home, who promised to come to present their dance. Then I set out again and arrived at the water hoist [Santo Domingo Pueblo]. From there I

---

[111] The informant forgot that the Meal Sprinkler was reporting and changed the style of his narration.

left again and reached the grass mat [Zia Pueblo]." "I came for
your foods, for your breads and paper bread," [he said].[111] They
promised to be there on the day before the close of the ceremonial.
"Bring your beads and pendants that we may buy from one another,
that is my purpose in coming here," he told them. "You are certainly
speedy, that is a great distance," they [the brothers] said to him.[112]
Next he set out towards the Black Mountain range again, and required much time before he arrived at its base. He went up to the
summit, where he found a narrow canyon and came to a waterfall.
Suddenly the Ye'i granduncle gave his call. He descended down into
the canyon and there called to him with his whistle. He [Valley Boy]
entered his [the Ye'i's] home where, in the rear of the room, the
Ye'i spread a robe for him. "Whence did you come, my grandchild?"
he said. It was then almost midday. "Under my direction the boughs
are to be lined up, that is your purpose in coming here," he said.
"Also that the Ye'i may dance, which will be my exhibit, for this
purpose you are here." From there he [Valley Boy] left and came
again to the hogan, where the other one met him. "On the closing
day we will be there," he said. Thus it happened that the two
returned to the [ceremonial place] and after their return, told of
themselves. It was then dusk, and he [older brother] told them to
practice dancing, but this was not done, they merely lay down
to sleep.

On the following morning they made another sandpainting,
they made the sandpainting of the Bridge. Late in the afternoon
it was finished, then medicine was again mixed in a bowl of water.
Then she [Older Sister] who sat on the sandpainting intoned
the songs. When these were concluded, he [her brother] pressed
her limbs, from the legs down, and her arms and her head. Thus
two nights of the ceremonial still remained. The sun set again
and they slept. On the following morning they again made a sandpainting, they drew the large tail feathered arrows, and were occupied with this sandpainting till the afternoon. Then they mixed
the medicine and foot liniment [chant lotion] in water again. Then
she again sat on the sandpainting, the songs were intoned and
finished again, after which he applied the proper portions of the
painting to her. Meanwhile large numbers had gathered, and the
Pueblo Indians [too], as the morrow would be the closing day.
"Tomorrow there will be no work, no sandpainting," she, over

---

[112] They pay him this compliment because they had originally preferred him to the
other Meal Sprinkler.

whom the ceremonial was held, said. "You will just chop limbs to be used for the brush circle." That was done. It was sunset. When it reached the horizon and disappeared over it, she announced, "Let it be done now! Take word to my granduncle, Talking God." "Where is he?" he [her brother] asked. "Here he is, nearby," [she said]. He went over there. "I will be there, my grandchild, return!" he said. He did, and soon he [Talking God] arrived here. "Strew meal around for it, my granduncle, wherever the branches are to be placed," [the brother told him]. He [Talking God] ran ahead, then turned back giving his call. Then he took out the meal and stood ahead of the brother, the latter standing behind him. "All of you who have moved here should help along," her brother said. This they did, they dragged the chopped limbs in place. Then he [the brother] intoned a song for him [Talking God] as he strewed the meal along. Following them, they stood the boughs upright, with the growing ends pointing sunwise as usual.

And wherever there were none [he would say], "Over there again, my granduncle," and would urge them to make it properly. Eventually the ground had become invisible and he [the brother] told them to build fires inside of it. Inside fires were built, as he urged them to move in and build fires. Great fires were built inside on both sides. Then it had become completely dark. "On the Red Mountain side people have their homes, inform them, they have arrows," he said. "Where shall they enter?" [they asked]. "Let them go into the hogan where the chant is conducted," [he said]. After some time they finally entered it. After the [center] fire was built he said, "Let the fire burn down first." In the meantime, he put down the basket in the rear interior [of the corral], then finished twenty-five songs. By that time little of the fire was left, so he went to the [ceremonial] hogan. Now some were standing here on the north side, while here on the south side, the first singer [dancers] to be stood. "We shall be first," said those who stood on the north side. "No, we are first," the south siders said. They [of the north side] had drawn many designs upon themselves by painting themselves with white clay and designing with charcoal, they had made mustaches for themselves. "Now then," they were saying as they started out, giving calls with their whistles. This group moved in, spreading their legs and creating nothing but laughter; they all laughed at them.[113] They left the corral.

[113] They stretch out their arms and legs as they stand, then make a leap ahead and again spread their legs. Father Berard remarked in a note, "Informant passes quickly over this exhibition of the so-called fire dancers and their vulgar antics."

Now two First Dancers left from [the south side] to enter. These two encircled the fire four times, then stood opposite where the baskets were turned down. "Where is the patient?" [they asked]. Then she sat down here, after he spread a robe for her, she sat down. Here the First Dancers sanctified her with the arrows [applied them to her limbs]. The two then left and returned to their places. Then the entire six of the group left for the corral, and danced four times around. Then they moistened their arrows in their mouths, and in this condition thrust them into their throats, then tremble-ran [short, quick, dancing steps] outside. The dancers Who-turn-it-white-again returned to the hogan, the First Dancers also returned there. "In days to come earth surface people will be directed hereby in their performances," they told her. So it happened that all of those Holy People were seen. After that he again intoned songs and concluded fifteen of them. At this point there was a call by the Ye'i, and when they came in, each one had a basket under his arm, while in the other hand they were carrying a basket tap as they danced around. This group danced four times around. Meanwhile he [the singer] put the basket down.[114] It certainly was a fine exhibition, they [the Ye'i] had much hair on their heads. Then he intoned a song while he [Ye'i] tapped his basket, and they danced with much spirit. Then they ceased and returned outside. The group again came in, four times they repeated this. Yonder he turned the basket down again, and dancing continued for them, then they would return. In this manner it was done four times, then they ceased and returned to the hogan.

Then it seems no specific order was observed. There was a group from Shootingway, whose exhibit was greatly spotted. Four times this occurred, the group danced around four times. Then he turned the basket down again. After they had done this four times the group went out [of the corral]. And now the Yavapai group entered. After they had danced around four times they left. They did not dance for her, none of this group were dancing for her. The group entered another time. Then the Mountain Sheep group entered, but only twice. Just twice the group entered then returned outside. Next the Turkey group entered twice then returned to the hogan. Next the Porcupine with Badger and Jumping Rat came in. These,

---

[114] The singer and his helpers in the corral do not tap their basket while an exhibition is going on, but wait until each new group has finished its act. It seems that the Ye'i tapped their baskets while they danced.

too, entered twice. By then time had passed well along towards dawn, when some people of the male branch of Mountain-Top-way entered. "You have not notified us," they said. They danced four times, then returned to the hogan. Another group of people who were strangers to them danced in, but it was learned that they belonged to Beautyway. "You have not informed us," they said. They only danced [for them?] again, and also four times, then returned to the hogan.

Now the big star [the morning star] had risen. Another group danced, in which was found to belong to Waterway. "You did not notify us," they also said. The group of the female branch of Shootingway also danced in. "You have not notified us," they said. "Of this same chant [Female Mountainway] none have danced in," she said. At that instant a group of people from Jet Black Mountain danced in. Their exhibit dancer happened to be spotted. A group of people from Young Spruce Round Hill danced in with young spruce. These danced around four times, then sanctified the patient again. By this time the dawn songs had been concluded over there, and when daylight had appeared with the conclusion of these songs, she [or he] said, "Cut the bough circle at the west, at the south and at the north." That was done.

When that had been done Valley Boy challenged the other to a footrace. "At midday, to be sure," He-who-lies-under-it said. "Let it be around Tongue Mountain [Mount Taylor]," Valley Boy said. Then Valley Boy went to the Pueblo Indians to tell them about it. These at once busied themselves with wagering beads and turquoise pendants, while on this side the Navajo wagered buckskins, beads and turquoise pendants against them. So it came about that there was much betting among them. Some people who came in were betting on Valley Boy. And the two set about to remove their clothes, then started out around the entire Tongue Mountain. They soon disappeared and were out of sight until late in the afternoon, when out in the distance a moving black spot appeared. "There Valley Boy is coming back," was said. Now their courses were side by side, but over a rolling country, so this He-who-lies-under-it would zigzag here and there on Valley Boy's track.[115] "Here Valley Boy is coming back," the Pueblos were saying. When there was little left of the race course, he ran after Valley Boy, overtook him, then He-who-lies-under-it slacked up somewhat to let the

---

[115] This caused the spectators to mistake him for Valley Boy at that distance.

other come. Then Valley Boy rubbed his leg against the other's imitating the cry of a fawn. And the other ran up close to him and got aside of him taunting him, "Get a move on you now, Valley Boy!" And they were one behind the other, Valley Boy was running behind, so he lost out and a wail went up from the Pueblos.

After that they finally dispersed. The one who had been patient of the chant sat among them. On top of the Wide Chokecherry, the two sisters met two nights after the singing over her. Then they told each other their stories. "I went this way [sunwise] around and returned, nothing was hidden from us," she said. "I too have done likewise. Those rough mountain peaks are not earth," she said. From there the two left to return, they returned to Red Mountain. "Where have you been my younger sister?" her brothers said to her.[116]

---

[116] The myth ends here rather abruptly because the informant claimed that he was not familiar with the account of the meeting of the two sisters.

Raised by The Owl

by River Junction Curley

Coyote Died

HE USUALLY PLANTED at Earth Shelf Place in the Sacred Canyon. He planted white dwarf corn and blue dwarf corn, and yellow dwarf corn and black dwarf corn, being terribly attached to it. Now and then he would merely return to his family at that Winged Rock [Shiprock Pinnacle, New Mexico]. There he had his daughter, a very pretty one, they say, his son also and his wife and himself, Coyote, First Scolder. So the four of them moved about.

Somewhere at the base of Spruce Hill [Gobernador Knob, New Mexico], Horned Toad had planted his field, it was learned. His corn was exactly like that owned by Coyote. In time Horned Toad matured some, when it happened that Coyote visited him. "For what reason did you steal this from me, which at that time was my corn?" he [Coyote] asked him. "That is my own corn," I suppose Horned Toad said. "I will swallow you," Coyote said. And he swallowed him, Horned Toad was swallowed, they say. He [Coyote] was walking around that corn of his. "Leave it alone," he said, "this is my corn," [probably he was speaking to birds]. Having settled that, he lay down inside of Horned Toad's home. And so it seems, the other was lying in his belly. "Shd!" he [Horned Toad] said to him. He spoke to him [Coyote] here from his belly. You should have

Recorded and Translated by Father Berard Haile. Edited by Leland C. Wyman.

seen him jump up! He ran out and looked around. "Who spoke, I wonder," he said and returned inside. "Shd!" he said to him again. He jumped up again, ran out and looked around in vain. He returned inside and lay down again. "Wonder what it was that called," he said. Again he [Horned Toad] called "Shd!" Again he [Coyote] dashed off and looked around in vain. He returned inside again. "Wonder who is calling," he said. "Is there any wonder about it, when one occupies a ghost's house?" he said. "I shall rebuild the hogan at another place," he said. Just then it said, "shd!" to him again, while he was lying on his back. He then looked up again and searched around in vain.

Then he turned his head this and that way, until his eye rested on his belly and he just remained quiet [listening]. "This green thing which is strung along here, what is it?" he asked [from his interior]. "That is my anus," he [Coyote] said. "What are these two blue things set side by side?" "Why! they are my kidneys," he said. "This big sack here what is that?" he asked. "Why that is my stomach," he said. "And this big thing here extending out lengthwise?" he asked. "Why that is my colon," he said. "These [cords] running side by side what are they?" he asked. "Why, that is my food pipe and windpipe running parallel to each other," he said. "And this tangled blue thing, what is that?" he asked. "Why those are my [green] intestines," he said. "What about this round thing set here, what is that?" he asked. "I don't know," he said.

"Anyway, what is it, I am asking you?" he [Horned Toad] said. "Why that is my heart" he [Coyote] said. "Even so, I am going to cut it off, in spite of you!" he told him. "No you won't! What if I run away with you?" he said. "Just the same, I am going to cut it off, that is settled!" he told him. "No you won't! I'll drop from a bluff with you!" he said. "Just the same, I am going to cut it off, that is settled." "No you won't, I shall plunge into the water with you!" he said. Directly he [Horned Toad] cut off his heart spoken of, and off he [Coyote] dashed. Somewhere outside, quite a distance away, he fell over. On his anus side the Horned Toad went out again and left quickly for home as [soon as] Coyote died. In time, however, he was again restored to life by those above the skies, Spotted Thunder and Left-handed Thunder, Spotted Wind and Left-handed Wind again restored him to life, they say.

So from there, it seems, he dashed home and returned to his family already mentioned. "My body is not at all well," he said. "No wonder! When people despise and hate a person [always], how can one be in good health!" he said. After that, time passed without

[his] taking food. After a time, he got so that he could not walk, then he could not get up, and in time he was speaking of his past.

"Whatever may happen to me, you must take good care of yourselves, my children, you must not feel discouraged, my children!" he said. "You must not go about weeping! What is to be done about it! It must be so and cannot be changed," he said. "Am I the only one that will die?" he said. "At any rate let her [his daughter] take a husband who is exactly as I am. She must take one whose looks are just like mine, who carries a mountain lion skin quiver on his person," he said. "Remember this with all your might! You must do exactly according to my words just spoken! As for me, I shall leave you for some unseen region! Shall I ever be seen again?" he said. "It just seems as though it were getting the better of me! Try as I may to make myself believe [the contrary], it is getting too much for me! Now it has reached a point beyond my endurance, therefore I am saying this, my children! What more shall I say to you! Do not go about crying, my children!" he said. "One should lead her children about carefully, my wife!" he said. "You will carry me up to a rack on a tree! On top of this you will place me, and whenever it happens that from above the worms fall and it is clear that I am dead this [death] will then take place. It can then be fired and will burn up with me," he said.

And so, I suppose, they set the rack on the tree for him and laid him on top of this. Up there they laid him, then left him and went home, merely looking over there now and then. But after four days, worms were falling down. "He must have really died," she [Coyote's wife] said. "That was the sign that it would happen, of which he spoke," she said. They were crying then, they say. "It must have been true what our late father was saying," they all said weeping. And since he had said, "set fire to it and let it burn up with me," she said, "Set fire to it my children!" And immediately she began carrying fire there and set fire to it. After that they left for home. Meanwhile the blaze started and a large volume of smoke went up! But when that son of his had looked back, he said, "My mother, it just seemed to me then as though my father had jumped down!" "You must not say that, my son! That father of yours is dead!" she said to her son.

And so from that time on they lived right in that neighborhood, suffering all sorts of hardship. As for the Coyote, he had jumped down in the smoke, moving away from them, and he too lived in difficulties. In this very manner four years had passed. But after four years some strange man unexpectedly came to them. The looks of this stranger seemed exactly like those of that late old man, when he came to them. "From where do you happen to be?" he said. "Oh, just around here! We go any old place," she told him. "After the old man that formerly led us unfortunately died, we go any old place," she told him. "I see! This is surely too bad!" he said. "Wonder what sort of things he said, he surely must have been a wise one," he remarked. "He didn't say anything in particular," she said. "What should he say? He said nothing at that time, he spoke nothing," they told him. "But you, from where do you come?" they asked him. "Oh, just from here! I camp wherever the sun sets on me." His travel-food happened to be a deer ham, and of this, he gave them some to eat. My, how grateful they were, expressing their thanks to him! After they also had prepared gray meal for food on his journeys, he left them.[117]

"Wonder from where this man came to us, my children. He certainly looks exactly like him, this stranger that came to us, my children!" she who was the [old] woman said. After four days, he again came to them, having deer meat for the road. "Really what did he say?" he asked. "He certainly used to be a wise one. He too, no doubt, said something," he again said. "He didn't say anything! Without saying anything [worthwhile], he died, unfortunately!" the woman said. And so again he left them for his home. Four days afterwards he again came to them, [carrying] deer meat as his food. Again he gave it to them. "Really what did he say? He certainly used to be a wise one! No doubt he must have spoken!" he said. "Yes he did speak at the time," she told him. "No matter what happens, one exactly like myself must lead you about, this he said to us." "Just as I was saying!" he said. "With him who carries a mountain lion [skin] quiver, my daughter must live, he said [and] after telling his daughter this, he caused us suffering [by his death]," she told him. Then she again made food for him of gray meal and cornbread [baked in ashes]. Again he left them, after which she [remarked], "How is it, my daughter, that the man is treating us so! He really does seem generous, much like your late father! You must live with one who is exactly like myself, who has looks like mine [you know] he told you at that time, my daughter," she said. "When he returns again you will go in to him, let him be our leader," she told her. She did not speak. "Why don't you speak, my daughter? You know your late father left no doubt about it when he spoke! Should one forget such

---

[117] Green corn roasted in heated pits is ground and furnishes "gray meal" for traveling. This is mixed with water to make a gruel (Albert Sandoval).

things?" she told her. "Well, where is he! As soon as he returns we will see, my mother!" she said.

After four days he again came to them and again gave them venison. And so, "How shall it be then, perhaps I ought to go outside," the woman said. She stepped outside and her daughter followed her out. "Tell him to make a brush circle!" she told her daughter. She entered again. "My mother says to tell you [to] make a brush circle over there," she said, "You shall lead us about, my mother tells you," she said. But he said, "Well, I hardly know what to say? I make a living with difficulty, but since my mother is pleading, I suppose I ought to make the brush circle," he said. So immediately he started out with one of the [stone] axes that were there, and with that he built a bough windbreak. That done, she went in to him there at sunset. And that night he, who was her father, had intercourse with her. From that time on, he began to lead them about and in this way he became her son-in-law and the woman hid herself from him. And so it seems he led them about as well as he could. In time, that daughter of his had become pregnant by him. In course of time her stomach bulged out and she was about to give birth, they say.

Now it seems that her father used to have a wart at the lower part of his head. And whenever she would begin to brush his hair and would feel along the back of his head, he would keep her away from that spot by saying, "A louse bit me here!" "Wonder why he says that," she thought. And when he tried to say, "here a louse bit me," she would feel around that spot and sure enough, at the lower back of his head was the wart. "How can this be possible," she thought. "He really does seem to resemble my late father himself!" she was thinking. So four nights passed with her keeping a close watch on him. Without saying a word about him, she was thinking, "that certainly is he himself." She then spoke of it to her mother. "My mother, it just seems to me that that is my late father," she said to her mother. "You must not say that, that father of yours is dead," she told her daughter. "No, my mother, he has every characteristic of my [late] father himself," she said. "You are wrong in saying this! What is there about him that makes you of this opinion?" the woman said. "Well, [all I can say is] he just looks like him," she said. "What about looking him over carefully? As an unfailing sign there will be a wart at the back of his head, if it really be he," the woman said.

She returned and there she again brushed his hair. Again she began to feel around at the back of his head. "Here a louse bit me," he said. "Let it bite!" she said and kept on feeling. Sure enough there was the wart! Very carefully she looked at it, then started back and went in to her mother again. "It is true, it is my late father himself, mother," she said. "Is it there? Did you carefully look at the wart back of his head of which we spoke?" she asked. "I looked at it carefully," she said. "It is the absolute truth, that this is my father [alive]. Why don't you believe me, mother?" she said. "It is truly my father," her daughter said. "Do you really mean this, my daughter?" she asked. "I am telling you the truth, mother! Just see for yourself! Go there, and take a look at him!" And so she ran over there and entered, [although] he was her son-in-law. At once she parted his hair at the back of his head. Although he strove to keep his hair from her, she parted it, and sure enough, at the back of his head was the wart! Then she looked at it carefully. "Man, you surely are a great one! Why, four years ago you died, there was no doubt about it!" she said to him. "Well, yes, it is quite true, I am he," he said. "You are surely a great one! What is there that you do not think of!" she said. "It is quite true," she said to him weeping.

After this happened she simply returned to his home. Meanwhile that daughter of his simply felt ashamed of him with her confinement approaching. In time she felt the movement of the child. Then she started out and went somewhere to a valley at a place called Anthill-covered-with-cactus [east of the Shiprock], being in labor. Here she gave birth and then kicked the child into the burrow of a badger. Then she started back home.

Old Man Owl Raised Him

SOMEWHERE IN A DRAW of Big Sheep [Hesperus Peak, La Plata Range], along a place called Cave-under-the-rock, old Owl Man had started on a hunt. He was hunting at Cactus Anthill when he heard a baby's cry. And so he went in search of it and soon [found] the baby crying right out on the smooth ground. When he arrived there he heard it inside of the burrow, and immediately took that baby out of it. He was then quite undecided what to do, [but] finally simply picked it up and returned home with it at Cave-under-the-rock.

Here old Owl Woman asked, "Where did you find this baby anyway? Whose baby have you?" the Owl Woman said. "It was lying down inside of a burrow, in a spot where nobody lives, it was just recently born when I picked it up. You will raise it, old lady, and take care of it!" he told his wife. "All right," she said "it shall be my babe, my son, my grandchild." And so, when he brought in rabbits, she would feed it with their broth and in this way the days began to pass on. In time, I suppose, it lost its tenderness, then got to be able to creep and later could stand on its feet. In course of time rabbit skins were sewed together and this furnished a rabbit robe in which he slept. Old Owl Woman loved him very much. In time he began to walk about and he [Owl Man] then made a bow and arrow for him. After a while he himself was able to go about hunting, and brought in rabbits and prairie dogs and wood rats, they say.

Meanwhile he got to be twelve years of age. She loved him much and called him babe, my grandchild, and had him sleep at her side. This made the old Owl Man jealous, and his jealousy led him to the opinion that he was committing adultery with her. So he departed from there and returned with him to the place of his birth. "Here is the place where you were born, here it was where you came into being. What you do about it is your own affair!" he told him. Then he left him and returned home, but he [the boy] stayed right there. "The fact is that your mother, your father, your grandmother [mother's mother] exist somewhere" old Owl Man had said when he was leaving him. "Why did he mention my mother, why did he mention my father, my grandmother to me," he was thinking and worrying about it as he went about. He spent the night right there. He camped at the place where he had been told, "you were born here."

Warnings

IN THE MORNING HE AROSE. He started out towards the east when he heard a noise in his trachea. He turned back and again made a start for the south, when his nose again made a sound. Again he turned back. "I wonder what this means," he thought. Again he made a start toward the west, but now his ear sounded [ringing]. Again he turned back and returned to his camp. Towards the north he again made a start, but [now] there was a twitching in his skin. Again he turned back and returned where he had camped.

In this manner it had happened four times when, right from the level ground, some young man arose before him. "In this direction, my grandchild, they moved from you," he told him. "Twelve years ago they moved away from you. As for me, I am your fetus bag liquid, your menstrual flux which once was, that I am, my grandchild. Your mother is living, your father exists, your grandmother is existing, my grandchild," he told him. He left not even a trace of himself. From there he started out, but had not gone very far when the sun set. He was staying right in that neighborhood when near him [he noticed] sticks lying in a circle which were gray with age and seem- ed to have been used for a brush circle. Here he camped for the night, they say.

At daylight he arose and at once made a start again for the east. But again there was that noise in his trachea. He turned back again. He made another start for the south, again there was the ringing in his ear and he turned back again. He made another start for the west, there was the tickling in his nose and he turned back to his camp. He made another start northward, again his skin pricked him. Going back again he returned and found a small stick lying there, which was the remnant of a burning. This arose facing him, in the form of a young man it faced him. "It is close by that your mother, your fa- ther, your granduncle, your [maternal] grandmother exist. In this direction they moved away from you, my grandchild," he told him. And so he started out again. He had not gone very far [when] again the sun set. Sticks gray with time still formed a circle, in the fire- place the ashes were still left, and here he spent the night.

At daylight he arose. At once he again made a start eastward, there was the same noise in his trachea, [and] he turned back again. He made another start for the south, again the ringing in his ear gave warning, and he turned back again. He again started for the west, there was the sound in his nose, again he turned back. He made another start for the north, his skin again pricked him [and] he turn- ed back again. Again it had happened four times. There was a very poor pot there with pieces broken out. At any rate this again spoke to him, in the form of a young man it happened to address him. "This direction [they took] from you [when] they moved," he said. "The fact is your mother, father, granduncle, grandmother are [still] exist- ing," he told him. And so again he started out. Without getting very far, the sun had again set, when there was a circle of dried boughs which had served as a windbreak and must have been a temporary shelter. The fireplace was there showing recent use. Right here he spent the night.

At daylight he again arose. From here he started out toward the east when again the noise in his trachea gave warning. He turned back again. He again made a start toward the south. Again his ring- ing ear gave warning and he turned back. Again he made a start for the west side [but] his nose gave warning and he turned back. He made another start for the north side, [but] again his skin pricked him and he turned back, and returned to his night's camp. There a cane, very poor one, again spoke to him and addressed him in the shape of a young man. "In this direction they [left you] and moved, my grandchild. Your mother, father, granduncle and grandmother moved leaving you," he said.

From there he started out again across the river and crossed at the [blue] banks of it. Here on the other side of the river, the sun had again set, when he came upon a windbreak whose boughs were still green. The footprints in the trails were [still] traceable. At this place he again spent the night. At daylight he started out again for the east side. Again there was the sound in his trachea. [He returned] and made another start for the south. His ear gave its ringing and he turned back. Again he started westward. His nose again gave warning and he turned back. Again he started northward. His skin pricked him somewhere and he returned back [to camp]. Just an old whisk broom again spoke to him in the form of a young man, "In this direction they moved leaving you, my grandchild. Your mother, father, granduncle, and grandmother moved away from you!" he told him. At once he started out again, without having covered a great distance. The sun had set on him again when it turned out that the moving had taken place recently. The boughs used were still fresh and of these a brush circle had served them as a temporary hogan. And right here he again spent the night, they say.

At daylight he again started out for the east. Again his trachea gave warning and he turned back. Again he started out for the south, there was the ringing in his ear, and he turned back again. He made another start for the west, his nose gave warning, and he turned back again. He made another start for the north, again there was pricking in his skin, and he returned back to his camp. And here the remnant of a broken-up stirring stick again spoke to him and happened to address him in the shape of a young man. "In this direction the moving away from you took place. Your mother, your father, granduncle and grandmother moved this way, my grandchild," he told him. From here again he started out. Without having gone very far, the sun had again set on him when closeby there was what had served as a hogan. Perhaps four days previously the moving had taken place, they say.

While camping there both of those Owls [spoken of] overtook him [most likely] for the purpose of killing him. Little Wind had come down upon him at his earfolds and was placed there to fit the coils of his ear. [So] it happened that he spoke to him from there. "That sound [which you hear] there, is the sound of one who wants to kill you presently, make him a sacrifice," Little Wind told him. Going out at once [he said], "Do not be saying that! Here is your sacrifice, I am now making it for you!" He made them a sacrifice of white shell. And so they did not kill him. "Now go on, return, the two of you, my granduncle, my grandmother!" he said to them. The two had not entered, but had given their call from the outside [and] right then ceased to give their call again. The two then left him, they say.

In time he went to sleep but happened to have a dream, in which he dreamt that many people had wanted to kill him and only with difficulty he reached safety. In the morning when dawn appeared he awoke. "What great thing is this that spoiled my sleep! What, I wonder, shall happen to me when I overtake them!" his thoughts were. And so his dream worried him. But Little Wind along his earfolds spoke to him again, "Do not be worrying over it! It will not happen! Although you had this dream it will not take place according to that, my grandchild!" he told him.

And now it was daylight, and this time he did not start out for the east, his trachea gave no warning. He did not start out for the south, there was no ringing in his ear. He did not start out for the west, his nose did not twitch. He did not start out for the north, there was no pricking of his skin. The several things, which at different times had spoken to him, which had told him, "this way the moving took place away from you," none of these now spoke to him. And so he was thinking it over. "So that is the thing called warnings! Had I not believed them, who knows where I should have gone! But since I started out those several times in accordance with my belief in them, you see, I have now overtaken them."

"Now then I have faith in the thing called noise of the trachea. Whenever I begin an undertaking and I hear this sound in my trachea, I would not proceed farther [to spite it]" he said. "Then too, if my ear should ring, I should go no farther," he said. "If my nose, too, should give a sound, I should travel no farther," he said. "Should there be a pricking of my skin I should not proceed farther, because a wonderful one has been placed on me, the Little Wind. A great one, too, old Owl Man, has raised me, a great one, old Owl Woman, has raised me, by spreading darkness upon me, by spreading skyblue upon me, by spreading evening twilight also upon me, by spreading dawn too upon me. Because in these I was raised. In the days to come, when earth surface people begin to come into being, they shall have faith in what I have here set down as a law, in trachea noises, in ringing of the ear, in nose sounds, in skin prickings, in frequent bad dreams, in all unusual happenings earth surface people should believe!" With these words he so ordained it.

He Became A Ute

THEREUPON HE BEGAN to track them. At the place where they had camped, he spent the night. Three nights before they had moved and he followed their tracks. Again there were signs of their camp and movement of two days before, and again he followed. Again there were signs of camp and moving of the previous day, and again he started out to follow. Again he found indications of a camp and moving that morning, the fires were still burning, and again he started out to follow. Where they had stopped to camp, he overtook them and entered. None of the people were absent. They were all there, his mother, his father, his granduncle, his grandmother, those brothers of his. And so he walked in to them, but he did not know them. They made no space for him, they say.

Meanwhile, it seems, they simply looked at him. And so at his earfolds Little Wind spoke to him, "That is the one there, that is she who gave birth to you, your mother," Little Wind told him. "That one there is your father, your granduncle. That one there is your grandmother, that is your brother," he said. "Now say relative to your mother, and to your father, and to your granduncle, and to your grandmother," he told him. The Little Wind told him this in a nice way. He then stepped towards his mother [who was sitting] there. "My dear mother, you are the one that gave birth to me. The castaway to whom you gave birth twelve years ago, this I am, my mother," he told her. Then he also stepped towards his father. He embraced him. "My dear father," he said to him. "My granduncle," he called him. He paid no attention to him. Then he also walked towards his grandmother. "My grandmother, of whom thou art grandmother, that one I am," he said to her. He then also walked to his brother. "My dear older brother," he said to him. They paid no attention to him.

Up to this time he had finished greetings, not one of them had called him relative. Thereupon he walked out and stayed right around there. "What is this thing that came to us saying my mother, my father, my grandmother, my older brother! He is not the kind to be trusted perhaps, they are saying about you," Little Wind whispered at his earfolds. After a while, when he vainly tried to call them relative, they talked about him right to his face, then they were saying that he ought to be killed. On that account he was very much filled with anger.

After a while that father of his said to him, "From where do you come anyway that you say this? Wherever your home may be, go back there! We do not know you," he told him. That hurt his feelings very much and on that account he was angered. "Let happen what may, I shall kill my mother and my father also," he thought. And so he shot down his mother and also shot his father. Having done that, he started off [in any old direction].

Behind him sounds of great excitement could be heard. "Where is that [scoundrel] that came here among us! Two people he has killed as you see! Had you done before this as told and killed him, this would not have happened to us," it was heard said. "Perhaps he will come in sight again," it was heard said. Thereupon a vain search for him was made. And to that shadow of his he spoke, "Something is being said about me perhaps, go there and get some news for me! Find out what is [actually] being said about me and tell me when you return to me!" he told it.

Accordingly it went there, while he remained where he was sitting. It arrived there, that shadow of his did. "Look out! look out! Curse the old thing that came among us! Look out!" could be heard. Children had been playing under a tree and two of these, he had killed. "Two children again he has killed, we found," the report came. From all sides the shouting of the people could be heard. They encircled him [his shadow] and pursued him. Right in their midst as they were encircled about him, he vanished from them. You should have seen how hard they searched for him, when suddenly he was running again elsewhere! "There he goes!" they cried and the crowd moved in his direction.

The people again encircled him and prepared to charge him. Just as the situation became critical for him, he again disappeared and they resumed their search for him in vain. "There he goes, there he goes!" they said, and again the crowd rushed towards him. The people again encircled him and again made ready to attack. And again, just as the situation was getting critical he vanished out of sight. In vain again they made a search for him. "There he goes! there he goes!" someone said again, and the crowd again rushed his way in pursuit of him. Much excited, the people surrounded him

again! Just as the situation was becoming critical he again vanished.
Again they made a vain search for him. "There he goes, there he
goes again!" someone said. This made it four times. He had again
vanished out of their sight. But he [shadow] had returned to that
place. "You have sent me into a very unsafe place. I was almost
killed! In spite of all you will be killed, they are saying about you,"
he [shadow] told him. "They are probably on the way now," he said.

Thereupon that shadow of his became himself again. At that
moment near him shouts again were heard. He dashed away from
there with every ounce of strength. He cut off one twig of hardwood [*Fendlera*], from which he scraped the bark. From that place
two [persons] started out. Nearby shouts again were heard. Together they dashed off leaving the tracks of two behind. The two came
again to a service-berry. From this he cut another twig, again scraped
the bark from it and three started out. Nearby shouts again were
heard and they started off on a run, leaving the tracks of three behind. Again they came to a wild currant and now you should have
seen them cut ever so many! When they had scraped them and
many people were coming into being, it was a sight to see this
number of people just like a crowd spreading out! After a while
they even cut main poles [of a hogan] and started moving away.
Again shouts were heard but their sound died out right there. But
the place [where the currant bushes stood] was much upset, one
could hardly tell which was the main spot [from which] they had
moved, there were [so] many tracks of poles, which had been dragged away. "There is no use, this is no ordinary person we are pursuing! It is enough! Let us turn back! He may do unpleasant things
to us!" it was said.

"That being so, we will just follow them to the top of the hill,"
it was said. They followed them then to the top of the hill. There
they were amazed to see that they had stopped moving, the place
was white with tents [from which] the smoke of many fires went up,
many groups of people could be seen with braided hair, who had
gathered there. It turned out, that they had become Utes, that they
had become Arrow People. This they saw, after which they started
back and arrived at their homes. "Not an ordinary one has done
this to us, we found, when right ahead of us he was making people!
In a short while there were signs of many moving and of wild currant [twigs] scattered about him, then of poles also being dragged
along, which left a deep trail in the soil, where they moved them.
And when we followed them to the top," he said, "the place was

white with tents side by side, many people braided-haired, were gathered in groups. You should have seen the smoke of these many fires," he said. "We just looked at them. A Ute had done this to us, he was one of the Arrow People we [now] know," they said. "So that is it! Well, that is the way it is, what is to be done about it!" it was said. "Let them [alone], let them have their homes where they are," it was said.

Then it seems, that Coyote was again restored to life from above the sky by Spotted Thunder, by Left-handed Thunder, by Spotted Wind and by Left-handed Wind. On the side of this one, Raised by the Owl, the story ends here, while stories about the Coyote are not yet at an end, but stories about him continue on.

References

ABERLE, DAVID F.
    1966   *The Peyote Religion among the Navaho.* Viking Fund Publications in
            Anthropology, No. 42. Wenner-Gren Foundation for Anthropological
            Research.

ALBERT, ETHEL M.
    1966   Introduction to Chapter 9, Expressive Activities, by Clyde Kluckhohn.
            In: *People of Rimrock. A Study of Values in Five Cultures,* Evon Z.
            Vogt and Ethel M. Albert, eds., Cambridge, Mass.

ARMER, LAURA ADAMS
    1953   The Crawler, Navaho Healer. *The Masterkey,* vol. 27, pp. 5–10.

ASTROV, MARGOT
    1950   The Concept of Motion as the Psychological Leitmotif of Navaho Life
            and Literature. *Journal of American Folklore,* vol. 63, pp. 45–56.

BAILEY, VERNON
    1931   *Mammals of New Mexico.* North American Fauna, Number 53. Wash-
            ington, D.C.

BERRY, ROSE V. S.
    1929a   The Navajo Shaman and His Sacred Sand-Paintings. *Art and Archae-
            ology,* vol. 27, pp. 3–16 (reprinted in *El Palacio,* vol. 26, pp. 23–38, 1929).
    1929b   Red Indian Sand-Paintings. *Discovery,* vol. 10, pp. 120–124.

COOLIDGE, DANE C., AND MARY ROBERTS COOLIDGE
    1930   *The Navajo Indians.* Boston.

CURTIS, EDWARD S.
    1907   *The North American Indian.* New York and Cambridge, England.
            20 vols.

CURTIS, NATALIE
    1907   *The Indians Book.* New York.

El Palacio
1923   Navajo Sand Paintings as Decorative Motive. Vol. 14, pp. 175–183.
1935   Vol. 38, pp. 72–73.

FISHLER, STANLEY A.
1953   *In the Beginning: A Navaho Creation Myth.* University of Utah Anthropological Papers, No. 13. Salt Lake City.
1956   Owl-Raised-Ute, An Origin Legend for Curing Sorcery. In: *A Study of Navajo Symbolism*, Franc J. Newcomb, Stanley Fishler, and Mary C. Wheelwright, Cambridge, Mass.

FOSTER, KENNETH E.
1964   *Navajo Sandpaintings.* Navajoland Publications, Navajo Tribal Museum, Window Rock, Arizona, series 3.

FRANCISCAN FATHERS
1910   *An Ethnologic Dictionary of the Navaho Language.* Saint Michaels, Arizona.

HAILE, FATHER BERARD
1938a   *Origin Legend of the Navaho Enemyway.* Yale University Publications in Anthropology, No. 17.
1938b   Navaho Chantways and Ceremonials. *American Anthropologist*, vol. 40, pp. 639–652.
1946   *The Navaho Fire Dance.* Saint Michaels, Arizona.
1947a   *Navaho Sacrificial Figurines.* Chicago.
1947b   *Prayerstick Cutting in a Five Night Navaho Ceremonial of the Male Branch of Shootingway.* Chicago.
1950   *A Stem Vocabulary of the Navaho Language. Navaho-English.* Vol. 1. Saint Michaels, Arizona.
1951   *A Stem Vocabulary of the Navaho Language. English-Navaho.* Vol. 2. Saint Michaels, Arizona.

HILL, W. W.
1938   *The Agricultural and Hunting Methods of the Navaho Indians.* Yale University Publications in Anthropology, No. 18.

———, AND DOROTHY W. HILL
1945   Navaho Coyote Tales and Their Position in the Southern Athabaskan Group. *Journal of American Folklore*, vol. 58, pp. 317–343.

KEARNEY, THOMAS H., AND ROBERT H. PEEBLES
1951   *Arizona Flora.* Berkeley and Los Angeles, California.

KLUCKHOHN, CLYDE
1960   Navaho Categories. In: *Culture in History*, Stanley Diamond, ed., New York.

———, AND DOROTHEA LEIGHTON
1962   *The Navaho.* Revised edition, New York.

———, AND LELAND C. WYMAN
1940   *An Introduction to Navaho Chant Practice.* Memoirs, American Anthropological Association, No. 53.

KRAMER, SAMUEL NOAH
1952   *Enmerkar and the Lord of Aratta: A Sumerian Epic Tale of Iraq and Iran.* Museum Monographs, The University Museum, University of Pennsylvania, Philadelphia.

LINK, MARTIN A., ED.
 1968   *Navajo: A Century of Progress.* Window Rock, Arizona.

MCALLESTER, DAVID P.
 1967   Review of *The Red Antway of the Navaho* by Leland C. Wyman, *American Anthropologist,* vol. 69, pp. 237–238.

MATTHEWS, WASHINGTON
 1885   Mythic Dry-Paintings of the Navajos. *American Naturalist,* vol. 19, pp. 931–939.
 1885a   The Origin of the Utes, a Navajo Myth. *American Antiquarian,* vol. 7, pp. 271–274.
 1887   The Mountain Chant: A Navajo Ceremony. *Fifth Annual Report, Bureau of American Ethnology,* pp. 379–467.
 1902   *The Night Chant, a Navaho Ceremony.* Memoirs, American Museum of Natural History, vol. 6.

NEWCOMB, FRANC J.
 1949   "Fire Lore" in Navajo Legend and Ceremony. *New Mexico Folklore Record,* vol. 3, pp. 3–9.

————, STANLEY FISHLER AND MARY C. WHEELWRIGHT
 1956   *A Study of Navajo Symbolism.* Papers of the Peabody Museum, Harvard University, vol. 32, No. 3.

————, AND GLADYS A. REICHARD
 1937   *Sandpaintings of the Navajo Shooting Chant.* New York.

O'BRYAN, AILEEN
 1956   *The Diné: Origin Myths of the Navaho Indians.* Bureau of American Ethnology, Bulletin 163.

OPLER, MORRIS E.
 1943   *The Character and Derivation of the Jicarilla Holiness Rite.* University of New Mexico, Bulletin No. 390.

PARSONS, ELSIE CLEWS
 1939   *Pueblo Indian Religion.* Chicago. 2 vols.

REAGAN, ALBERT B.
 1934   A Navaho Fire Dance. *American Anthropologist,* vol. 36, pp. 434–437.

REICHARD, GLADYS A.
 1939   *Navajo Medicine Man.* New York.
 1944   *The Story of the Navajo Hail Chant.* New York.
 1970   *Navaho Religion: A Study of Symbolism.* Bollingen Series XVIII, second edition, Princeton, New Jersey.

RUSSELL, FRANK
 1898   An Apache Medicine Dance. *American Anthropologist,* vol. 11, pp. 367–372.

SAPIR, EDWARD, AND HARRY HOIJER
 1942   *Navaho Texts.* Iowa City.

SPENCER, KATHERINE
 1957   *Mythology and Values: An Analysis of Navaho Chantway Myths.* Memoirs, American Folklore Society, vol. 48.

STEVENSON, JAMES
 1891   Ceremonial of Hasjelti Dailjis. *Eighth Annual Report, Bureau of American Ethnology,* pp. 229–285.

UNDERHILL, RUTH M.
  1956   *The Navajos.* Norman, Oklahoma.

VOGT, EVON Z.
  1960   The Automobile in Contemporary Navaho Culture. *Selected Papers of the Fifth International Congress of Anthropological and Ethnological Sciences,* pp. 359–363, Philadelphia.

——, AND ETHEL M. ALBERT, EDS.
  1966   *People of Rimrock: A Study of Values in Five Cultures.* Cambridge, Mass.

WHEELWRIGHT, MARY C.
  1946   *Hail Chant and Water Chant.* Santa Fe, New Mexico.
  1951   *Myth of Mountain Chant and Beauty Chant.* Museum of Navajo Ceremonial Art, Bulletin No. 5.
  1956   *The Great Star Chant.* Santa Fe, New Mexico.

WORTH, SOL, AND JOHN ADAIR
  1970   Navajo Filmakers. *American Anthropologist,* vol. 72, pp. 9–34.

WYMAN, LELAND C.
  1952   *The Sandpaintings of the Kayenta Navaho.* University of New Mexico Publications in Anthropology, No. 7.
  1957   *Beautyway: A Navaho Ceremonial.* Bollingen Series LIII, New York.
  1959   *Navaho Indian Painting: Symbolism, Artistry, and Psychology.* Boston.
  1962   *The Windways of the Navaho.* Colorado Springs.
  1967   Big Lefthanded, Pioneer Navajo Artist. *Plateau,* vol. 40, pp. 1–13.
  1970a   *Blessingway.* Tucson, Arizona.
  1970b   *Sandpaintings of the Navaho Shootingway and The Walcott Collection.* Smithsonian Contributions to Anthropology, No. 13.
  1971   *Navaho Sandpainting: The Huckel Collection.* Second edition, Colorado Springs.
  1972   A Navajo Medicine Bundle for Shootingway. *Plateau,* vol. 44, pp. 131–149.
  1973   *The Red Antway of the Navaho.* Second edition, Santa Fe, New Mexico.

——, AND FLORA L. BAILEY
  1943   *Navaho Upward-Reaching Way: Objective Behavior, Rationale and Sanction.* University of New Mexico, Bulletin No. 389.
  1944   Two Examples of Navaho Physiotherapy. *American Anthropologist,* vol. 46, pp. 329–337.
  1964   *Navaho Indian Ethnoentomology.* University of New Mexico Publications in Anthropology, No. 12.

——, AND STUART K. HARRIS
  1941   *Navajo Indian Medical Ethnobotany.* University of New Mexico, Bulletin No. 366.

——, AND CLYDE KLUCKHOHN
  1938   *Navaho Classification of their Song Ceremonials.* Memoirs, American Anthropological Association, No. 50.

——, AND FRANC J. NEWCOMB
  1962   Sandpaintings of Beautyway. *Plateau,* vol. 35, pp. 37–52.

Index